LON OF 1000 FACES!

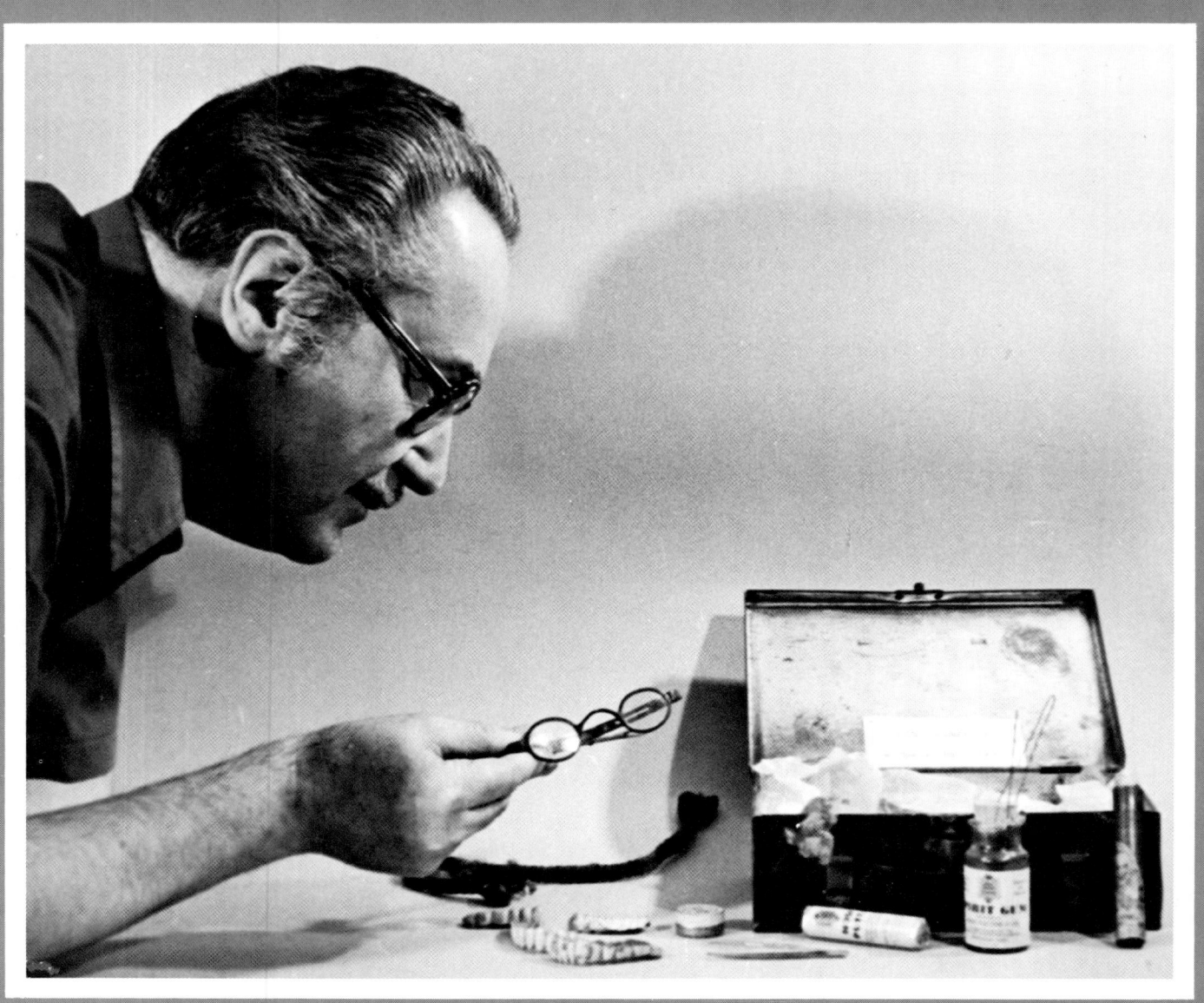

Chaney's #2 Makeup Kit & Paraphernalia.

LON OF 1000 FACES!

Forrest J Ackerman

Morrison, Raven-Hill Company
Beverly Hills, California
Pangbourne, Berkshire, England

LON OF 1000 FACES!
Copyright © 1983 Morrison Raven-Hill Company
All Rights Reserved

Printed in The United States of America
First Printing 1983

DEDICATED
To the Greatest Chaney Fans I Know:

Robert G. Anderson, Ken Anger, Robert Arthur, Rick Baker, Rudy Behlmer, Robert Bloch, Ronald V. Borst, Ray Bradbury, David Bradley, Vivien Burgoon, James Cagney, Stanley Caidin, R. Wright Campbell, Cal B. Champion, Paul Clemens, Bill Cobun, Rich Correll, Luigi Cozzi, Dik Daniels, Walter J. Daugherty, Gary Dorst, Lotte Eisner, Oscar G. Estes Jr., Eldon K. Everett, William K. Everson, Steve Fobert, Brian L. Forbes, Mark Frank, Georges Gallet, Luis Gasca, Brandi Gifford, Lee A. Gladwin, Don Glut, Don Grollman, Al Grossman, Tammy Hajewski, The Hamptons (Silent Movie Theatre, Los Angeles), Bruce and Pam Hanson, Curtis Harrington, Hugh Hefner, Ro Kim, John Kobal, Pat LaBrutto, Celia Lovsky, George Mitchell, Bill Nelson, Jim Nicholson, Bill Nolan, Charles Nuetzel, Randy Palmer, Flavia Paulon, Tom and Terri Pinckard, Dr. Donald A. Reed, Philip J. Riley, Jean-Claude Romer, Angus Scrimm, Sam Sherman, Roman Soldier, Hank Stine, Lamar D. Tabb, George Turner, Bill Tuttle, Ron Waite, Bill Warren, Doug Wright; and to my Maternal Grandparents GEORGE AND BELLE WYMAN, who took me to All the Chaney Films 1922 (age 5½) to 1930; and to Mary Philbin, heroine of the Opera who unmasked Erik the Phantom; and to the Widow of Chaney Sr. and the Widow of Chaney Jr. and Senior's three Grandsons and All the Great Grandchildren *and* Most Especially to
LON, *DON* AFTER MIDNIGHT:
CHANEY!

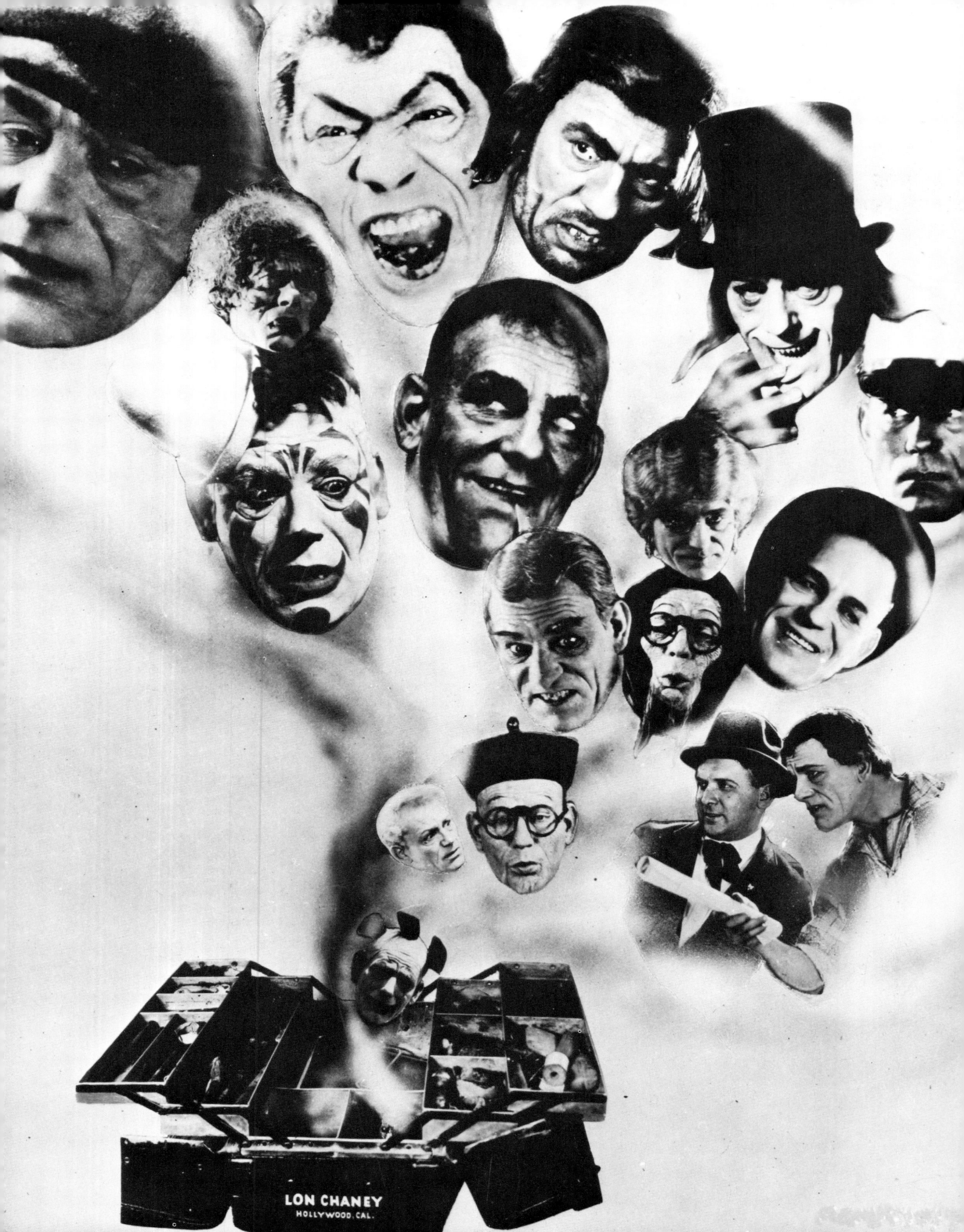

17 of his thousand faces. By the time you finish the book you should be able to identify all of them.

LON CHANEY
THE MAN OF A THOUSAND FACES

THE SCREEN'S GREATEST ACTOR

From a Chaney fan's scrapbook. Note autograph.

ACKNOWLEDGMENTS

Layout and Design:
Douglas E. Holdaway

Typography:
Reference Publications, Inc.

Artwork by:
Cover:
Chaney & Makeup Kit (Oil Painting): Ro Kim
Chaney as the Clown: Bill Nelson
Chaney as the Hunchback: Ron Cobb
Chaney as the Phantom: Bob Juanillo
Chaney as the Vampire: Bob Zraick

Back Cover:
Chaney as the Clown: Bill Nelson

COPYRIGHTED MATERIAL copyright © 1958, 1962, 1965 by Warren Publishing Co. © 1976 Metropolis Publications. Ray Bradbury excerpt from *Playboy* article "Death Warmed Over", © 1968 by HMH Publishing Co. Inc.; reprinted by permission of Ray Bradbury. Bloch piece by permission of Robert Bloch. Cobb painting, permission of Ron Cobb. Phantom and Vampire paintings by permission of Electric Lemon Records and courtesy of Verne Langdon (Forrest J Ackerman agent for Juanillo). Bill Nelson pieces courtesy Bill Nelson.

COVER ARTIST Hyang Ro Kim, a Morrison, Raven-Hill "discovery", was born in Seoul, Korea in 1941...and 7 years later started painting in oils. He has painted professionally in Japan, France and currently the USA—Southern California. Many celebrities have commissioned portraits from Ro: George C. Scott, the late William Holden and Jim David (the latter of *Dallas* fame; Ro's portrait of him appears in the Ewing livingroom in the TV show), Judy and Diana Canova, and numerous others. He is currently creating the cover for a book about Forrest J Ackerman, "Mr. Science Fiction".

Kimo F. Kaawa was born in Maui, Hawaii and came to the Mainland USA where he attended Brown University and the Rhode Island School of Design. He continued his studies in Spain and France and took up sculpting in Italy, after which he moved to England where he worked at the famous Madame Tussaud's Wax Museum in London. He returned to New York where he became an international makeup artist for the Max Factor Co. Later, in California, he continued with the Charles Revlon Co. For the past seven years he has been Director of the Hollywood Wax Museum, for which he has sculpted exhibition pieces at the same time creating wax figures for movies and TV such as THE MAN WITH BOGART'S FACE, *The Munsters' Revenge*, and films for Walt Disney Productions and Mel Brooks Productions. He recently founded Original Monkart Creations in North Hollywood where he specialized in unique sculptings and decors. His figure of Lon Chaney Sr. as The Phantom of the Opera was created in homage to the Man of 1000 Faces for the occasion of the celebration of Chaney's 100th Birthday at a Los Angeles theater.

GRATEFUL ACKNOWLEDGMENT is made to the following individuals, institutions, publications and motion picture studios for their assistance and/or use of their materials in the creations of the volume:

Academy of Motion Picture
   Arts and Sciences Library
Wendayne Ackerman
Alhambra Theater
John E. Allen
Robert G. Anderson*
Niels Augustin
James Babcock
A.S. Barnes & Co. Inc.
Lori Birmingham
Jerry Bixby
Robert Bloch
Bluebird-Universal
Robert V. Borst
Ray Bradbury
David Bradley
Eddie Brandt
Bressler
Buffalo Times
Lon Chaney Jr.
Maude Cheatham*
Cleveland Press
Collier's
Homer Currie*
Dorothy Curtis
Gray Daniels
Walter J. Dougherty
Dayton Daily
Oliver Dernberger
Dorothy Donnell*
Mitch Evans
Eldon K. Everett
F. & M. Enterprises
Faces, Forms, Films
Famous Monsters
Brian L. Forbes
Freulich*
Tammy Hajewski
Evan Hayworth
Jimmie Horan
Milton Howe*
Cortlandt Hull
Stephen Jochsberger
John B. Kennedy*
Ro Kim
John Kobal
L.A. Examiner
Dan Levitt
Loew's State Theater
Ruth Harriett Louise
MGM Studios
N. Michaels
Motion Picture
Motion Picture Classic
Movie Star News
James Muir
Bill Nelson
Paramount-Artcraft
Picture Play
Picture Show Library
Mary Ellen Rabogliatti
Philip J. Riley
Elza Schallert*
RKO Studios
Will Rogers
Bob Scherl
Richard Sheffield
Signature Films
Roman Soldier
Hank Stine
Theatre
Tony Tierney
Universal-International Pictures
James Warren
Warren Publishing Co.
Alan White
Belle Wyman
George Wyman

---

*If you are an asterisked individual, a complimentary copy of this volume will be sent you by the author upon request. Forrest J Ackerman, 2495 Glendower Ave., Hollywood, CA 900027.

ABOUT THE AUTHOR...

THE (ACKER)MAN OF 13 FACES

FORREST J ACKERMAN has appeared off and on in films since 1947 from extra to cameo role to bit player (sixth billing in AFTERMATH). He has played Basil Rathbone's assistant (QUEEN OF BLOOD), "bad Dr. Beaumont" (DRACULA VS. FRANKENSTEIN), Technician #3 (THE TIME TRAVELERS), himself in SCHLOCK and THE HOWLING, the curator of the last museum on Earth in World War 3's AFTERMATH, but is better known as editor of the pioneering filmonster magazine *Famous Monsters* (since 1958) and a seminal force in the fantasy film field since *1932*. In tandem with Boris Karloff he was awarded one of the *first* two Ann Radcliffe awards (for Gothic excellence); received the *first* Science Fiction, Horror and Fantasy Hall of Fame Award; the "Trixie" (Fritz Lang Award) from the Academy of Science Fiction, Fantasy and Horror (a critics' award) and three International Hugos (Germany, Italy, Japan) in addition to the first Hugo (the Oscar of the science-fantasy genre). He is the author of the widely acclaimed MR. MONSTER'S MOVIE GOLD and during 1983 expects to see published BEAUTIES AND THE BEASTS, THE FRANKENSCIENCE MONSTER (revised and enlarged tribute to Biris Karloff and his films) and the companion to MR. MONSTER'S MOVIE GOLD. This book is a work he has dreamed of producing for a quarter of a century. No library, college, Chaney fan, film buff or cinema student can afford to be without it.

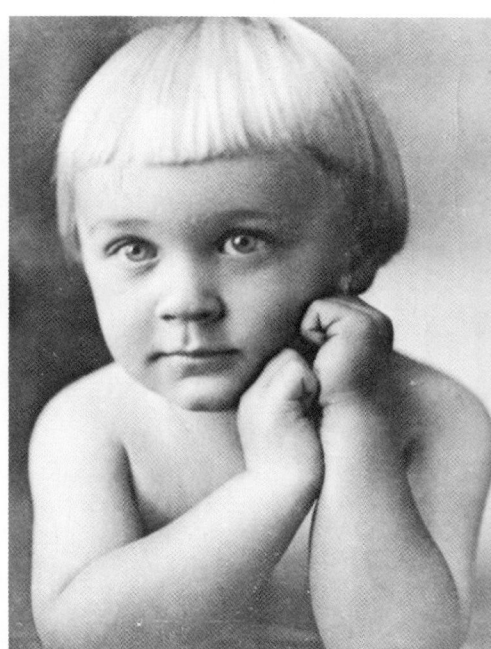

TABLE OF LONTENTS

THE STAR SINISTER	10	Forrest J Ackerman
THE CLOWN AT MIDNIGHT	22	Robert Bloch
LON'S LIFE: Real & Reel	23	Eldon K. Everett & Roman Soldier
THE UNCANNY MR. CHANEY	40	Homer Currie
CHARACTER ACTOR #1	43	Milton Howe
THE FACE THAT LAUNCHED A THOUSAND SHRIEKS	44	Forrest J Ackerman
WHY I PREFER GROTESQUE CHARACTERS	47	Lon Chaney Sr.
HIS FACES, HIS FORTUNE	49	John B. Kennedy
COMING ATTRACTIONS	52	Slides, Stills, Etc.
LON AGO & FAR AWAY (The Primeval Films)	56	Stills
MAN OF MANY MOODS	78	Stills
ORIENTAL INTERPRETATIONS	79	Stills
CRIPPLED (But Not Handicapped!)	82	Stills
LON GLAD	84	Stills
LON SAD	88	Stills
LON MAD	89	Stills
LON CRAZED	92	Stills
GRANDPARENTS OF THE 80s MAY REMEMBER THESE FILMS OF THE MID-20s: The Hunchback of Notre Dame; He Who Gets Slapped; The Tower of Lies; The Monster; The Road To Mandalay; The Unknown; Mockery; Tell It To The Marines; Laugh, Clown, Laugh; While the City Sleeps; The Big City; West of Zanzibar; Thunder; Where East is East; The Unholy Three (both versions)	98	Stills
MAD HATTER	203	Stills
BEHIND LON CHANEY'S MASK	206	Elza Schallert
MY DARKEST HOUR	209	Lon Chaney Sr. & Maude Cheatham
JUST PLAIN LON	210	Stills
I PANICKED THE PARIS OPERA HOUSE AS ERIK	213	Kenneth Strickfaden
THE PHANTOM & I	214	Ray Bradbury
BEHIND THE SCENES	215	Stills
CANDIDS	218	Stills
LAFF, LON, LAFF	225	Stills
CURIOSITIES & RABABILIA	230	Stills
MY FATHER—LON CHANEY	237	Lon Chaney Jr.
HIS LIFE FOR HIS ART?	238	Dorothy Donnell
DEATH OF THE IMMORTAL	241	History
"DON'T STEP ON IT!" (Reincarnation) Bela Lugosi, Boris Karloff, Walter Huston, Lon Chaney Jr., Carroll Borland, Jean Hersholt	247	Stills
LON & SON	270	Vincent Price
MISCEL*LON*EOUS	271	Stills
ADVERTISEMENT FOR MYSELF	278	Forrest J Ackerman
LETTER TO AN ANGEL: Fiction	280	Forrest J Ackerman

Top to bottom (left to right) The Ackermonster of the Opera by Bill Nelson; Ron Cobb's Hunchback of Notre Dame, Quasimodo' Bob Juanillo's Erik (Lugosi's Dracula Ring); Chaney Jr.'s Life Mask (left end, middle row), Chaney Sr.'s "London" top Hat; Lon Lives in the Ackermuseum of Fantasy'Filmemorabilia in Hollyweird/Horrorwood.

Mirror, mirror, in his hand, who was the greatest in the land? Lon was!

THE STAR SINISTER

STRANGE INTERLUDE. It has been an unusual period in my life, vicariously immersed day and night in the life of another. Lon Chaney was alive for the first 14 years of my life; he has now been dead over half a century.

I feel like an ancient alchemist, a sorcerer, out of the dust and clay of browning brittling photos of a long gone yesterday, a time as remote as 20 lustrums (his birthdate: 1883), reassembling Lon Chaney. Recapturing his personality from pictures and posters and pressbooks and articles and clippings. Giving the simulacrum of life to a man I never met, 53 years a corpse in his unmarked crypt.

I hope I prove worthy of the task I have set myself.

Once the work is done, I think it will prove to be the definitive book for eternity. Not that it couldn't be improved on but the major accumulation of material has been completed and the best we could hope for, should there be future, revised editions, would be refinements, a few photos from certain titles where they exist in large quantities being replaced by stills from films on which photos are still missing. If anyone out there in the audience by some miracle has any information or pictures on such Chaney films as BACK TO LIFE, BY THE SUN'S RAYS, THE CHIMNEY'S SECRET, THE CRIMES, THE DEAF MUTE TALKS, THE FALSE FACES, THE FORBIDDEN ROOM, THE GILDED SPIDER, A NIGHT OF THRILLS, PARTNERS OF THE NIGHT, THE PIPER'S PRICE, THE PIPES OF PAN, PLACE BEYOND THE WINDS, PUBLIC ENEMY #5, THE RESCUE, THE SCARLET CAR, THE STRANGE MIND (or is it THE STRONGER MIND?), STRONGER THAN DEATH, THREADS OF FATE, THE TRIBE OF TRAITOR, THE WRONG SIDE OF PARADISE or any other obscure title, please *run*, do not walk, to the nearest matter transmitter and expedite the material to this Chaney acolyte so that such finds may be shared with the world of Lonophiles.

AND NOW, I'll direct your attention to the following tribute to Lon Chaney which I prepared for the Halloween issue of *Famous Monsters* back in 1973. I pretty well said it all then. I can think of nothing further to add now.

Forrest J Ackerman
1313 Chaney Way
Lon's Angeles
Londay the 13th, 1983

LON AND FJA

I NEVER MET LON CHANEY (Forry Ackerman speaking). Boris Karloff, yes; Bela Lugosi, Peter Lorre, among the old-time all-time Greats. And at least I *saw* Colin Clive, both alive and dead.

I've met his son but Lon Chaney Himself, alas, no.

But as an image on the screen, Lon Chaney Sr. was one of the earliest people in my life to make an impression on me; a lifetime impression. I was only seven when my wonderful maternal grandparents took me to see Lon Chaney in THE HUNCHBACK OF NOTRE DAME.

At eight my Chaney treat for the year was HE as the Clown in HE WHO GETS SLAPPED, while at nine it was a four-star year with the Man of A Thousand Faces portraying a Mad Scientist in THE MONSTER, a Ventriloquist and Old Woman in THE UNHOLY THREE, a pathetic Demented Old Man in THE TOWER OF LIES...and, his crowning achievement, his shining hour—THE PHANTOM OF THE OPERA. It was a memorable year for me, 1925.

Came '26 and with it two Tod Browning films featuring Chaney, THE BLACKBIRD (a cripple) and THE ROAD TO MANDALAY (a one-eyed outcast). Incidentally, it was of his role in the latter that it was erroneously reported that "he covered one eyeball with collodion to simulate a cataract." I have tracked down this POTENTIALLY VERY DANGEROUS MISINFORMATION— I'M TOLD A PERSON COULD BE BLINDED BY PUTTING COLLODION IN THEIR EYE—and it was in the December 1953 issue of *Films in Review* magazine that it was published. I will not embarrass the author of the article by naming him. I do not know if the error was corrected in a later issue—I certainly hope so. Unfortunately, in all innocence it has been repeated in *Famous Monsters*. But I wish to take the opportunity HERE AND NOW to hopefully correct ONCE AND FOR ALL the wrong information about Lon Chaney putting collodion in his eyes. *never!* He may very well have used collodion—a sticky liquid consisting of guncotton dissolved in ether—to contract skin on his face to form artificial scars. But in an eye? Uh-uh! Don't ever try it. Try the thin membrane from the inside of an egg, instead, if you feel you *must* emulate Lon Chaney.

MIME MARCHES ON

1927 was a busy year for "Mr. Fear":

He made raw recruits tremble before his gruff bark in TELL IT TO THE MARINES (with Warner "Fu Manchu" Oland).

He played a dual role of elderly Chinese and his *ancient* Mandarin father in MR. WU.

He sacrificed his own arms for the hoped-for charms of Joan Crawford in the circus melodrama directed by Tod Browning, THE UNKNOWN. I saw this film once again, after more than 45 years, in Belgium last year, and the original thrill was still there. Norman Kerry, who was menaced by Lon in THE PHANTOM OF THE OPERA, was again his rival in THE UNKNOWN.

In MOCKERY Chaney was a half-witted Russian serf who was cruelly mistreated. In the cast was Ricardo Cortez, who about ten years later would appear with Boris Karloff in THE WALKING DEAD.

And the real treat for '27—Tod Browning once again behind the megaphone—was LONDON AFTER MIDNIGHT, with Chaney in the dual role of the detective-hypnotist and the ghoulish creature twisted in body and mind.

I saw every one of the pictures so far named—*and at the time they were first released*. I heard of THE MIRACLE MAN (1919) and finally sometime in my teens saw a revival of it. I stress this fact, not to brag or to make anyone feel envious, but because, after I wished a "Happy Birthday, Dear Phantom" to Lon Chaney Sr. in *FM#98*, pointing out that, had he lived, 1 April 1973 would have been the 90th celebration of his natal day, for some reason a highly critical fan wrote me a real put-down, a sharp-toothed piece of fangmail saying he doubted I had ever seen more than a handful of the Chaney films to which I "knowingly" referred. Whereas the truth of the matter is that I saw, as fast as they arrived at my local theater, every movie Lon Chaney made from THE HUNCHBACK on, with (admittedly) the possible exception of THE NEXT CORNER, 1924, which if I *did* see it, I regret I don't remember. And in later years I caught up with THE SHOCK, SHADOWS, THE TRAP and—one that knocked me for a loop, it almost qualifying as political science fiction—THE PENALTY, where he plotted to take over San Francisco with a city-wide organization of criminals. In the latter he was kind of a legless Dr. Mabuse.

I don't think I'll ever live long enough to understand why a few soreheads have to periodically pick on me or challenge my credentials. I don't claim to be the world's greatest authority on Lon Chaney Sr.—Robert Bloch, with his eidetic memory, has probably seen every bit as many of Lon's films as I, perhaps even more—but, along with Phil Riley, Tammy Hajewski, Bill Nelson, Verne Langdon, Robert G. Anderson (author of "Faces, Forms, Films: The Artistry of Lon Chaney"), George Mitchell (who did a Career Article on Chaney) and Rudy Behlmer, I'm pretty sure I'm one of his most devoted *fans*.

HIGHLIGHTS FROM THE SCRAPBOOK

As is common knowledge, I have some of Bela Lugosi's own scrapbooks. I have thick files of newspaper clippings on Boris Karloff. Scholars and authors frequently consult me to extract information from the source material I have on the latter two departed greats as well as living artists of the macabre and outstanding or obscure monster, sci-fi, horror and/or fantasy films.

Let's suppose, now, that you have come to the Ackermuseum (Grislyland West) to research Lon Chaney Sr. You already know from *FM#1* and 100 (the reprint of "Alice in Monsterland"), nos. 8, 27, 31 and 32 and *Monster World* #10, most of the basic background on The Star Sinister. So instead, let's finger through my files, thee and me, and see what we find of mutual interest.

Re WEST OF ZANZIBAR: Lon Chaney is said to appear as "a paralyzed, vengeful Nemesis, ruling a savage tribe as a 'white voodoo' in order to work out a monstrous revenge in the wilds of an African jungle." Chaney is seen as "Dead Legs Flint", former stage magician paralyzed by the man who stole the love of his wife, and trailing that man through the perilous wilds of the Belgian Congo in Africa. (From the Sunday *Oregonian,* Portland/OR, 25 Nov. '28.)

Re THE BUGLE SOUNDS. A Chaney film never made but announced as "The most ambitious production of Lon Chaney's career. Something new in the way of adventure films". It would have shown him being killed in an act of heroism, capturing an enemy cannon.

Re Lon Chaney himself by Herbert Cruikshank in *Motion Picture Classics* for March 1929: The big car careened through the imposing portals of the Metro-Goldwyn-Mayer studios by leaps and bounds. Which was exactly the manner in which sundry mere pedestrians gained the comparative safety of the walks. One of these persons, togged out in horn-rimmed specs, a checkered cap and a green tie, missed a fanny-full of fenders by an act of God and the flexible spine of an acrobat.

"Look out," I giggled to the gleeful driver. "It might be Lon Chaney!"

Imagine my embarrassment. It was.

Yep. Lon Chaney himself, in person, and not The *Hunchback* of Notre Dame, The *Phantom* of the Opera or *Mr. Wu*. At first I thought he was disguised as a human being. But he wasn't. He's just that way naturally. Very much so.

Now Lon Chaney doesn't look it. I mean he doesn't look like Lon Chaney. That is, of course, the Chaney who makes us marvel by being minus a few arms, legs, eyes or other parts which habit has accustomed us to expect in *homo sapiens.* In fact, the most astonishing discovery about Chaney is that he possesses a Barrymore profile. Perhaps a secret shame at this first caused him to seek concealment behind putty noses and crepe hair. He's the kind of guy who'd hate to have a Barrymore profile. Which, in itself, makes him unique among movie actors.

Re THE BLACKBIRD: Lon Chaney has placed himself in the foreground as one who can accurately analyze any human soul and any human emotion. This is one of the finest characterizations to Chaney's credit. He doesn't resort to heavy makeup to put over his character. Even when he appears as a cripple, he shows how he merely throws his shoulders and hips out of joint and hobbles on crutches.

As clever as Chaney is, Tod Browning's direction is just as remarkable. In the delineation of his English characters and haunts his interpretation rings true. He has a born storyteller's gift of entertaining narrative—for he wrote the story.

It is one of those crooked affairs that is filled with suspense. Excellent entertainment and so mystifying that we'll wager you'll like to see it again. Don't pass it up. (From *Photoplay* magazine, courtesy of Dan Adams.)

Re THE ROAD TO MANDALAY: Oh-oh! (FJA) speaking). We'll have to let the *Films in Review* writer off the hook, the one who in 1953 reported that Chaney had put collodion in his eye to create the effect of blindness in this picture, for here in a 1926 edition of *Motion Picture Magazine* is the same misinformation, over a quarter of a century earlier: "As *Singapore Joe*, Chaney is required to have one dead eye. He consulted eye specialists galore and finally discovered that he could achieve the desired effect by coating the eye with collodion. Incidentally, he can only keep this in his eye about ten minutes at a time." A split second, I understand, would be more like it, the instant intense pain would be so great, and almost certain permanent eye damage would be the immediate result. So don't try it!

Re THE HUNCHBACK OF NOTRE DAME and LAUGH, CLOWN, LAUGH: Lon Chaney knows human nature. And he profits thereby.

Everyone of us is curious. We cannot get away from this failing. Chaney, after years of disappointments and discouragement, awakened to the fact that the great American public (and the great public of any other country, for that matter) is essentially curious.

Do you remember how we marveled over his makeup in THE HUNCHBACK OF NOTRE DAME? How it was a nine-day-wonder? From this time on, Chaney has kept his public guessing. His pictures may be good, bad or indifferent but what does that matter? The curious public, young and old, go to see them and marvel again and again on "how he does it."

LAUGH, CLOWN, LAUGH came here to Dubuque, Iowa, the other day. The publicity agent of the theater showing the picture, exploited Chaney's use of a mysterious lacquer process by which he erased all wrinkles and appeared as a 21-year-old boy in the opening scenes. Enormous crowds viewed this picture, partly because of the plot but chiefly out of curiosity.

I feel quite safe in predicting that as long as Chaney continues to keep the crowds guessing, he will be one of the greatest box office attractions on the screen.—Auleen Bordeaux, *Motion Picture* magazine, Jan. '29.

HERE THERE BE CHANEY

It has been years since we published our original Chaney Filmography. We now bring it up to date with *20* additions supplied by the late "Roman Soldier" (a pseudonymous friend who provided me with copious amounts of incredible lost fantasy film lore and regrettably died without revealing his identity to me). Each of the "Roman Soldier" additions is italicized. Most of his then-unique titles have since been discovered and published by Robert G. Anderson in his fine "Faces, Forms, Films" book, to which he himself added 22 further titles or additional pieces of information and his material too we have incorporated in *italics*.

The 17 Previously Unrecorded Chaney Pictures come to us courtesy of BOB ALLEN of Canada, friend of a FRED TRAVERS, the latter a gentleman who may be in his 90s, who, when he was a youngster, "would list the title of the film and the star, Lon Chaney, whenever mom or dad or brother took him to a Chaney preview or he went to a Saturday matinee" and as a consequence has no doubt one of the greatest, rarest Chaney scrapbooks in existence. We cannot thank BOB ALLEN and FRED TRAVERS enough for sharing this exciting information with our readers and making this important information available for scholars of the present and researchers and cinemaphiles of the future.

THE CHANEY CORPUS

A
- ACCUSING EVIDENCE (new discovery)
- ACE OF HEARTS *(from book "The Purple Mask" by Gouverneur Morris)*
- ALAS AND ALACK
- ALL FOR PEGGY
- ALL THE BROTHERS WERE VALIANT
- ALMOST AN ACTRESS
- The ALTAR OF FRIENDSHIP
- ANYTHING ONCE (see The MAVERICK)

B
- *BACK TO LIFE*
- The BIG CITY
- *BIRCH IS SOFT
- BITS OF LIFE
- *BLACK SHADOWS
- The BLACKBIRD
- A BLIND BARGAIN (see THE OCTAVE OF CLAUDIUS)
- BLOODHOUNDS OF THE NORTH
- BOBBIE OF THE BALLET
- BONDAGE
- *The BOSS OF POWDERVILLE* (same as The GRAND PASSION)
- BOUND ON THE WHEEL
- BROADWAY LOVE
- A BROADWAY SCANDAL *(see MY PARISIAN SWEETHEART)*
- BY THE SUN'S RAYS

C
- The CHIMNEY'S SECRET
- *COMMAND PERFORMANCE
- *The CRIMES

D
- *DANGER—GO SLOW*
- *DAREDEVIL JACK (serial)*
- The DESERT BREED
- *The DEAF MUTE TALKS*
- DISCORD AND HARMONY
- *DOLLAR DEVILS
- A DOLL'S HOUSE
- DOLLY'S SCOOP
- *DYNAMITE JOEY

E
- The EMBEZZLER
- The EMPTY GUN
- The END OF THE FEUD

F
- The FALSE FACES *(from book of the same name by Jos. Louis Vance)*
- The FASCINATION OF THE FLEUR DE LIS
- FAST COMPANY
- FATHER AND THE BOYS

FELIX ON THE JOB
FIRES OF REBELLION
FIRES OF VENGEANCE *(see FLESH AND BLOOD)* (E.K.E.)
The FLASHLIGHT *(see The FLASHLIGHT GIRL)*
The FLASHLIGHT GIRL (same as The FLASHLIGHT)
FLESH AND BLOOD *(see FIRES OF VENGEANCE)* (E.K.E.)
The FORBIDDEN ROOM
FOR CASH
FOR THOSE WE LOVE

G

The GIFT SUPREME *(from book of the same name by Geo. Allan England)*
The GILDED SPIDER
The GIRL IN THE CHECKERED COAT
*GIRL IN THE RAIN
The GIRL OF THE NIGHT
GIRL WHO DARED
The GIRL WHO WAS AFRAID OF LOVE (E.K.E.)
The GRAND PASSION *(see The BOSS OF POWDERVILLE)*
The GRASP OF GREED (based on H. Rider Haggard's novel, "Mr. Meeson's Will")
The GRIND
The GRIP OF JEALOUSY

H

HE WHO GETS SLAPPED
HELL MORGAN'S GIRL
HER BOUNTY
HER ESCAPE
HER GRAVE MISTAKE
HER LIFE'S STORY
The HIGHER LAW
The HONOR OF THE MOUNTED
The HUNCHBACK OF NOTRE DAME

I

An IDYLL OF THE HILLS
IF MY COUNTRY SHOULD CALL
IN THE SERICE OF THE KING (Director) (E.K.E.)J
*JUST ASK HARRY

K

The KAISER, BEAST OF BERLIN
*KICK IN
The KING'S KEEPER (new discovery, 1915)

L

The LAMB, THE WOMAN, THE WOLF
LAUGH, CLOWN, LAUGH
The LIE
The LIGHT IN THE DARK
LIGHTS AND SHADOWS
The LION, THE LAMB, THE MAN
LON OF THE MOUNTAINS *(or is it LON OF THE LONE MOUNTAIN?)*
LONDON AFTER MIDNIGHT

M

MAID OF THE MIST
A MAN'S COUNTRY
The MARK OF CAIN
The MASK *(see WOLFBREED)* (E.K.E.)
The MASK OF LOVE
The MAVERICK

The MEASURE OF A MAN
The MENACE OF CARLOTA *(or is it THE MENACE TO CARLOTTA?)*
THE MILLIONAIRE PAUPERS
A MINER'S ROMANCE
The MIRACLE MAN *(from novel of same name by Frank L. Packard)*
MOCKERY
The MONSTER *(based on play of the same name by Crane Wilbur)*
A MOTHER'S ATONEMENT
MOUNTAIN JUSTICE
MR. WU
MY PARISIAN SWEETHEART (same as BROADWAY SCANDAL)
*MY UNCLE HE...

N
The NEXT CORNER
A NIGHT OF THRILLS
NOMADS OF THE NORTH

O
The OCTAVE OF CLAUDIUS (same as A BLIND BARGAIN; adapted from novel "The Octave of Claudius" by Barry Pain)
The OLD COBBLER
OLIVER TWIST
*ONE MILLION IN JEWELS
The OUBLIETTE
OUTSIDE THE GATE
OUTSIDE THE LAW
*OVERLY UNDERHANDED
The OYSTER DREDGER

P
PAID IN ADVANCE
*PARTNERS OF THE NIGHT
PAY ME
The PEDDLER (director) (E.K.E.)
The PENALTY
The PHANTOM OF THE OPERA
The PINE'S REVENGE
The PIPER'S PRICE
The PIPES OF PAN
PLACE BEYOND THE WINDS
POOR JAKE'S DEMISE
The PRICE OF SILENCE
*PUBLIC ENEMY #5

Q
QUINCY ADAMS SAWYER
QUITS

R
The RANCH ROMANCE *(or is it A RANCH ROMANCE?)*
RED MARGARET, MOONSHINER
REMEMBER MARY MAGDALEN
The RESCUE
*RETURN OF JOHN JUSTIN
RICHELIEU
The RIDDLE GAWNE
The ROAD TO MANDALAY
ROSE OF THE NIGHT (same as The WICKED DARLING)

S
The SCARLET CAR
The SCARLET LETTER

The SEA URCHIN
SHADOWS
The SHERIFF OF LONG BUTTE (new discovery, 1915)
The SHOCK
The SIN OF OLGA BRANDT
STAR OF THE SEA
STEADY COMPANY
The STOOL PIGEON
The STRANGE MIND
STRONGER THAN DEATH
SUCH IS LIFE

T

The TALK OF THE TOWN
TANGLED HEARTS
TELL IT TO THE MARINES
THAT DEVIL BATEESE
THREADS OF FATE
THUNDER
The TOWER OF LIES
The TRAGEDY OF WHISPERING CREEK
The TRAP (see *WOLFBREED* and *The MASK*) (E.K.E.)
TREASURE ISLAND
*The TRIBE OF TRAITOR
TRIUMPH
The TRUST

U

UNDER THE SHADOW *(or is it UNDER A SHADOW?)*
The UNHOLY THREE (Silent) *(from book of the same name by Clarence A. Robbins)*
THE UNHOLY THREE (Talking) *(from book of the same name by Clarence A. Robbins)*
The UNKNOWN
The UNLAWFUL TRADE

V

VENGEANCE OF THE WEST
VICTORY
The VIOLIN MAKER
VIRTUE ITS OWN REWARD *(or is it VIRTUE IS ITS OWN REWARD?)*
VOICES OF THE CITY

W

WEST OF ZANZIBAR
WHEN BEARCAT WENT DRY
WHEN THE GODS PLAYED A BADGER GAME
WHERE EAST IS EAST
WHERE THE FOREST ENDS (E.K.E.)
WHILE THE CITY SLEEPS
WHILE PARIS SLEEPS
The WICKED DARLING *(see ROSE OF THE NIGHT)*
WOLFBREED *(see THE TRAP)* (E.K.E.)
The WRONG SIDE OF PARADISE

■ ■ ■

HOLLYWOOD REVUE of 1929, previously included in the Chaney Filmography, has been removed as your Editor recently had the opportunity to see the film again and established that Chaney does *not* appear in the picture, only a musical spoof segment inspired by him called "Lon Chaney's Going To Get You If You Don't Watch Out!"

A "CHANEY FREAK" SPEAKS

In my position as Editor of **FM**, receiving approximately 500 fan letters a month, I have observed for 15 years the enduring phenomenon of fans, especially females, passionately attached to the screen image of someone long dead such as Bela Lugosi. They react to him as though he were still alive; there are admirers of Lugosi as fanatically devoted to the deceased Dracula as to his living incarnation, Christopher Lee.

So I thought it would be interesting to get a firsthand account from a young lady who spends an inordinate amount of time thinking about a man who left life nearly 50 years ago but looms larger than life to her in her daily activities. An unusual human document is:

MY MASTER
by
Tammy Hajewski

Permit me to introduce myself. I am known as The Lon Chaney Freak. It's an accurate name for I can say in all honesty that I have existed two years now for the sole purpose of digging up little particles of information on this gentleman who continuously denied his own existence between the films he appeared in.

You know, if somebody had mentioned Lon Chaney Sr. to me in 1970, I would have stared at them stupidly and inquired, "What's a Lon Chaney?" This year I'm afraid that my friends are warning everyone I come in contact with not to breathe Word 1 about my subject to me lest I deafen them with Chaney talk.

But this isn't supposed to describe the life and times of the Man of 1001 Faces. I take it for granted that you wouldn't pick up an issue of **FAMOUS MONSTERS OF FILMLAND** dedicated to Lon Chaney if you either didn't know something about him to begin with or didn't aim to find out something about him from it.

You're probably closer to him than you think already. Who hasn't heard of the Phantom of the Opera? The Hunchback of Notre Dame? Chances are, if Chaney hadn't made them, hadn't once portrayed the demented organist or the pathetic bellringer, you wouldn't know them. You wouldn't think of the timeless celluloid masterpieces you do when you hear those names.

No, I'd like to try to write about the miraculous charm of Lon Chaney...of a man who used to literally become people who were misunderstood...

Being an over-emotional sentimental fool from way back, I crumpled like a piece of aluminum foil under the spell of Lon Chaney's Hollywood biography, THE MAN OF 1000 FACES. It still chokes me up, even though I've seen it 13 times. I'm not far from the day when I shall begin worrying about the strange thrill I get from maliciously picking out the many small departures from truth it contains as I watch it.

While this most humble disciple stubbornly maintains that her Master would turn over in his crypt if he ever found out about James Cagney's reproductions of some of his best known makeups, she is quick to assure any budding Chaneyphile that the MAN OF 1000 FACES is no less than a great movie and that it is *the* place to start discovering Lon Chaney.

Now I'm proud to say that I possess researching abilities which, with regard to thoroughness, can be likened to laser light. But even though I've achieved Freakhood, my failure to uncover any really useful references to Chaney *anywhere* in the *entire* city of Baltimore has made a hideous blotch on my record of fact-finding successes. I must admit, though, that wherever I have sought Lon Chaney, whether I was victorious in my search or not, I have stumbled upon a Beautiful People...that is, someone well worth coming to know better. As it turns out, I not only have to my name a right good-sized heap of the Master's treasures worth a small fortune but also the friends he's helped me find...worth a large one.

Don't think for one minute that my hard-won collection simply sits there vegetating. Quite the contrary. I often hear its anguished cries of exhaustion from over-use begging me to let it gather just a *little* bit of dust. Teacher I ain't but speaker I am and whenever I get a chance to talk Chaney to any someone or group of someones, I do. Still, I can never think of words to achieve the same effect as placing a photograph of Chaney's peasant Sergei, taken from a movie called MOCKERY, next to one of Singapore Joe from THE ROAD TO MANDALAY; Quasimodo, the Hunchback of Notre Dame; Erik, the Phantom of the Opera; and perhaps the vampire from LONDON AFTER MIDNIGHT; asking my audience how many people posed for these pictures, then quietly stating that all of the characters are truly one and the same person.

Do YOU think it odd for me to be madly attached to a man who died 14 years and 2 months before I was born? Well, at any rate I do definitely hope with all my heart that when you see some of the people Lon Chaney Sr. has brought to life, you come to consider him as wonderful and awesome and magnificent a creator as I do.

FACE -1001

In the Tammy Hajewski article just ended, Ms. Hajewski spoke casually of the thousand and *one* faces of Lon Chaney. It was not a mistake. In the 32d issue of **FM** we printed a feature so popular that we repeated it at the end of 1968: FACE 1001. That was five years ago and as we realize that many of our readers were only anywhere from three to eight years old then and may never have seen the famous article, we reprint it now (in slightly abridged form in order to fit our format). It was by the great Hollywood Star portrait photographer Clarence Bull as told to Raymond Lee, child star and later book author.

One afternoon Lon dropped into my studio for a chat about makeup and the importance of lighting on grease-paint and putty. He never stopped experimenting and demanding the best in every character he created. As we talked and light began doing strange things to the clown face, I took off my glasses and wiped them. Suddenly in the criss-cross of shadows I was startled by another face...that of Jesus Christ!

The lines around the mouth being drawn down by nails of the cross...the lips sagging with drops of blood...the eyes reaching out into a space that was terrifying.

I began to shake.

THE FACE BEHIND THE MASK

"Clarence, you cold?"

Lon Chaney was about the kindest man you'd ever know. He was fingertip sensitive to every emotion whether inside or out. He could read thoughts as easily as lips.

I coughed and stood up, stretching, and then I said quietly,

"Lon, I just saw Christ's face behind that clown makeup!"

In those silent days this was the most silent I had ever experienced.

As I stared at the "Man of a Thousand Faces", again I saw the Savior behind the white mask. Tears in the eyes. The lips parted in thirst. One of the Seven Last Words trying to break through the cracks in the skin.

Then a heavy shadow fell through the window and the clown looked up for another slap.

Lon walked to the window and seemed to speak to the shadows outside in the street.

WHEN LON WAS LITTLE

"Clarence, as a little boy I remember a picture of Christ which used to hang in our livingroom. Just the head on the cross. I'd study it for hours, watch what the light did to it, what the shadows tried to out do. And some times the thought startled me like a voice: "Some day, Lon, if you're a real good boy, maybe your face will be remembered like His!"

The telephone rang. It was for Lon. They wanted him on the set. We made an appointment for the following Monday. I watched the clown sag into the shadows outside and I wondered, Would he let me some day take his portrait as Christ...?

At the next sitting I completed the advance stills for "He" and just as Lon was about to leave, he said gently, "Clarence, I know you are a sensitive yet level-headed fellow. I've been thinking a lot about what happened last week. I've even been working on the makeup. Do you think it would be out of line for the monster to pose as Christ?"

I had tears in my eyes when I put my arms around Lon Chaney and replied, "They tell us He is in all of us. Some of us find Him in strange ways. You name the day!"

Lon was quite nervous that day. He had decided to make up in my studio. He wanted no one to know what he was doing. I cancelled all appointments and locked the front door. I set up my camera and waited.

Slowly a figure walked across my studio and sat before my camera. In the shadow it could have been any man. As I switched on my lights it was the Christ who suffered little children to come unto Him...

THE UNBELIEVABLE RESULTS

The next day Lon and I looked at the prints.

It was incredible!

Lon smiled. A rare thing to see a smile on those lips which generally showed only sneers and fangs. It seemed a fulfillment of something.

Lon and I were in another world for that suspended moment. Suddenly one of the louder voices from the Publicity Department burst into the room. I had forgotten to lock the door.

"What's new, boys? Lon cooking up another shocker? I don't know how you keep topping them. What's this?"

He grabbed the print from Lon and stared at it.

"Hey, fellows, we aren't that hard up for material!"

Lon's fist clenched.

"Say, who posed for this? A new contract player trying to be different, huh? Well, kind of a new slant, but I don't think the public will buy this Bible stuff."

I started to speak. Lon shook his head.

"It's something I was working on with a friend. Just an experiment."

"Mind if I use your phone, Clarence?"

Lon and I just sat looking at each other as the voice rattled on.

DEATH OF A PHOTO

The photos were never shown to any one. Lon even suggested I destroy them. But I couldn't do this. The publicity man's comments had done something to Lon. He smiled just before he left and said, "We had our moment, that no one can take from us. Thanks for everything, Clarence."

I put the photos in a dead file that only I knew about. The years passed on and Lon and I had many exciting photo sessions but the Christ image was never mentioned.

Time was a deceiver in those days when sound was poking its head into the silent screen. But there was tradition and one of the most enduring came every Christmas. We all chipped in and in teams went around with baskets and presents to our fellows who didn't have our share of worldly goods.

I will never know why I went to the dead file that Christmas week. As I looked through it I suddenly realized the Christ photos were missing. I searched every possible file. The Chaney stills were gone. There had been some improvements in the building, the files had been moved many times, but no one had access to them but me. I was sick at heart.

At the Christmas studio party, also a tradition, I could hardly look Lon in the face. He wasn't a party man and stayed just for greetings. Watching him leave the stage I wondered what could have happened to those photos? How could they have escaped from my own files? "God Bless Ye Merry Gentlemen" sung by a studio chorus didn't cheer me any.

THE SMALL HIDDEN HOUSE

I can't remember who I made the Christmas rounds with. I know there were three of us and we had a prepared list of folks to visit. As we went from house to house my spirits rose at the smiles we brought to surprised faces. It was warm in Los Angeles that Christmas Eve and quite a contrast to the Montana yuletides I had been born to.

Our last basket. A small house way back on an empty lot. A few eucalyptus trees tried to hide its size. We churned up dust as we drove up. A faint light through the window as if it would burn out any minute.

I knocked at the door. You could smell the oily eucalyptus leaves. You could hear the knock repeated inside. I tapped again. The door opened and a boy of ten and a girl of five behind him stared at me.

"Merry Christmas!" we all chimed.

A young woman appeared out of the gloom. I thought she would cry as we handed her the things but the laughter of her children as they opened their presents stopped that.

A branch of a eucalyptus tree nailed to a piece of wood rose from the table. Pieces of colored paper and bits of tin-foil were its only decoration. At the base of the sprig a smattering of cotton. But gradually the gloom had movement and then I saw on the mantel a vigil light in a red glass cup burning before a picture. It was the warmest glow I had ever seen.

THE RETURN OF LON CHANEY

The mother saw me staring at the vigil light and began talking in broken English and gesturing to the mantel. The boy came up and took her hand and said in very good English, "My mother is trying to tell you how much she thanks you but most of all she says she knew we would have a good Christmas because of the picture."

I looked at the picture.

"You see, sir, my papa, before he was hurt in the accident, brought it home and said it would always protect us."

I moved to the wall. Gazed at the red circle outlining the face. I couldn't believe it! Lon's face...Christ's face...the red circle glowing about it almost making it move...

"Where did your father get this picture?"

"He used to work at the movie studios and one day in the trashcan he found this picture of Our Lord. And he said it was the most beautiful he had ever seen and he knew it would always protect us."

I knew the answer before I asked the question, "Where is your father now, son?"

He smiled again.

"In heaven, sir, with Our Lord."

MAN OF MANY VOICES

The following year was a busy and revolutionary one for the motion picture world—1930. Pictures talked! Sound had arrived. Silence was dead. Confusion reigned. My beloved stars crowded my studio in sessions mounting almost to hysteria as they wondered how long they would burn bright with voices.

I had seen Lon sparsely that year. Always something to interrupt us. I knew some day I had to tell him about that Christmas Eve.

READYING FAMOUS VAMPIRE ROLE!

DRACULA was next on his list and he was giving this fabulous monster all the experience of his many years scaring the daylights out of movie fans.

The lasttime I saw him was in August and only passing in the street outside the studio commissary.

"Lon, I know you're awfully busy with your new picture, but there is something I must tell you. How about having coffee with me in my studio about three?"

He agreed and then took off.

HE NEVER KNEW

But Lon Chaney never came at three that afternoon.

He never called.

I waited—waited for hours. It was completely unlike him. He had never been late for an appointment before.

Several days later I heard he was ill at home. I meant to call on him but the schedule was always crowding, crowding time and life.

August 26, 1930, Lon Chaney died of cancer of the throat. He had spoken only once on the sound screen and would never speak again.

And I had never had the chance to speak to him about the Christ picture. His inspiring portrait, greater than life, that lived after his death—and may live to this day.

■ ■ ■

THE CLOWN AT MIDNIGHT

By Robert Bloch

Editor's Note:

The portions of Mr. Bloch's article pertaining to Lon Chaney Sr. have been excerpted and are reprinted herewith:

When I was an eight-year-old I saw Lon Chaney in THE PHANTOM OF THE OPERA—and gazed upon the face of naked fear. A couple of years ago I attended a revival of the same film. And despite the flickering flaws of this dated melodrama, the scene where Chaney is unmasked exerted the same monstrous magic upon a modern audience.

Since the 1925 version of THE PHANTOM, Hollywood has arrayed itself in nose-putty and fright-wig hundreds of times. And yet only a score of genuinely shivery efforts have actually emerged from the studios—and practically none for 15 years following World War Two.

If censors have a distorted idea of what constitutes real horror, audiences seem to retain more than their share of misconceptions. In film after film the great Lon Chaney played a succession of cripples and deformed men; he earned a deserved reputation as "The Man of a Thousand Faces". But aside from his role as the Phantom in PHANTOM OF THE OPERA, Chaney seldom played outright "monster" roles. Usually he sacrificed his life for the heroine. Yet to the public Chaney was a maker of "horror movies".

We who cherish the creeps will continue to haunt the local cinema for shocks and shudders and the wholesome release of fears as old as humanity. Where our search will lead, I don't know. It may be that we'll discover the ultimate cinematic horror in a clown. Years ago Lon Chaney said:

"A clown is funny in the circus ring but what would be the normal reaction to opening a door at midnight and finding the same clown standing there in the moonlight?"

That, to me, is the essence of true horror—the clown...at midnight. ■

A LENGTHY EXAMINATION of horror films and censorship bearing this title was published in 1960 in *Rogue* magazine, at that time perhaps *Playboy's* nearest competitor, and twice since in the pages of *Famous Monsters* magazine. The author, Robert Bloch, introduced himself in these words:

Horror is my business.

The insurance agent peddles protection and security—I sell terror and dread. The doctor guards your heart; I devote my professional skill to inducing failure in same. Some people live by their wits; I live by scaring you out of yours.

For the past 27 years [now 46] I've been a professional writer of horror fiction for magazines, books, radio and TV shows. And when I'm not creating nightmares of my own, I spend my spare time investigating the nightmares of other people—namely the so-called "horror" movies being foisted off on the public via TV and theater screens.

ROUND-EYED CHILDREN clutching "monster" magazines and long-haired aesthetes who haunt half-filled art theaters and attempt to endow silent films made to entertain with the perfumed odor of artistic triumph—are they the only ones who still remember Lon Chaney?

True, matronly barflies and grizzled freighthandlers with calloused hands and rheumy eyes sometimes grow reflective when the TV breaks down—and then the conversation turns to Saturday matinees when kids screamed at Elmo Lincoln rassling lions; when young girls gasped at Louise Glaum wrapped in a leopard skin—and then, with an unholy awe, they talk about Lon Chaney.

A book might be (and has been) written about the twisted hunchbacks, the sinister chinamen, the bugeyed vampires and the legless freaks with which Chaney frightened a generation—but such a book ignores the mild-mannered song-and-dance man whose life and career spanned the entire infancy of the movies and whose death injected the final tocsin of doom into those golden days when a night at the show was an adventure.

April 1, 1883. Colorado Springs, Colorado. The west is still wild. Wyatt Earp is free-wheeling in Tombstone. Dirt roads and horses-and-buggies. And Emma Ken-

LON'S LIFE AND FILMS

by Eldon K. Everett and Roman Soldier

nedy, in Colorado Springs, is the mother of two daughters and a son. They are all deaf-mutes.

Grandma Kennedy, a woman of unfailing spirit, has formed the Deaf and Blind Institute of Colorado, born of her own misfortune. Her assistant is a young man named Hugh Herbert, who edits the institute's paper the *Colorado Deaf and Blind Index*. Her eldest daughter marries Herbert. The youngest daughter marries a mute barber named Chaney. The union is blessed with four children: John, Lon, George and Caroline. Lon was born on April 1, 1883. Like the other children, he is normal.

One day, when Lon was in the 4th grade at Lincoln School, he returned home to find his mother on the floor, completely paralyzed, struck down by inflammatory rheumatism. His brother John had already quit school to go to work and, now, confronted by this new tragedy, Lon also left school and went to work in a bakery.

It was a close-knit family and, even with the handicaps, they seem to have been happy. Lon worked in the bakery for four years, then, at 13, he left Colorado Springs to act as a guide on Pike's Peak. Returning home at the end of the Summer of 1899, he found that his brother John had been hired as the manager of the Colorado Grand Opera House.

Lon went to work in the theater as a prop boy and later recalled seeing such luminaries as Richard Mansfield (in his famous *Dr. Jekyll and Mr. Hyde* role, one wonders?), Lew Dockstader and Nat C. Goodwin in the touring companies that passed through Colorado Springs that year.

Things slacked off during the winter, so Lon became a call-boy at a mining exchange, then went into drapery and carpet-laying, decorating the Antlers Hotel, which many years later displayed a placard in the fading lobby announcing that the threadbare hangings had been erected by movie star Lon Chaney.

Chaney apparently possessed quite an aptitude for the trade, leaving Colorado Springs to work for three years in Denver for the drapery house of Cordtez and-Feldhauser; but the addiction to greasepaint lured him back. His brother John sent for him, offering him a role in the comic opera *Said Pasha*, being staged in Colorado City, and Lon came back home.

The show was so successful that they followed it with *The Mikado* and John got

23

Unknown films, unknown date

backing to take the company on the road with *Fra Diavolo*. Lon played comedy leads. Business committments kept John in Colorado City, so we find Lon Chaney, at 18, on the road managing a show troop for $12 a week.

Young Chaney was something less than a success as a theatrical entrepreneur, and after a short time Holmes bought the company from the Chaneys, keeping Lon on as an actor. Things improved and the company toured the Indian Territory, Kansas, Missouri, Nebraska, the Dakotas, Minnesota, Arkansas and Texas.

The company traveled in its own leased caboose car with a woodstove. Bookings began to fall off and they spent a hungry Christmas 1903 stranded in Florida. A few more bookings got them north again but the company finally folded in Chicago.

Lon was able to join the company of a show called *The Cowpuncher* as second comedian for $14 a week but shortly after going off with it the understudy for the leading lady somehow managed to shoot him in the hand when a prop gun got loaded with live shells and 1905 found him on the road with a touring company of *The Beggar Prince*.

In Champaign, Ill., the company's prima donna came down with laryngitis and the manager ran in a local girl (his wife's sister). The girl was a pretty blond named Myrtle Steadman, who several years hence was to become a picture star for Selig.

Again Lon was stranded with a company that busted—this time in Columbus, S.C.—but William Craston, the Canadian impresario, wired them fare to book them through Canada to Vancouver, B.C. They played a repertoire that included *The Royal Chef* and *A Knight For a Day* but the company busted again in Canada and Lon landed back in Chicago.

The next company Chaney joined featured a pretty young ingenue named Cleva Creighton. They were married during the tour and some months later, in Oklahoma City, Lon Chaney's only child arrived prematurely. It was February and they were living in a rickety cabin on the shores of freezing Belle Isle Lake.

The company moved on to its next date and Lon got a job as a carpetlayer. Somehow they got enough money together to get back to Chicago. The baby, Creighton Tull Chaney (Lon Chaney Jr.), recalled that during those early days he often slept backstage in a cotton-lined box with holes punched in the lid.

Things were rough in Chicago. Sometimes Lon could get work as a stagehand but most of the time he had to rely on the generosity of an old theatrical friend who was playing piano in a saloon. Lon would bum a nickel for a beer, eat a sandwich from the free lunch and then smuggle enough out in his pockets to take home to his wife.

Lon Jr. recalled a Christmas Eve during this period: "Dad put most of his precious 25¢ into the gas meter. Then he started out for the free lunch. Then he did his dance and picked up small change. Meanwhile he filled his overcoat pockets with pretzels and sandwiches. Do you know what else he did when we got home? After I was asleep, he went out, broke a limb off a park tree, fixed it in a box in our room and spent the whole night making tree decorations out of a roll of red crepe paper he had bought for a few pennies. He told me afterwards he made the paste out of cold baked potato and water."

Finally they got a break. Lon was signed as stage manager with the touring company of *The Girl in the Kimono*. The second comedian was Lee Moran, remembered for his many silent film comedies. Together, they worked their way to the West Coast.

His brother John had also stayed in the business and at this time was managing a theater in Los Angeles. Through his brother's recommendation, Lon (who divorced but still had the baby boy with him) went to work in the Olympic Theater on Main Street—seven shows a day, seven days a week, for $35 a week.

Newsman Harry Carr, who knew him well, later recalled: "Behind the scenes was an assistant stage director who was something of a genius at makeup. His job was to see that the scenery was ready, the girls were ready and they had their tights on straight. This was Lon Chaney, later the movie star. To his last day, he never changed. His best friends as a movie star were the ham actors who had been with him in Pop Fisher's stock house. When any of them came to his parties in evening dress, he tore off their shirts and gave them bathrobes in which to dine!"

After six months he went across the street to the Grand Opera House Co., with lead comedians Roscoe (Fatty) Arbuckle and Robert Z. Leonard. Lon played Germans, Jewish comics, chinamen and everything—five characters on one bill.

He was so successful here that he was signed by Kolb and Dill as stage manager for *The Rich Mr. Heggenheimer* and took the show on the road. In San Francisco he staged *45 Minutes from Broadway* for the Alcazar Stock Co., starring Bert Lytell (later a film actor); then took over the Savoy Theater for Kolb and Dill.

This was late in 1910 and Lon was playing in *Hoity-Toity*, a musical comedy, in a temporary theater that had been erected after the earthquake. Clarence A. Locan, who met him during the run, recalled that he used to heat the baby's milk over the same little alcohol stove he used backstage to melt his greasepaint.

His best friend at this time was Clinton Lyle, and together they were sparking two of the girls in the show, Hazel Hastings Bennett and Flo Emerson. They each married one of them, too—Lon tying the knot with pretty dark-haired Hazel in 1912.

With a new wife to support, Lon began looking for work and returned to Los Angeles. Lee Moran (of *The Girl in the Kimono*) was now working at IMP (Universal) making one-reel comedies in a ramshackle building behind a horse corral at Sunset and Gower.

Lon went to work in the Joker comedies in 1912 for $3 a day, working with Moran, Louise Fazenda, Max Asher and Gale Henry. Some days he worked and some days he didn't. Finally, in 1913, he got his first picture credit, in a forgotten opus called *Poor Jake's Demise*.

The first dramatic role Chaney was ever able to recall was a picture in 1913 called *The Bloodhound of the North*, in which he played a mountie. He once recalled: "I alternated between comedies and one-reel westerns at Universal. We slapped pictures together in two days to a week. I must have been in at least 100. Only a few names stick. I remember a Joker comedy called *Back to Life* and another called *Red Margaret*, [RED MARGARET MOONSHINER]. I was a moonshiner hidden among the rocks in that one. The chief thing for me was that I got $3 checks daily."

It was on 4 March 1914 that Joseph de Grasse was hired to head the Universal Victor Co. with J. Warren Kerrigan. De Grasse had directed films for Lubin and Pathe in the east, and apparently Chaney joined the company almost immediately.

In June he is listed as the author of a film called THE TRAGEDY OF WHISPERING CREEK, released on the U's Bison program; then went on to play a Mexican bandit in a western called HER GRAVE MISTAKE, a Nestor release, in July.

Kerrigan was transferred to another Universal Company and de Grasse began production for the Rex company with THE GIRL WHO WAS AFRAID OF LOVE. Pauline Bush was the leading lady and although Chaney wasn't credited he almost certainly worked on the film.

It was in July 1914 that—hot on the heels of THE PERILS OF PAULINE and THE ADVENTURES OF KATHLYN—Universal began production of a now-forgotten serial called THE ADVENTURES OF FRANCOIS VILLON. Directed by Charles Giblyn, this historical spectacle was based on a series of stories by George Bronson Howard being published simultaneously in a fiction magazine.

A full-scale replica of the Bastille was built at the then-under-construction Universal City and a cast of several hundred extras was used in the lavish production. The first episode was a three-reeler called THE OUBLIETTE, directed by Giblyn, with Lon Chaney as Bertrand de la Payne.

The second episode, THE HIGHER LAW, continued with Chaney in the same role but he was absent from the two final episodes—THE 90 BLACK BOXES and MONSIEUR BLUEBEARD (two reels) because "Uncle" Carl Laemmle had decided to use the expensive sets for another film. (After the first four episodes the serial was discontinued. Audiences preferred the slam-bang action of the U's Grace Cunard-Francis Ford episodes to the historical experiment.)

The new epic was a four-reeler called RICHELIEU, directed by Allan Dwan, using the same sets and costumes. It was quite a landmark for September of 1914 and featured Lon Chaney as Barados.

Following the historical craze, Lon and his associates returned to de Grasse's Rex company, and that same month saw Lon's first favorable review: "Never have Pauline Bush and Lon Chaney been seen to better advantage than in HER ESCAPE, the most recent of Joseph de Grasse's productions, written especially for the Rex company cast by Mr. Chaney, who plays the role of heavy lead. Laura Oakley, as 'The Salvation Army Girl', is worthy of particular mention."

They began to knock them out at the rate of one a week, and what remarkable films they were! VIRTUE ITS OWN REWARD was a drama in a garment factory with Lon and Pauline, followed by THE PIPES O' PAN (Joseph King was an artist in this one, Lon the heavy)—"the model's abbreviated attire will undoubtedly raise the old question of just what constitutes art in such matters. This will shock some observers," said a reviewer.

Then came LIGHTS AND SHADOWS, a drama about a theatrical boarding-house, with Chaney and Bush (Critic: "This offering is peculiar in construction and, while not uninteresting, contains much of a semi-morbid character"). And the week after brought a peculiar fantasy called THE STAR OF THE SEA. Lon played the hero, a rough fisherman. A widow poses in the altogether for a statue of the Madonna, and in an unforgettable sequence, her lover (Lon) tries to smash the statue. Miraculously, the eyes of the statue open and a tear trickles down the face. Lon, converted, clasps the widow in his arms, and all is forgiven.

Then, in December, came THE LION, THE LAMB, AND THE MAN, in which Pauline and Lon were two sides of a modern triangle, and there was a flashback to prehistoric times, where all three of them skulked around in caveman makeup.

1915 started off with Bush, Chaney and Dowlin in THE SIN OF OLGA BRANDT, MEASURE OF A MAN (a Mountie picture), and SUCH IS LIFE. Review of the latter: "This story, located in a theatrical boarding-house, is so interesting the observer wishes there was another reel. All the types are good: the slavey, the burlesque man, the matinee idol and the girl looking for her first engagement. The entire cast is pleasing..."

The same cast went into WHERE THE FOREST ENDS (along with a rare appearance by director de Grasse as an actor) and the nameless critic of the *World* said: "The girl dresses in wild grapevines and dances over the hills. The artist lures her to the city but when her moral awakening comes, she flees back to the mountains."

Following the formal opening of Universal City on 3/3/1915, Lon went into MAID OF THE MIST; then a slum story, GIRL OF THE NIGHT (Lon was the hero for a change); and AN IDYLL OF THE HILLS (about some moonshiners. Critic said: "Lon Chaney does a good piece of character work in this one").

On the strength of his work with the Rex Co., Lon was now promoted to director of the Victor Co., starring the U's resident matinee idol J. Warren Kerrigan. (Kerrigan's twin brother, Victor Kerrigan, was head of the Universal ranch.) Kerrigan had just flexed his muscles in a multiple reel epic called SAMSON, that was cleaning up, and this was quite a step up for Lon.

In June 1915 he directed Kerrigan in a costume epic called IN THE SERVICE OF THE KING. He also directed himself in a one-reeler called THE PEDDLER, from a scenario by Milton M. Moore, who worked on the lot in the special effects department.

Lon was unhappy directing Kerrigan, and the front office was unhappy with the one-reeler, declining to release it. The next Kerrigan epic was THE OYSTER DREDGER, for which Lon also wrote the scenario (at $25 per reel).

He directed for Kerrigan for six months and during this time also worked all over the lot. In later years he was to recall working in a couple of Jeannie MacPherson films but couldn't recall the titles. His name doesn't appear in the credits of any of these pictures but he stated later that he played a hunchback for the first time in one of them and that they were the most rewarding parts he had played up to that time.

He was building quite a reputation and on 19 June 1915 he and Pauline Bush were leading the Grand Parade at the Static Flasher's Ball. Among other films he made during this period were STEADY COMPANY, a slum story with Pauline; THE TRUST, in which he played a burglar; and BOUND ON THE WHEEL, described as "Life in a poor factory district."

The Chaney boy, Creighton (Lon Jr.), was being sent to school by this time. He recalled, years later, sitting on the wooden bench at Hollywood and Vine during vacations, waiting for the studio buses to come and pick them up to take them to the lot. During those summers of the 'teens, the boy would hitchhike up to Bakersfield Calif., and pick 'cots for 3¢ a basket to earn his spending money.

In July 1915 de Grasse took the Rex Co. up to Fallow's Camp in San Gabriel canyon. The company now consisted of Cleo Madison, Arthur Shirley and Lon Chaney. They made MOUNTAIN JUSTICE, QUITS, THE PINE'S REVENGE (forest rangers), THE SHERIFF OF LONG BUTTE and then climbed to the 7000 foot level in Bear Valley to make THE KING'S KEEPER.

They came down out of the mountains and rounded out the year with a Graustarkian romance: THE FASCINATION OF THE FLEUR DE LYS, and a couple of undistinguished films called ALAS AND ALACK and A MOTHER'S ATONEMENT.

It was at the beginning of 1916 that the Universal program was reorganized. At that time there were seven or eight U releases a week—a Rex, a Joker, a Nestor, a Bison, a Gold Seal, a Victor, etc. The new policy called for the addition of a couple of feature-length (five-reel) big budget "Bluebirds", to help sell the one- and two-reelers to exhibitors.

1914, title unidentified

1914, title unidentified

1915, THE RESCUE

1915, unidentified

1915, unidentified

1915, unidentified

1915, problem picture: I have two copies of this still. On the back of one someone has written at some time FATHER OF THE BOYS and on the back of the other, THE PRICE OF SILENCE. In other PRICE OF SILENCE photos he has a mustache; in this picture he does not. Not necessarily proving anything, as he could have a mustache in part of THE PRICE OF SILENCE and a clean-shaven upper lip in the other. However, in this case I'll opt for the photo being from FATHER OF THE BOYS. (Elsewhere it's recorded as FATHER *AND* THE BOYS!)

De Grasse and his wife, scenario-writer Ida Mae Park, were selected to make the Bluebirds, and they chose as their star Louise Lovely, a beautiful blond girl from Sydney, Australia, whose real name was Louise Carbasse.

Chaney was assigned to the Bluebird company at the magnificent sum of $100 a week. The Bluebirds were made exclusively at Universal City and Lon was to learn his trade inside out in his years at the U.

The first Bluebird, early in 1916, was THE GRIP OF JEALOUSY, a drama of the old south with Chaney as a brutal slave-driver. This was followed by THE GRASP OF GREED, based on H. Rider Haggard's *Mr. Meeson's Will*. This was one helluva picture with a buried treasure on a desert isle, and the map tattooed on Louise's fair white back.

Next was DOLLY'S SCOOP, a crime drama called THE GILDED SPIDER, and then Louise was replaced by a little dark-haired actress named Dorothy

1916, THE PRICE OF SILENCE

1915, FATHER OF THE BOYS (?)

1916, THE GIRL IN THE CHECKERED COAT. (Chaney: inebriated man in top hat).

1916, TANGLED HEARTS

1916, THE PRICE OF SILENCE

1917, DANGER—GO SLOW.

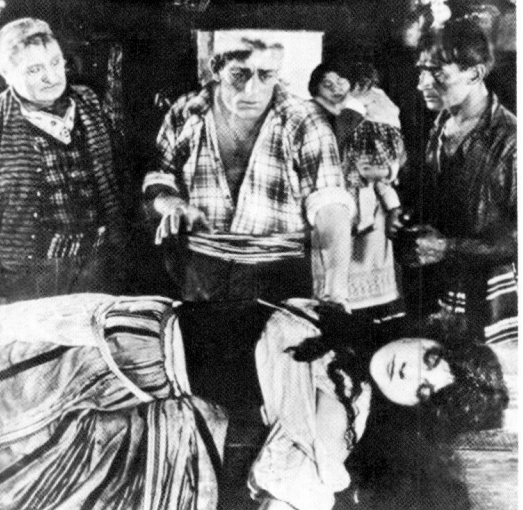

1917, THE GILDED SPIDER

1917, THE GILDED SPIDER

Phillips. In July 1916 de Grasse made IF MY COUNTRY SHOULD CALL, then went up to Bear Valley to make PLACE BEYOND THE WINDS, THE PRICE OF SILENCE, THE PIPER'S PRICE, THE WRONG SIDE OF PARADISE and then, in 1917 HELL MORGAN'S GIRL, a spectacular reenactment of the Barbary Coast and the San Francisco Earthquake, all with Chaney.

De Grasse's wife, Ida Mae Park, directed them in THE FIRES OF REBELLION, THE FLASHLIGHT GIRL and an adaptation of Ibsen's DOLL HOUSE. Chaney made a one-reeler called THE MASK OF LOVE with Pauline Bush, then went on to make THE GIRL IN THE CHECKERED COAT, THE RESCUE and BONDAGE, all Bluebirds.

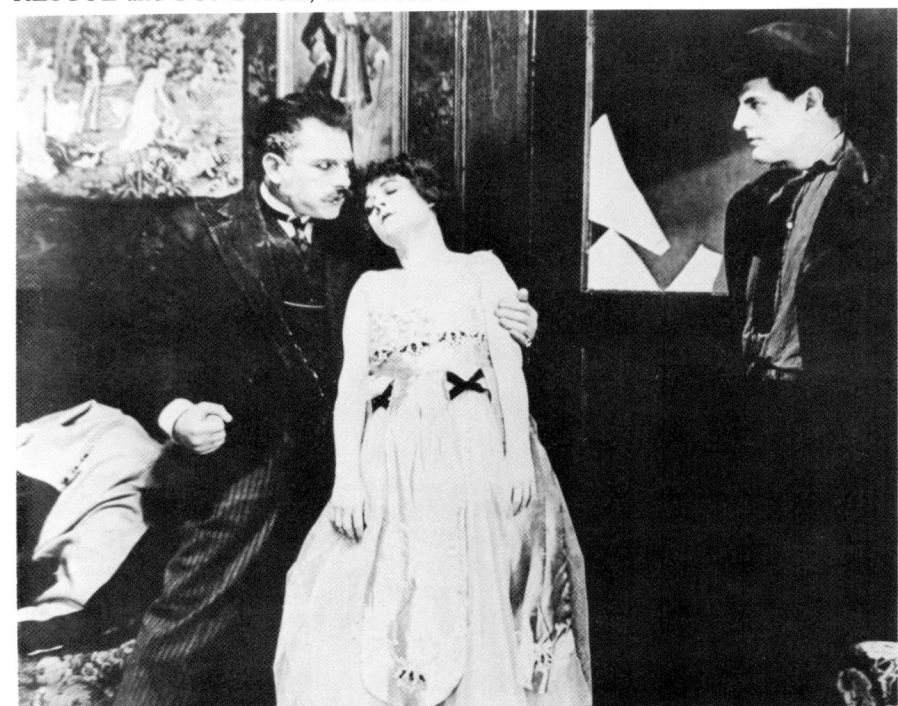

1917, FIRES OF REBELLION

1917, THE GIRL IN THE CHECKERED COAT

Chaney was working steadily but the parts got smaller and more uninteresting. Finally he went to the studio manager and demanded a raise to $125 a week. All he got was a suspension. He went back to the Bluebirds and made TRIUMPH but de Grasse got transferred to the Franklyn Farnum Co. and Dorothy Phillips went on a vacation.

In September 1917 he was working the lot again. He was in THE MAVERICK, then in a western called PAY ME!; ANYTHING ONCE; then a two-reel western called THE EMPTY GUN, directed by de Grasse.

In THE BOSS OF POWDERVILLE he was an old restaurant keeper; in THE SCARLET CAR, a bank cashier; in December 1917, after BROADWAY LOVE and THE GIRL WHO DARED, Chaney again demanded a raise and went on suspension.

By March 1918 he was back at Universal again, chastened and unhappy. He made MY PARISIAN DARLING with Carmel Myers for de Grasse, then went into FAST COMPANY. After a North Woods drama called THAT DEVIL, BATEESE, he left the U again.

His first outside venture, early in the year, had been a propaganda film called THE KAISER—BEAST OF BERLIN, a classic of its type produced by and starring Rupert Julian, for Renowned; but this was backed by Uncle Carl, and Lon probably got the role through the Universal's office. (Also in the cast were Nigel de Brulier and Elmo "Tarzan" Lincoln).

In July 1918 he took an engagement with Triangle and played the leader of a gang of outlaws in William S. Hart's RIDDLE GAWNE. It was an undistinguished part but Chaney always credited it with being the foundation of his later career in films.

For a few months Chaney survived by being hired by friends. Dorothy Phillips put him in THE TALK OF THE TOWN; then came DANGER—GO SLOW with Mae Murray, directed by Robert Z. Leonard, who had been in vaudeville with Lon and Fatty Arbuckle years before.

Then he got a break. He went into THE WICKED DARLING, a crime melodrama Tod Browning was making at the U in late 1918. Browning, who was later to be known almost exclusively as "Chaney's director", had been acting for

1917, Unknown

1918, THE KAISER, "THE BEAST OF BERLIN"

HELL MORGAN'S GIRL

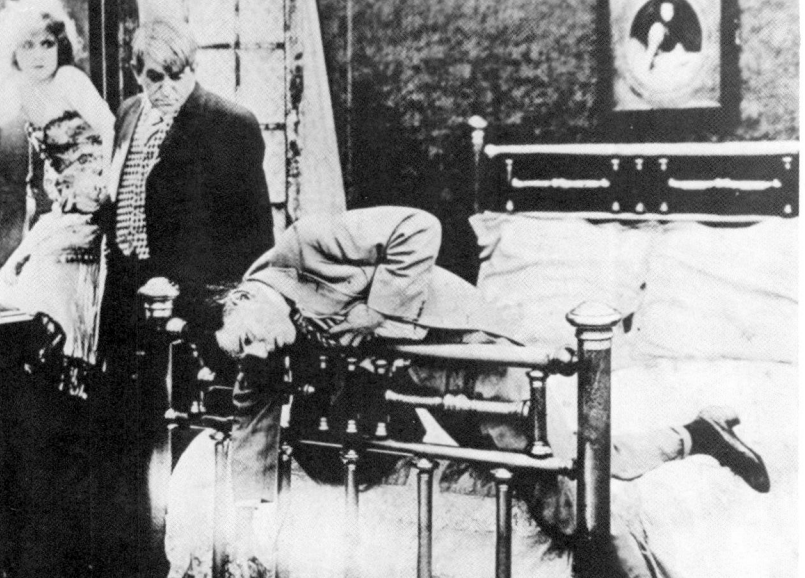

1917, Unknown

about six years, including a bit as "The Racing Car Owner" in INTOLERANCE.

Of THE WICKED DARLING a reviewer said: "The entire cast cooperates with some of the best character work shown on the screen in a long time; Lon Chaney as 'Stoop' and Spottiswoode Aitken as 'Uncle Fadem' being especially good."

In January 1919 Chaney went into THE FALSE FACES at Paramount. Based on a Louis Joseph Vance story, this had the Lone Wolf (H.B. Walthal) working for the British Intelligence Service. Lon played Eckstrom, the German superspy who had been Michael Lanyard's arch-enemy even before the war.

Following this, Maurice Tourneur formed a company to make "prestige" pictures, with a resident company including Jack Holt, Wallace Beery, Seena Owen, Bull Montana and Lon Chaney. Chaney played character parts in Joseph Conrad's VICTORY and TREASURE ISLAND, filmed at Tourneur's studio in Culver City, then left to rejoin Dorothy Phillips at the U for a melodrama called PAID IN ADVANCE.

Things were beginning to break for him. In June 1919 he made a western about the California gold rush for an independent studio, Robertson-Cole. This was A MAN'S COUNTRY, with Alma Rubins, and Chaney played a gambler named "3-Card Duncan".

1918, RIDDLE GAWNE

It was in July and August of 1919 that Lon Chaney's screen career may properly be said to have begun. With more than 100 pictures already behind him, he heard of the problems that George Loane Tucker was having casting a character part for a new film, and Lon decided to go after it.

Tucker was the fair-haired genius of the silent pictures; the original phototype of Irving Thalberg, one might say. Like the later Thalberg, he died young and left a legend behind him. He had joined the Universal staff in 1913 and early showed a remarkable talent for both directing and administration. He produced the infamous TRAFFIC IN SOULS, the first important "white slave" film, and while it made a great deal of money, the stink that it stirred up resulted in its being banned in many cities. Tucker was "exiled" to England. When he returned to America after the war, he started casting a story by detective writer Frank L. Packard. It was called THE MIRACLE MAN.

The story was an unusual one, revolving around a gang of crooks who convince an evangelist that he has the power to heal with his hands, and then proceed to milk

1918, RIDDLE GAWNE

the suckers who came for the cure. Thomas Meighan and Betty Compson had been cast as the leads but the most difficult role was still open.

This was the part of "Frog", one of the crooks who posed as an amputee but who was really just a contortionist. Tucker had been testing professional acrobats and circus freaks, all without success. Chaney later recalled that he practiced for almost two weeks, with his legs strapped up behind his knees, before getting a test with Tucker.

The rest is history. Chaney got the part and the critics ignored the fine performances of the rest of the cast to marvel at Lon's incredible characterization.

Within weeks, he was one of the most sought-after character actors in the industry. Early in January 1920, when heavyweight champ Jack Dempsey arrived in L.A. to make the Pathe serial DAREDEVIL JACK, A.H. Giebler visited the Brunton studios. Chaney, who was a lifetime fight fan, was there shooting the bull with

1918, THE WICKED DARLING

1918, THE WICKED DARLING

1918, RIDDLE GAWNE

1919, THE FALSE FACES

Dempsey, and Giebler spent more time interviewing Chaney than he did the Champ.

In February, Lon was signed by Goldwyn to make THE PENALTY. He had drawn $125 a week on THE MIRACLE MAN and was now drawing $500 a week with Goldwyn, only to discover later that production head Abe Lehr had been willing to go as high as $1500.

Reporter Giebler visited the set in March. "I watched Wallace Worsley making THE PENALTY by Gouverneur Morris, and the Gouverneur was right there on the set to see how it was done. THE PENALTY is the play in which Lon Chaney has a legless part. Lon is 'Blizzard', a wicked old devil who is a newspaper vendor on a street corner in the daytime and a king of the underworld and power in crooked politics at night."

The role offered plenty of scope for characterization. Blizzard was cured of his insanity by a blood-clot operation at the end of the film but was shot and died with great gusto. In a final scene, Lon appeared smiling, showing the audience he really *did* have legs of his own.

Photoplay commented: "Lon Chaney...(as a)...legless wonder, bending his legs back at the knees and strapping them against his thighs. You can see the strap arrangement, and you know that the long coat conceals his feet, but you are extremely interested in watching him try to fool you....rope-ladders hang below peek-hole windows that the legless one may climb up like a misbegotten spider to take a look around."

Lon next went into an independent, THE GIFT SUPREME by *"Scientifiction"* Pioneer George Allen England, for Macaulay Photoplays, playing a bit, then, in July 1920, he went to Tod Browning's OUTSIDE THE LAW, with Priscilla Dean and Wheeler Oakman.

Browning wrote the scenario of this crime Meller but although Lon only received third billing, the picture was designed as a vehicle for the makeup talents he was beginning to display. He played two parts: one was the heavy, "Black Mike Sylva",

TREASURE ISLAND (1920)

and the other was a villainous chinaman, "Ah Wing". In a double exposure at the end, Lon (as Sylva) shot "himself" (the chinaman).

Before this film went into release, Lon completed NOMADS OF THE NORTH for First National. This was a James Oliver Curwood story with Betty Blythe and Lewis Stone; Lon played the hero, Raould Challoner, in one of the few "straight" roles he was to enjoy from there on in.

In July 1921, George Loane Tucker died. The funeral was held on a Sunday, with an orchestra playing Tschaikowsky's "Pathetique" and Beethoven's Fifth Symphony in the background. The first and last reels of THE MIRACLE MAN were shown, and Lon Chaney and Joseph Dowling, from the picture's cast, gave short tributes to the deceased. Also present were Mary and Jack Pickford, Douglas Fairbanks and Robert Brunton.

Chaney signed with Universal in September 1921, to receive star billing in a series of Universal Jewel productions. Robert Thornby was assigned to direct the first of these films, a picture known variously as WOLFBREED, THE MASK and THE TRAP.

Whether Chaney was out to get his own back on the U or just wanted too much control is difficult to say. The film began with Grace Darmond, who was then replaced by Dagmar Godowsky. The original script was by Lucien Hubbard* but after a couple of weeks of production, Chaney refused to go ahead with the picture, and through the intervention of studio manager Irving Thalberg, he wrote a new script himself that he liked better.

The final product was released almost a year later as THE TRAP, costarring Alan Hale, with Lon as the hero in an adventure yarn of the northwoods. Needless to say, with audiences panting to see Chaney as various assorted freaks, it was hardly a howling success. It was the only picture he made under his Universal-Jewel contract.

His next film was BITS OF LIFE for First National. This was a four-part film directed by Marshall (Mickey) Neilan as an experiment. Each of the four stories had a different cast and Lon appeared in the section called HOP, as a chinaman who nearly kills his wife (Anna May Wong) because she presents him with a baby girl instead of a boy.

A month later he was back at Goldwyn, with Worsley again directing him in another Gouverneur Morris story, ACE OF HEARTS. Lon was the leader of a gang of Bolsheviks who got noble and blew himself and his cohorts up at the end of the picture to save the girl, Leatrice Joy.

Goldwyn then gave him a bit part as a gambler in a scenario by Perley Poore Sheehan called FOR THOSE WE LOVE, with Betty Compson, and Lon then took off to spend Christmas 1921 in New York City.

He returned to California to complete THE NIGHT ROSE for Goldwyn. This was pretty strong stuff—so strong, in fact, that the film was banned in its entirety by the New York State censor Board and wasn't shown anywhere in that state.

It was a seamy crime melodrama, with Leatrice Joy and Cullen Landis, and the loss of revenue from New York state hurt it badly. Exhibitors elsewhere were advised: "Play up Chaney and make it clear just what the picture is, since the title is so deceptive. Always link 'Underworld' with the title announcement."

On loan from Goldwyn, Chaney next went into FIRES OF VENGEANCE (FLESH AND BLOOD), being produced at Universal City for young Sol Lesser's Western Pictures Exploitation Co. Jack Mulhall and Noah Beery assisted as Lon played the hero—who was also an ex-convict who had escaped and was hiding in San Francisco's Chinatown.

Chaney was by now receiving top billing on his pictures but he still found time to wander idly around town, studying "types", and he never missed the Friday night

---

*Hubbard later scripted and directed Jules Verne's part-talking two-color MYSTERIOUS ISLAND of 1929.

fights at Hollywood Legion Stadium for over ten years. He regularly had a reserved second row seat, and Leo Guild recalled: "One night a new sports announcer introduced him from ringside. He was mobbed and bothered for autographs all during the fights. The next week he had his seat changed and wore a disguise. He was safe again for several years!"

In September 1922 he signed the contract with Universal for THE HUNCHBACK OF NOTRE DAME, then went on in the meantime to make several other films, beginning with QUINCY ADAMS SAWYER for Goldwyn. Lon played the heavy in this all-star comedy in which he costarred with Louise Fazenda, Hank Mann, Elmo Lincoln, Blanche Sweet and Barbara La Marr.

Next came THE LIGHT IN THE DARK for First National, a peculiar film that was lensed in an early *color* process. It was a vehicle for Hope Hampton, with E.K. Lincoln as the hero and Lon as a crook. Lincoln (no relation to Elmo) found the Holy Grail in a lost valley in Africa. He brought it back and after such mysterious sequences as a flashback of Launcelot and Elaine, it changed the lives of all the principals.

In October he was filmed for *Pathe Screen Snapshots #10*. This one-reel short showed Doug Fairbanks, Mary Pickford and Charlie Chaplin on the set of the United Artist picture; ads also said, "Lon Chaney is also shown, making up for various types of characters."

He was grinding them out almost as fast as the good old days at Universal. He made OLIVER TWIST for First National, playing Fagin to Jackie Coogan's Oliver; then made SHADOWS for Preferred Pictures—a fascinating crime epic with Lon as chinaman "Yen Sin" and the lovely Marguerite de la Motte as "Sympathy Gibbs".

Then it was back to Goldwyn for A BLIND BARGAIN with Worsley directing. This was one of the earliest of the straight "horror" films, with Chaney in a dual role—that of the villainous mad doctor and his creation, the mute, whimpering apeman.

Rounding out 1922, he made ALL THE BROTHERS WERE VALIANT for Goldwyn, playing the hero's brother in a drama of the sea.

Production on THE HUNCHBACK OF NOTRE DAME began at Universal City in January 1923. Chaney took Wallace Worsley with him, as well as Perley Poore Sheehan, to revise the script. Budgeted initially at $750,000, it literally used a cast of thousands, and the exterior sets for the Cathedral de Notre Dame were said to be the largest built for a picture since Griffith's INTOLERANCE.

Carrying around 20 pounds of makeup on his face, wearing a rubber suit and strapping himself all over with wires to play the deformed Quasimodo, Lon created a character that no one who ever saw could forget.

During the nearly six months he worked on this film, others that he had ground out during 1922 kept appearing. Hodkinson released WHILE PARIS SLEEPS, an unpleasant film directed by Maurice Tourneur, who had had Chaney under contract in 1919 but had done nothing about it. Much of the action took place in a waxworks, with Chaney chasing the heroine all over the landscape. Lon was a demented artist who tortured his subjects with electric shocks.

Then there was a drama called THE SHOCK, with Virginia Valli, and Chaney was a crippled crook again—this time in a story about the San Francisco Earthquake.

In September, Lon traveled with the film to New York, where THE HUNCHBACK OF NOTRE DAME was premiered at the Astor Theater. A throng of usherettes in 17th Century high-pointed caps and laces showed patrons to their seats in a theater hung with tapestries, setting the mood of the picture.

How did they like it? "An outburst which did not lessen until Lon Chaney, the star, had been half-pushed, half-dragged onto the stage that he might stutter his thanks in the din of hundreds voicing their approbation!"

"Lon Chaney, the star!" He had come a long way. He returned to Los Angeles a star of the first magnitude. He made an undistinguished Spanish love story for Para-

1923, WHILE PARIS SLEEPS

mount, THE NEXT CORNER, with Dorothy Mackail and Ricardo Cortez, and then signed with Universal for THE PHANTOM OF THE OPERA.

Chaney's parents had by now moved to Los Angeles and the boy had been sent to live with his grandparents. At 16, Creighton Chaney was attending Hollywood High School with Fay Wray and Joel McCrea. He was six feet tall and weighed 225 pounds. He was turned down by the football team but was then invited by some of the other students to come with them to the studios and work as an extra on weekends to pick up a little extra money.

When Creighton broached the subject to his father, Lon went right through the roof. Not only did he dislike the idea of his son becoming an actor, he went so far as to transfer the boy from Hollywood High to a business school. Chaney Jr. recalled: "His ideal of someone to look up to was the head teller of a bank. He wanted me to become someone like that. So I went to business college, graduated and got a job with the General Hot Water Heater Corporation."

Chaney spent the greater part of 1924 working on THE PHANTOM OF THE OPERA. The film itself turned out to be unsatisfactory and what success it had it owed to Chaney and his reputation alone. The production went on and on. Lon's father was dying during the production and Lon was refused time off to attend the sickbed. Most of his time between shots was spent on the phone checking his father's condition.

Then he had a fight with the director, Rupert Julian, and refused to speak to him during the last few weeks of filming. All communications between the two were carried out back and forth by cameraman Charles van Enger.

Portions of the film were shot in the primitive red-and-blue Technicolor process, then scrapped. A whole episode with Chaney as Erik drowning in an underground lake was filmed and then discarded. Mob scenes with several hundred extras storming the phantom's lair were shot and then discarded. The entire love interest story was changed with Norman Kerry introduced in some scenes as Mary Philbin's suitor.

Carl Laemmle saw the rough cut and disliked the whole film. He ordered in a new director, Edward Sedgewick, and Sedgewick contributed such things as a bunch of comedy sequences with Chester Conklin. It was almost a year after production started that the film was finally released, and whatever the critics said, it did a land office business.

1925 and 1926 brought a long succession of peculiar roles. Greta Garbo had just arrived from Sweden with her director, Victor Seastrom, who directed Chaney in HE WHO GETS SLAPPED, an old Pagliacci story with Lon as the clown, and a cast that included Norma Shearer, John Gilbert and the 14-year-old Loretta Young.

Then came THE MONSTER for Metro and he was teamed again with director Tod Browning. They made THE UNHOLY THREE, with Chaney playing the ventriloquist Prof. Echo, and doubling as a nice little old lady who led a gang of circus freaks including Harry Earles (a midget) and Victor McLaglen.

Lon made TOWER OF LIES for Metro, then rejoined Browning for THE BLACKBIRD, a crime drama in which he played both a crook and another of his amputee roles; and together they proceeded to THE ROAD TO MANDALAY, in which Lon played a bald heavy with a cataract in one eye (he stuck egg-white inside his eyelid for that one).

Chaney and Browning next began a picture called THE UNKNOWN. Lon's costar was a young actress named Joan Crawford. Joan has recalled: "Here was the most tense, exciting individual I'd ever met, a man mesmerized into his part. Between pictures when you met him on the lot you saw a grave mild-mannered man with laughing black eyes who seldom laughed, but when he did, his laughter was irresistible. When he worked it was as if God were working, he had such intense concentration.

"It was then I became aware for the firsttime of the difference between standing in front of a camera and acting. Lon Chaney's concentration, the complete absorbtion he gave to his character, filled all of us with such awe we never even considered addressing him with the usual pleasantries until he became aware of and addressed us.

"He was armless in the picture—his arms strapped to his sides—and he learned to eat, even hold a cigaret, using his feet and toes. He was in a world of his own, a world in which he'd had those arms amputated for the love of a gypsy girl who abhors men's arms.

"And when he returns to the circus, he finds her—me—in the arms of the strong man! He kept them strapped that way for five hours, enduring such numbness, such torture, that when we got to this scene, he was able to convey not just realism but such emotional agony that it was shocking...and fascinating!"

After this film, Clarence A. Locan was talking to him and Lon said: "I can't play these crippled roles any more. The trouble with my spine is worse every time I do one and it's really beginning to bother me!"

He was starting to take things easier. Most of his weekends were spent on camping trips in the Sierra and late in 1926 he took a vacation trip to Seattle with Hazel, traveling incog. While attending a vaudeville show, he was amazed to see "Lyle and Emerson" on the bill. It turned out to be the same Clinton Lyle and Flo Emerson they had known in San Francisco before the movies, and Lon brought them back to Los Angeles.

Chaney would spend his evenings at home, playing Russian Band with Lyle, Eddie Gribbon, M.K. Wilson and his chauffeur, John Jeske. He liked to cook and at various times served up things like raw spinach salad and avocados with caviar.

His greatest avocation, however, was simply walking the streets of Los Angeles, studying people. Dressed in old clothes, wearing horn-rimmed glasses and a dusty cap, he spent long hours in skidrow movie houses, looking for unusual "types".

Browning directed Chaney in LONDON AFTER MIDNIGHT, with Lon as a bulging-eyed vampire, his eyes pushed out by a wire run inside the eye lids; in WEST OF ZANZIBAR (a still exists of Chaney in a "duck" suit, with no arms and legs, in a dream sequence in this film. It was cut before release and Browning later used the makeup for Olga Baclanova in FREAKS); THE BIG CITY (reunited with Betty Compson); and WHERE EAST IS EAST.

In TELL IT TO THE MARINES Chaney scored a great success in a straight role as a tough sergeant in the leathernecks; and in MR. WU he returned to his Chinese characterizations.

During the Summer of 1928, Chaney and his wife went to New York City. It was ostensibly a pleasure trip but Chaney had been suffering from a recurrent throat ailment and he wanted to consult with several specialists.

His hobby was photography and he owned both a Filmo and a Graflex, shooting hundreds of feet a week, having it developed at the MGM labs at Culver City. During the New York trip he met Mayor Jimmy Walker and shot some pictures of him on the City Hall steps. He told a reporter: "The best thing I do is thread my camera on horseback!"

Early in 1929 he and Hazel did a broadcast over KNX in Los Angeles, reminiscing about his early days in pictures. His well-modulated voice made him a natural for the new "talking pictures" but he refused to make a talkie, claiming "They haven't been perfected yet."

In July the studio announced that Lon Chaney was sick for the *firstime* in 17 years. He was no longer able to pose for publicity shots but his $400-a-week salary continued.

Universal tried to get him on loan from MGM that Summer to make a film called THE RETURN OF THE PHANTOM (of the Opera) but MGM refused to loan him out, and cast him in a film called THE BUGLE SOUNDS. The studio wanted to make it his first talkie but he refused. He began the film but was forced to stop by illness. Wallace Beery replaced him and Beery talked. Chaney went to Yellowstone after "pneumonia" and a "tonsil operation".

Another Chaney vehicle, BROTHER OFFICERS, was turned over to Fred

Niblo to make with another star. Chaney protested and came back to begin it—as a silent—under the title SGT. BULL. He also began preparation for filming a Gaston Leroux novel, CHERI-BIBI.

Again illness forced him to quit. Still the company retained him signing him to a new contract for 5 years early in 1930. The contract called for him to receive one million dollars during the first three years.

One often hears that had he lived Chaney would have played FRANKENSTEIN and DRACULA. His exclusive contract with MGM would have rendered that unlikely but he did make one final picture for Browning: THE UNHOLY THREE, his only talkie, a remake of his silent success.

Chaney was feeling better and was back on the lot. He was also having a feud with John Gilbert, whose career was tumbling down with the advent of talkies. Lon brought his wife and some friends down to tour the studio one day and Gilbert had left standing orders not to let *anyone* on the set while he was performing. "What's the matter with Jack?" Lon complained. "He's just doing a job, like any of us!"

Browning began preparing a remake of OUTSIDE THE LAW (it was made with Edward G. Robinson) and Warners tried to get Chaney on a loanout to make a talkie of THE MIRACLE MAN (it was made with Chester Morris and Boris Karloff).

During the Summer of 1930, Lon was in New York again for more throat treatments. He must have known by then that it was cancer but no word of it ever appeared in the press.

In October he went into a hospital in Los Angeles. He woke up one day and listened to the radio for several hours. Then he asked the nurse if it would be alright for him to smoke. She told him he's have to ask the doctor.

He was worried about his voice. He arranged a signal with her that he would use if his voice failed: One finger—I can't talk; two fingers—*bad trouble*.

That night she checked his room and saw that he had one finger raised. "Try to speak!" she urged. "Try to speak!"

Lon Chaney smiled, raised two fingers, then closed is eyes. The Man of a Thousand Faces was dead.

He lies in an unmarked crypt in Forest Lawn in Glendale, Calif. His eulogy was delivered by Col. H.S. Dyar, USMC Chaplain.

His $550,000 estate was left mostly to Hazel. His first wife, Cleva Creighton Bush, received $1. His chauffeur, John Jeske, got $5000, and his surviving brother and a sister, along with his son Creighton, divided the insurance of $275,000.

Hazel married the chauffeur, and the boy, Creighton, changed his name to Lon Chaney Jr. and played heavies in serials during the 30s, joined Lugosi and Strange in following in the famous footsteps of Karloff's Frankenstein monster, created his own niche in the pantheon of horror film classics with his sympathetic characterization of Larry Talbot, the reluctant Wolf Man; made an indelible mark as simple-minded Lenny in the mundane movie OF MICE AND MEN: and received an Ann Radcliff Award from the Count Dracula Society in recognition of his contributions to the horror movie genre. Then, "appropriately", on *Friday the 13th*, 1973, the man who was Kharis the Mummy, Count Alucard, "The Indestructible Man", died of heart failure...ironically contributed to by seven years of fighting cancer of the throat, the same fatal malignancy that finally took its death toll on his legendary father:

LON CHANEY SR.
The Man of A Thousand Faces.

THE UNCANNY MR. CHANEY

By Homer Currie

NO HUMAN FACE can hide any secrets from Lon Chaney.
In mastering the art of theatrical makeup, he has learned what the lines mean—the little telltale lines with which your character is written all over your face.

When the world and his wife walk past Chaney in the street, they might as well have their secret sins and shortcomings printed on a banner.

"I would never trust that man at the next table," said Chaney while we were sitting in a cafe one night at dinner.

"Why not?"

"He is cruel."

"Cruel? Well, he looks genial. He laughs all the time."

"Yes, that's the trouble. I know him by his laugh. I am distrustful of a man who laughs too readily. Especially am I distrustful of a man whose mouth still stays fixed in a grin after he has stopped laughing; and the man who laughs with a noise but does not laugh with his eyes. You can see at once that this man is laughing, not from merriment, but with a purpose."

Another man came by and stopped to speak to us. He was a writer of much ability; but luckless. One of those fellows of whom people say: "Why doesn't he ever get anywhere. You are always expeting him to make a hit but he never really lands."

"That's easy," said Chaney. "The trouble with him is that he needs a manager."

"How do you know?"

"Well," said Chaney, "let's look him over. He has large and rather gentle eyes; from that I know he has sympathy and kindliness.

"At the corner of his eyes—the outside corner—he has a little full place—almost a lump. If the eyes are level, and not too far apart, I have always found that this signifies great human sympathy. If the eyes are too far apart, or if they slant, this lump is very likely to denote deceitfulness.

"You will notice that this man has a slight impediment in his speech—a wavering of his words: also that he chops off his words as though he were clipping cheese with a knife. From that I know that he is very irritable; and that his thoughts pour out faster than he can find words to tell them.

"On the other hand, his jawbone isn't hung right. It looks firm and determined in front, but at the corner where it fastens on, it hasn't the square big hinge that it should have.

"That man has ideas that come in absolute gushes; but he lacks the ability to say

No; and the ruthlessness to make people pay for his ideas. He scatters his stuff around like birdseed on a windy day. His ideas come faster than he can dispose of them."

I mentioned a certain very famous face. Chaney almost shuddered.

"That man has them all fooled," he said. "He is gentle and mild and suave and cultured when you talk to him. To me his face shows a horrible character.

"His large fleshy nose shows a ruthless sex instinct. He has the puffs at the corners of his eyes which are too large. Combined with small eyes that have a distinct slant they indicate deceit. He has a weak chin and a mouth that is simply a slit in his face. Underneath his polished exterior, he is a voracious and ruthless hunter. He is without mercy and without honesty."

"If you had to make up for the character of a thoroughly greedy money-mad man, how would you do it?" I asked.

Mr. Chaney hesitated. "Beyond the fact that I would give him a few straight lines of determination, I don't think I could register this character with makeup," he said. "It is mostly in the manner of acting.

"The man who advertises his greedy and avaricious character, to me, does it with his eyes. They seem to be always hunting for something. I have also noticed that a man avid for money usually has a way of opening his lips when money is mentioned. It is an expression of thirst. I have always noticed, too, that such men have a nervous way of hitching up their chairs closer and closer to the person to whom they are talking when money is mentioned."

I told him that I always thought the great money kings were supposed to have very tight-shut mouths.

"That," he said, "is true. It is true because they are not greedy men. It isn't money they want; it is power. In another age, they would have been knights on horseback swashing around the world with big two-handed swords. Our conditions of life being what they are, they use the weapon they have at hand—money."

Just then there passed a young actress whose future is problematic. I asked him if she would ever get anywhere in the world.

"I am afraid not," he said. "She is a love child—not a determined woman."

"Where does she show it?"

"She has a cute little pug nose; this shows both a sense of humor and a volatile disposition—fond of excitement and joy. She has wide-open, soft dark eyes: that shows she has a very tender, warm heart. She has a kissing mouth, with full, soft, red lips of passion. Her jaw lacks firmness; her long artistic hands indicate a lack of steadfastness."

Mr. Chaney qualified this. "The long hand," he said, "is likely to denote either the occult or the artistic disposition. Unless these instincts are coupled with other hand qualities, they are likely to make anyone a straw blown about in the wind of impressions. Unless an artist has a business man concealed in his character, he is never steadfast."

I asked him how I could know a villain the nexttime I saw one.

"Are there really any villains?" he countered.

"What about Fagin in OLIVER TWIST: you make a great character of that part."

"Fagin wasn't a villain. He was a very warm-hearted man. He loved Oliver Twist with a true and beautiful tenderness. He did all he could for him—according to his own lights—which was to make him a great thief. There is something wistful and beautiful about Fagin.

"He was a man of strong character too. He ruled Bill Sykes by his superior brain and his salesmanship."

"Salesmanship?"

"Certainly, salesmanship. that was the keynote of his character. He had the ability to convince the brutal Bill Sykes of his superiority; and that is the heart and soul of salesmanship. He made Bill accept his ideas. He sold Bill his superior mind."

"What about Bill Sykes? Wasn't he a villain?"

"He was a man of terrific physical force—used in the wrong way. All the Bill Sykes of this world are not big brutes, however. Some of the men of overpowering brutality are small and weak-looking. The far-famed brutal jaw is not a sign or guide.

"Take, for instance, Bull Montana, who has the roughest face in Hollywood. Bull is a big, tender-hearted baby. He has the softest heart and gentlest nature of almost any man I have ever known. Bull simply couldn't force himself to do anything mean or cruel. On the other hand, one of the cruelest criminals I have known—a killer by instinct—has a delicate face."

"Suppose," I said, "that a man offered you a tremendous business proposition which meant a huge, towering success for you if it succeeded; and failure and ruin if it didn't. What would you look to see in that man's face?"

"It wouldn't be so much in his face," he said; "I would pay more attention to his manner.

"If it meant as much to me as you say, I would want to be sure, first of all, that he had an absolutely definite idea that was completely and soundly thought out.

"If he took a long time to tell it; or if he began to pull papers out of his pocket and scribbled on them; or if he began drawing figures on his hands to illustrate his points, I would draw back. I would want him to look me straight in the eyes, and tell it in a few direct sentences, and not gesture too much.

"If he got that far, I would look to see if he had honest, open eyes, coupled with a determined jaw."

I asked Chaney if it was true that a man who couldn't look you in the eyes was a rascal.

"I don't claim to be a psychologist," he said, "I only can judge from my own experience. I think that is the biggest pipe dream in the world. Many men are very self-conscious and do not look you in the eyes for that reason. Other men have learned a trick of confusing you. If you want thoroughly to throw someone off his balance, look him straight in the eyes as he begins to talk; then shift your eyes to his mouth or his head."

He went on to say that he had been studying the eyes of the Chinese. "They have a curious characteristic. A Chinaman sees, but he does not look. You never have the sense of his eyes traveling over to meet you—as you often do with a white man.

"I think this is due to racial training. For centuries the Chinese have practised the arts of indirection. They do everything in a roundabout way. If they come to buy a horse, they begin by inquiring for the health of your honorable family. They speak of their best loved children as little brats, and so on."

"What about walks?" I asked. "What does a man's walk tell you?"

"The opposite of what it seems to tell many people. I have always learned to believe that a man who walks with a snappy, quick, flat-footed walk is not a determined character at all—he is seldom sure of himself. The man of determined character comes down on his heels."

We spoke then of a famous star who has the most peculiar eyes on the screen.

"Did you ever notice," he said, "that they never seem to be in focus; she never seems to be really looking at you—always beyond you; on the other hand, you seem always to be looking into her eyes—and seeing nothing.

"They are, however, deepset eyes. And they are a little close together; they always give you the impression of listening.

"To me they tell this: that she is not thinking for herself—although she is a shrewd, self-contained girl. That listening look in her eyes tells me that she is under the influence of someone—possibly her family. There is a cautious look there—as of a something withheld. And a look of pain. Just as a guess I should say that she has had a bad time with some love affair; and has resolved both to take warning nextime and to be very sure there isn't any nexttime."

"But," he added ruefully, "women are so hard to guess."

■ ■ ■

HE DOESN'T like to be interviewed! He growls at the fan writers and threatens to tear them limb from limb. After hearing these reports, aperson feels just like Little Red Riding Hood when he strolls in to get an interview with Lon Chaney. I walked in a half hour late to meet this bugaboo man of the interviewers.

I timidly excused my tardiness and prepared to have my eyes torn from their sockets. "You ask the questions and I'll answer them," said Lon. To Chaney the whole interviewing process appeared to be a matter of answering questions. I learned that he had encountered various writers who wanted to know how he combed his hair and why? they wanted to know if he loved his mother and why? they wanted to know if he liked somber colors or organdies and pinks.

He sat on the desk in the little office, assuming a resigned attitude of boredom. I had arrived at a very unfortunate of story. He has wondered and observed, and he knows life. He is an intense realist, and a great admirer of von Stroheim. Dress suits and formal parties are Lon's greatest aversions. He would rather talk to a longshoreman than the most publicized social lion. To him the most interesting people in the world are not those who wield the monocles and lorgnettes in the social spotlights. They do not understand him. He is a student of life in the raw and creates his characters as an artist would create a portrait.

All of Chaney's characterizations are composites. He combines the mannerisms of several characters he has known into the one he is to portray for the screen. He even makes a physical composite of the character, drawing upon his observations of the past. The big overcoat with the large, cheap fur collar and the form-fitting lines which Chaney wore as the yegg in THE UNHOLY THREE was a replica of a coat used by a high-class crook. Chaney had

CHARACTER ACTOR #1

By Milton Howe

time. Lon had just been handed a publicity questionnaire to fill out. Some of the questions were:

What is your favorite breakfast food?
What is your favorite car?
What is your favorite tobacco?

Chaney had handed the sheet back marked, "What of it?" He said he could visualize a line something like this. "Eat Lon Chaney's favorite breakfast food and grow to look like the Hunchback of Notre Dame".

His aversion to publicity is not modesty. It is business. To be interviewed, exposed and exploited in the wrong manner is like pulling the beard off Santa Claus in his opinion. He takes the attitude exemplified in H.L. Mencken's famous line to the effect that kings lost their prestige with the public when they put on pants ... the illusionment was gone.

Two hours later we emerged from the little office. I had met the bear of the interviewers and had emerged intact. I had gone in with the intention of getting Chaney to give me a character analysis of various stars, and discovered that Chaney, himself, had never been properly analyzed.

He possesses one of the keenest minds in the motion picture business. Lon has not traveled the road of life through the pages of a book. His lot has been that of a good many of our great writers and artists; to be thrown against the hard realities of life at an early age with but a few years of schooling. Gorki, Jack London and John Masefield are but a few who earned their positions after years of battering and suffering. All were vagabonds. Chaney's life story is that kind

met the gangster several years ago during his wanderings. The fellow was the leader of his gang and was considered one of the fashionably dressed men of his profession. He drew on men of like type for additional color for the character.

Chaney spends weeks studying a character. His mind will roam back to his childhood days in search of a man who, in a way, parallels the one he is to do on the screen. In his study of characterization Chaney has acquired the ability to read a character by his face. There are a few simple rules known to everyone, such as a protruding chin signifying determination, and a receding forehead denoting low mentality. Lon has delved deeper into the lines of the face and can judge a person very quickly by the contours and general makeup of the face and head.

I asked him to give me a reading of some of our well known stars, but he declined because of the serious consequences that might be involved in a critical review of a star's face. He also thought it a very unprofessional thing to do. I was about to ask him to give me a reading on the profile of Rex, the King of Wild Horses, but on second thought I remembered that Elinor Glyn had diagnosed Rex. We didn't have a picture of Rin-Tin-Tin and I was the only handy object, so Lon looked at my pan and said I had criminal instincts. We quit our chatter about analysis right here and switched the conversation to screen characterization.

The fact that the public is no longer interested in the beautiful but dumb ingenue accounts for the growing popularity of the character men and women, according to Lon. Chaney is the king of the character players and draws more money per week than 80% of the stars. He is not paid for his beauty but for his ability as an actor and painter of human characters.

Chaney is not stinting in his praise of the work of his fellow players. He paid high tribute to Raymond Hatton, Tully Marshall, Wallace Beery, Louise Dresser and Gloria Swanson. He did not speak of these people in condescending sense. He sees all their pictures and he learns from them. He classifies Gloria Swanson as a character player. Her work in THE HUMMING BIRD brought the true Gloria to the screen at least, in Chaney's opinion. She was not just a thing of beauty but a living human character. She gave a marvelous screen portrayal. It was an entirely different Gloria and that is why the public liked her, says Chaney. Pola Negri was the real pioneer in the field of characterization among the women stars. People were amazed at her work in PASSION because she disregarded all the conventionalities of the feminine star...she came to the screen without a marcel and forgot that she was supposed to be beautiful.

As a motion picture personality, Lon Chaney does not want to be known. He does not want to be stamped and classified. He does not want people to go to the show to see Lon Chaney the same person they saw last week. He wants to be an entirely different human each time he steps before them on the screen. That is one reason why he does not wish the public to become acquainted with him through publicity or the usual out-of-studio pictures. The Lon Chaney of private life he keeps in the background. The only Chaney he wants known is the man who bows to his audience in a different characterization each time he appears.

■ ■ ■

THE FACE THAT LAUNCHED A THOUSAND SHRIEKS

By Forrest J Ackerman

LON CHANEY, film historians would try to make us believe, was born in Colorado Springs on 1 April 1883 but we will not be April Fooled!

They pretend that, in Los Angeles, on the 26th of August, 1930, his throat aflame with cancer, he was taken by Prince Sirki to Valhalla; but we know better!

Lon Chaney never died!

So much for the warped imaginations of those who would try to deceive us and say that a god can die! They are the stone hearts, who would deny that the power of Wendy's plea to the fairies could save the life of Peter Pan; and their greatest curse should be to ban them from the privilege of ever again seeing another Lon Chaney picture.

It was in the eventide of the Dark Ages that a kindly witch met a great magician in chameleon's skin and they were married by a gnome-king. Together they sired a *wunderkind*, a wondrous kind of changeling child the like of which the mundane world had never known before, and they named this strange-ling L'han Shayn-nii, which in the tongue of the Ancient Ones of the Black Forest meant "the one with face of wax and body that twists like the vine."

For hundreds of years L'han practiced his art of pantomime and was known by many names in many places through the passing centuries while all the while he waited patiently for Motion Pictures to be born and grow strong enough to record the magic of his mimicry. Then (cleverly) he told producers, publicists, newspaper reporters that his parents could neither hear nor speak, for who would attempt to check on his origin with a Mother and Father who were deaf-mutes?

By now he was known no longer by his fey-name of L'han Shayn-nii but by his film name: Lon Chaney.

Soon he would be known in 3000 tongues as "The Man of a Thousand Faces".

THE FALSE FACES was one of Chaney's early makeup jobs, followed the same year (1919) by his rigorous role as Frog, the contorted beggar, "divinely" healed in THE MIRACLE MAN. In four roles the following year, he was blind in one (the wicked pirate of Robert Louis Stevenson's adventure classic, TREASURE ISLAND) and legless in another, THE PENALTY, in which he played a crippled criminal whose body ended in knee-stumps.

In 1921 he essayed two oriental parts, the first that of a Chinaman in Tod Browning's OUTSIDE THE LAW, and another slant-eyed menace in BITS OF LIFE with Anna May Wong. 1922 saw him as a Chinese again in SHADOWS, and the same year he was both unwhole of body and mind in FLESH AND BLOOD, and played a mad scientist and simian beast-man in A BLIND BARGAIN.

In 1923 he shook audiences in THE SHOCK, an earthquake spectacle, and once again was a crazed savant, this time in the company of John Gilbert in WHILE PARIS SLEEPS.

Then—

Quasimodo!

THE HUNCHBACK OF NOTRE DAME! The first of his two most celebrated characterizations, and one of his most painstaking—and painful. Chaney did more than merely make himself up, he empathized himself into the very valence of Quasimodo, threw himself or grew himself or somehow got himself inside the very soul of the pathetic demented bell-ringer of the Parisian cathedral. The mound of malformed rubber that he attached to his back bent his spine under a weight of 70 pounds. On his chest he wore a breastplate and shoulder pads similar to those of football tacklers. A harness fashioned of leather joined the front and back "armour" in such a manner that he could not have stood erect under any circumstances. Over this cumbersome and uncomfortable foundation he wore a rubber suit, tinted flesh color. Tufts of animal hair were affixed to chest and back. Modeling putty molded his face into a misshapen horror and a set of false teeth worn over his own accentuated his repulsive appearance. An uncombed bird's-nest of a wig topped his disguise, which he donned daily over a period of almost three months!

Grueling, ghouling!

Blind in one membrane-covered eye, tongue darting nervously in and out of his ugly mouth like a serpent's fang, he scuttled like a beetle in the dark corridors of the cathedral or crouched with his silent friends, the sculptured gargoyles of the parapets. Crazed but kindly unless tormented, at last he revolted against the crowd who had jeered at his cruel torture, and scalded his enemies with torrents of molten metal cascading from red-hot pots from on high in his eyrie sanctuary.

Charles Laughton later played Quasimodo, and very well; and, still later, Anthony Quinn was an effective Modo named Quasi; but neither interpretation had the stamp of authority of Chaney's.

1925 was Lon's top horror year, with THE MONSTER, wherein he played Dr. Ziska, who gained his victims by arranging auto accidents on a dark and lonely stretch of road near his underground laboratory.

...top horror year with his *dual* role in Tod Browning's UNHOLY THREE...

...with his characterization as the mind-warped one of THE TOWER OF LIES.

...and then—

His crowning achievement as the mad musician imagined by Gaston Leroux, the deranged organist "whose face was so hideous that he was forced to haunt the innermost depths of the Paris Opera." Roberta O'Toole, one critic who admitted "I shrieked right out loud in the theater and buried my head unashamedly on my husband's chest when Mary Philbin slipped the mask off Chaney as he sat playing the organ," described the impact of his portrayal in these indelible terms:

His outraged visage was horror incarnate: bulging, bloodshot eyes fatigued with violet semicircles beneath them; the grotesquely exaggerated mounds of the cheekbones; the hooked-up, flaring, porcine nostrils; the rotted, jagged teeth, like the rim of an enameled tin can top opened with a ragged knife; the scraggly strands of dead gray hair hanging like soggy serpentine from the incredible pyramid of a head....

And the thought may well have crossed the nostalgic mind of Ray Bradbury that if the great artist Gustave Dore had painted the picture of Dorian Gray, and Henry Frankenstein endowed it with life, it would have been Lon Chaney as The Phantom.

Today we say, "Is it a bird? Is it a plane? No—it's Superman!" But 55 years ago, when Lon Chaney was at the height of his power, the warning cry was: "Is it a spider? Watch out! Don't step on it—it may be Lon Chaney!" And with good reason, for anything that crept or crawled across the silver screen (or even *flew*, as in the case of the bat-man of LONDON AFTER MIDNIGHT) was quite liable to be L.C., the Master of Make Believe.

In 1926 he played a Jekyll-Hyde type role in THE BLACKBIRD and, covering one eye with a coating of egg-white, simulated a cataract to play the part of a semi-blind outcast in THE ROAD TO MANDALAY.

In '27 he played *three* Chinese roles in MR. WU; an armless freak in THE UNKNOWN whose feet took the place of his hands, complete to throwing knives with deadly accuracy with his toes; and a human vampire in Tod Browning's LONDON AFTER MIDNIGHT, wherein his face was bone-white with eyes popping like olive pits out of hard-boiled eggs and teeth that resembled the ends of ivory spikes.

And the last film he ever made, THE UNHOLY THREE, was a talkie remake of his silent hit which Tod Browning had directed from the book by Tod Robbins. In THE UNHOLY THREE Chaney was a sideshow ventriloquist in the company of "a long, lizard-like figure" called The Human Skeleton; Madame Fatima, "a mountain of purple, painful flesh with small pig-like eyes;" and Tweedledee, a dwarf just a shade over two feet tall, whose "little round, shoe-button eyes could flash and his soft, chubby face writhe into a terrible mask, suddenly transforming his expression into that of a murderer". The audiences of 1930 were electrified when the "Man of a Thousand Faces" spoke in four different voices during the same film.

Such was the *reel* Lon Chaney, the star of the scary and the scarry. Had he lived there seems little doubt that he would have become the monster of FRANKENSTEIN, the menace of THE INVISIBLE MAN, Im-ho-tep the 3700-year-old MUMMY, and, instead of Bela Lugosi, would himself have played the role he created in LONDON AFTER MIDNIGHT in the sound version of it called MARK OF THE VAMPIRE.

What of the *real* Lon Chaney? A biographer, George Mitchell, tells us:

His movements were quick but graceful, he was high-strung, even nervous, and somewhat grim. His dark eyes, deeply lined face, and cynical mouth, made him seem hard-boiled. He despised weakness and believed in decency.

He was the second of four children. Due to the bedridden state of his ill Mother he was withdrawn from school in the fourth grade to help care for her. In his teens he began his theatrical career as a stagehand and scene painter. He was married when he was 19 and the following year was born his only child: Creighton Tull Chaney, known as Lon Chaney Jr. of WOLF MAN, MUMMY, etc. fame.

The first picture on which he got screen credit was POOR JAKE'S DEMISE in 1913. In 1915, besides appearing in 25 pictures, he directed 6 shorts, the last being THE CHIMNEY'S SECRET, which he also wrote as well as acted in.

Once he became world-famous and was besieged for interviews, he became retiring and declared: "Between pictures there is no Lon Chaney."

Between pictures there is no Lon Chaney—there is the clue, the reason we have not seen a new Lon Chaney film since they say he died 53 years ago. He has been resting, giving his son and actors like Boris Karloff, Bela Lugosi, Peter Lorre and Christopher Lee a chance. What is 53 years between pictures to a man who has lived for hundreds? Undoubtedly he is waiting for just the right part, the greatest monster role of them all, in which to make his comeback appearance.

Comeback?

Lon Chaney has never been away, in the hearts and minds and memories of those who knew his greatness.

Today he should appear to be about 100 years old.

Be kind to the next centenarian you meet—he may be the legendary Lon. ■

WHY I PREFER GROTESQUE CHARACTERS

By Lon Chaney

IT WAS PURELY by chance that I became associated with screen characterizations that required the use of grotesque makeups. I began my so-called career on the stage, that is if one may dignify the little shows in which I appeared as "the stage". In turn I was the hero, the villain, the spear carrier, the stage-manager and the stage-hand. In fact, I still retain my card in the stage-hand's union and it is one of the few things of which I am really proud.

All during the time that I was traveling about the country with repertoire and one-night stands, the thing that interested me most was makeup. It was not merely the applying of grease-paint and putty noses to the face but mental makeup as well. I wanted not only to look like the character portrayed but to attune my mind to his. Even when I was a boy, the hero or juvenile roles did not interest me. I felt that there was a greater field in characterization; nor was it the stereotyped characterizations that interested me. If I played the role of an old man, I tried to crawl into the old man's mind rather than merely build up a putty nose and don white whiskers. Even in the makup I attempted to avoid the conventional. For example, whenever I was given an old man's role to play I tried to inject into it some distinctive mannerism, a limp, perhaps, or a drawn arm or maybe just a slight nervous twitch of the face; anything, in fact, to take the character out of the lesson-number-52-in-makeup—old-men class.

Anyone who has had the amazing experience of roadshow work knows how every hour of the day and many of the night are full but I still managed to spare the moments for makeup, experimenting by the trial-and-failure method, discarding one idea, elaborating upon another.

One day I found myself in the small California town of Santa Ana. I discovered myself stranded with the company with which I had been connected. The members of the troups disbanded to go their separate ways. I had only a few dollars and could not even start walking to another town because there were no towns to which I could walk.

Someone, however, told me of a gold mine. At Universal City there was a motion picture studio where they hired men to ride horses before a camera and gave them five dollars a day for this. In my financial condition five dollars a day seemed a fortune, so I took what capital I had and invested in a ticket to Universal City.

I discovered that the rumor was a fact, that they *did* hire men to ride horses and gave them five dollars a day. My experience along this line was limited. However, I could stick on a horse, and I found that I had a more or less steady job.

To the cinema I had, heretofore, given no thought. As for its being my life's work—that seemed preposterous. But as I now found myself in this new game, I attempted to discover what possibilities it held for me. What sort of makeup would register before the camera? Obviously one could not use the same kind as one used on the stage but instead of makeup becoming limited in the new medium, rare, unique possibilities opened up.

I used to stand before my mirror—stand being the correct word during those first days when I was a centaur—and apply the makeup, keeping in mind the possibilities and the limitations of the screen.

Finally I got a chance to do comedies, which put me in more direct touch with the camera. Then one day I secured a cameraman and a camera and tried to put into practice some of the things that had evolved during the time I had experimented. When the studio began casting for THE MIRACLE MAN, I asked to be given a chance to play the role of the "Frog". In the pictures that followed, THE PENALTY, HUNCHBACK OF NOTRE DAME and the more recent ones such as MR. WU, THE UNKNOWN and MOCKERY, I have tried to play roles that admitted of different characterizations.

I prefer these parts, not merely because I like to play with makeup but because I feel that they give me a wider scope. The care and the time given to the actual putting on of makeup is sometimes tiresome and I have often envied the actors who played "straight" and allowed themselves 15 minutes in their dressingrooms before going on the set, while I took hours just to get ready. The makeup is, I hope, merely a frame for the picture, and it is the picture with which I am concerned. It is not morbidity that made me turn to the type of role with which I have become identified. I hope that I shall never be accused of striving merely for horrible effects. True, the smashingly dramatic appeals to me more than intimate stories of everyday life. I always respond quicker to a vivid dramatic situation than to a quiet theme. If I did not it would not be this type of role that interests me.

Grotesqueries as such do not attract me; it is vivid characterization for which I strive. I want my makeup simply to add to the picture, to show at a glance the sort of character I am portraying. But I want my roles to go deeper than that. I want to dig down into the mind and the heart of the role. But as a man's face reveals much that is in his mind and heart, I attempt to show this by the makeup I use; and the makeup is merely the prolog.

I have little patience with tricks and mechanical devices as such. They are useless unless they advance the story. There are many freak makeups that I might evolve but I would not wear them unless to some definite purpose. In THE UNKNOWN I contrived to make myself look like an armless man, not simply to shock and horrify you but merely to bring to the screen a dramatic story of an armless man, or rather one who pretended to be so.

I play unusual characters not for the sake of applying grotesque makeup but always to advance the drama of a startling plot.

■ ■ ■

HIS FACES, HIS FORTUNE

By John B. Kennedy

THEY WERE trying to make Lon Chaney mad. It was during the final shot for the grand climax of a cowboy melodrama, and Chaney, the villain, was supposed to "register" rage.

Again and again the young unknown (he *was* unknown then, for this was in 1921) made an effort to look properly angry. But he simply couldn't do it.

Suddenly the director cupped his hands. Sharp, staccato and fierce were his words—epithets which, if photographable, would never have passed any board of censors, anywhere. He called Chaney a bum, incongruous ham and much, much worse. Chaney lifted his brow-barred face, paling beneath a two-ply coat of studio bronze. With a snarl he flung himself forward.

The director backed away from the camera, Chaney lunging at him. Then the camera man stepped between them with a broad smile, slapped the infuriated actor on the back and uttered:

"Bully. That's a pip!"

Dazed, Chaney saw the ruse. And a few weeks later millions of movie fans in hundreds of theaters also saw it to the accompaniment of pine pianos; they hissed appropriately, never realizing that this high-point of rage was genuine.

It was the one little incident needed to convince Lon Chaney, christened Alonzo, that his face was really his fortune. Movie folk talked about that rush of rage and it became a text on the ham lots for ambitious actors hunting their degrees in film villainy. From that time on Chaney was tagged as the man who could make his face behave in any way he wanted.

He had broken into the screen game after hamming his way through vaudeville and stock companies, with the usual post-public-school preliminaries of baggage smashing, scene shifting and tab showing at county fairs. He started with Universal at $5 a day, paid up boarding-house debts contracted while he was with stranded shows, and bided his time to emerge. Now he makes more money making faces than any other man in the world.

"Nobody had ever dreamed in those early days," he says, "that the motion pictures provided a better field for character portrayal than the spoken stage, and this notwithstanding the handicap of silence. We were content to plod along doing the oldfashioned Wild West stuff with horses and revolvers playing the principal parts, until the demand to screen popular works of fiction was felt, and there followed that the demand for actors who could give effective characterizations of the varied roles."

He got his first big chance with Tom Meighan in THE MIRACLE MAN. Anybody who read the book or saw the picture will realize the terrible task imposed upon the fake cripple in that play. Meighan, as the adventurer from the underworld, was out to exploit the old, blind New England hermit. Chaney, in the role of confederate, had to be the subject of the first miracle. The role necessitated Chaney's twisting his body and distorting his face like a paralytic in acute agony. He had to drag himself along a stony road like a spineless dwarf for 200 yards before a camera planted on the porch of the hermit's mountain shack. The director of this scene had to bar nonprofessional outsiders, permitted to watch it at first in order to swell the number of spectators called for in the book. Three times natives spoiled the picture by taking Chaney's realism at its face value and rushing to aid him in his distress.

Nowadays the public is more sophisticated. A man could blow his brains out before a movie camera on any Main Street without anybody's attempting to interfere with the "shot".

Lon Chaney's reputation as a portrayer of the odd was made by that punishing role of the paralytic. This contortionism of Chaney's—reduction of his naturally powerful limbs to withered legs, apelike, hanging arms, while twisting the torso into acute disproportion—is the more marvelous because there is nothing freakish about him. Every digit on feet and hands is normal. He isn't even double-jointed.

The trick of holding the limbs and trunk, head and neck in grotesque attitudes while repeated camera shots are made is, of course, painful—although Lon Chaney admits nothing of the sort. But men and women who have worked with him—Tom Meighan and Betty Compson, for example—can testify that Chaney earned his effects through physical agony, especially when physical distortion was long sustained.

Following THE MIRACLE MAN Chaney's next famed picturization was Fagin in OLIVER TWIST. Jackie Coogan played Oliver. Chaney, naturally, did not make his appearance in the picture until the scene in the thieves' kitchen showing Fagin rehearsing the Artful Dodger and Oliver in pocket-picking. Little Coogan's Oliver was his first role of large consequence. He was excited about it, nervous.

On the first day for trial shots of the kitchen scene, Chaney swooped down on the studio in his grotesque makeup, bowl-backed, evil-faced, greasy of beard and with half-bare legs. Jackie ran screaming away. Not until he saw Chaney light a cigaret and remove the beard to make better adjustments could the child star be calmed.

As the central character in THE HUNCHBACK OF NOTRE DAME and the Phantom in THE PHANTOM OF THE OPERA, Lon Chaney had to sustain difficult makeup longer than in any other roles save one, the cripple in the dual part of bishop and burglar he played in THE BLACKBIRD. This piece added little to his fame, although his performance was perhaps of a higher quality than any he has ever given. He declares it was the toughest job he ever undertook.

For entire days, with few rests, he had to keep the pose of a victim of hemiplegia—a man with one side of his body stiff from paralysis. The least muscular movement on that side of the body would have been detected by the camera, would have spoiled the picture. Scenes had to be shot endlessly of such simple incidents as opening a door because some slip of normal, healthy motion obtruded. For weeks after the film was made, Chaney confesses, he found himself involuntarily assuming the attitudes of a muscle-bound paralytic.

In THE HUNCHBACK he didn't use the ordinary padding that stout burlesque comedians employ as shock absorbers for kicks fore and aft. An anatomist carefully designed from deformed life a hump of plaster, which was rigidly strapped to Chaney's back. Throughout the play he had to maintain his posture at a painful crouch.

"There are tricks in my peculiar trade that I don't care to divulge any more than a magician will give away his art," he confided, if refusal to rend the veil can be construed as confidence. "In THE PHANTOM OF THE OPERA people exclaimed at my weird makeup. I achieved the death's head of that role without wearing a mask. It was use of paint in the right shades and the right places—not the obvious parts of the face—which gave the complete illusion of horror.

"Since falling heir to the odd and ugly roles of drama in pictures, I'm supposed to have evolved some magic process of malforming my features and limbs. It's an art but not magic."

In real life Lon Chaney is an ordinary-looking man, the right side of middle age, whose face would fit any prosperous business man alert for more prosperity. He is married and has one son.

"My experience as a stage manager, which was wide and varied before I jumped into the films, taught me much about lighting effects on the actor's face and the minor tricks of deception. These I have been able to put to use in achieving weird results on the screen. I've never worn a mask in my life, save at Halloween parties. It's all a matter of combining paint and lights to form the right illusion."

Most successful makeup is a matter of improvisation. Chaney can't tell you now what he'll do to his face if he should put, say, Brasson's Leper or Marquis' lovesick India-rubber Man on the screen tomorrow as he put Hugo's Hunchback on yesterday. Broad horror of line is achieved by exaggerated grayness, and the bumps and scars of the hunchback role were made by channels and hummocks of paint—just as the nose was plug-ended by molded greasepaint.

But Chaney has a problem more difficult, for instance, than Arliss in OLD ENGLISH to transform a smooth, well-kept face into a shriveled mask, for footlights do not slaughter effects with the ferocity of the Kleigs. In terms of poundage it means that the movie character actor has to carry twice as much paint poundage on his face as the footlights player and to mix tones more intricately to counterbalance the glare and the normal, necessary, lurid movie makeup.

And in roles like THE MIRACLE MAN, where shots were made in the bright sunlight, makeup is most difficult, for the sun searches out all unnaturalness, favoring only dark blue tones as dermal evidence of ill-health or malice.

"I was," he says, "ambitious, at first, to become a director. Barnstorming had sickened me with the acting side of the profession. I took screen jobs merely as a stepping stone to the megaphone; but when my salary started jumping after every part I played the lure was too great." So he remained an actor—and he's glad of it.

"Prettiness on the screen in men and women is important," he says, "and unfortunately it leads all Main Street belles and backwoods sheiks to imagine that Hollywood is yelping for their looks. But the good-looking have little chance to get character roles. That is why there is so much opportunity for homely souls like myself who are not ornamental.

"The plain man and the plain girl have more chance in the movies now, I'd say, than the collar models and the beauty pageant winners. Pulchritude is becoming more and more conventional and expected. Its opposite, which predominates in real life, is beginning to govern the screen, which has to pattern itself to the great world it portrays.

■ ■ ■

COMING

ATTRACTIONS

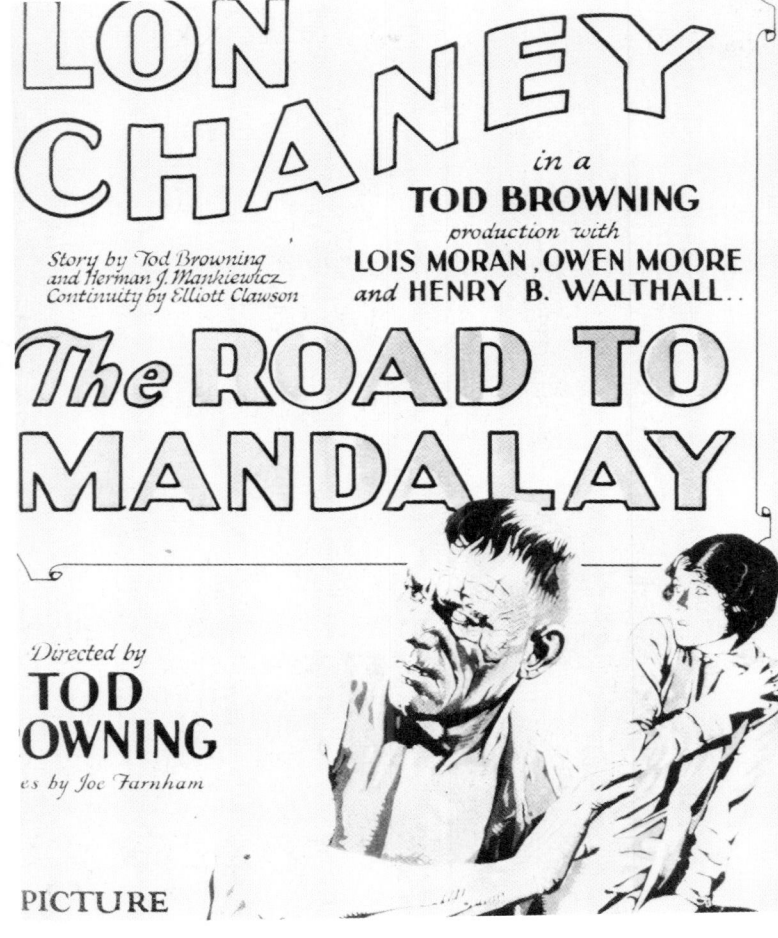

1916
FATHER OF THE BOY

The Primeval Films

LON

VODVIL 1912

ANCIENT HISTORY. These are the motion pictures in which Chaney appeared as long ago as *67 years*, the primeval movies that led, bit by bit and characterization by characterization, to his...prime evil films: THE UNHOLY THREE...WEST OF ZANZIBAR...LONDON AFTER MIDNIGHT...MR. WU...THE HUNCHBACK OF NOTRE DAME...*THE PHANTOM OF THE OPERA.*

As a matter of fact the first photo—the earliest I have—preceeds even his celluloid appearances. It appeared 17 May 1912 in a newspaper and his dancing partner in the vaudeville act was identified as "Mlle. Vanity".

1917
PAY ME

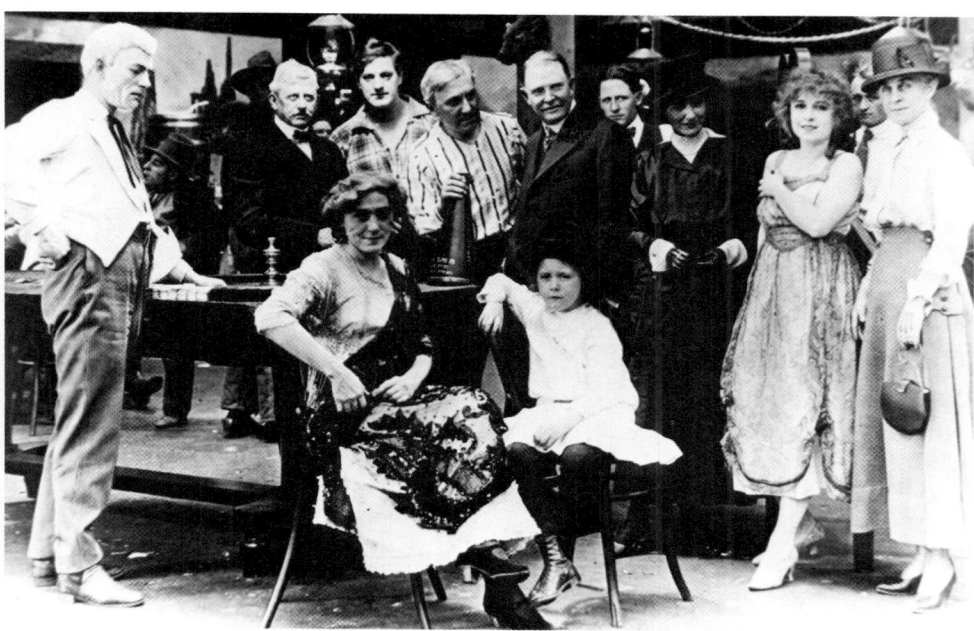

1917
PAY ME

1917
PAY ME

1919
THE MIRACLE MAN

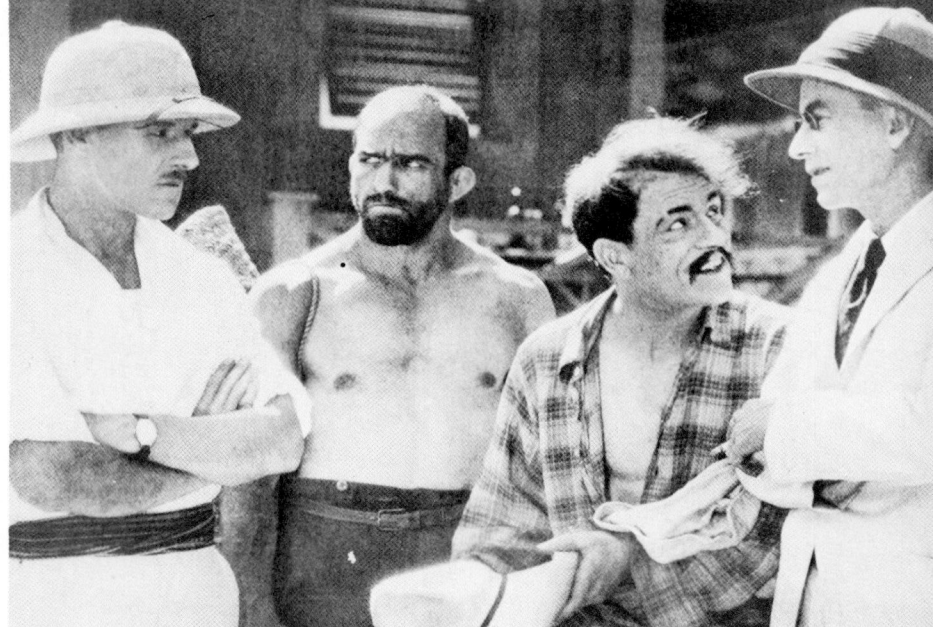

1919
THE MIRACLE MAN

VICTORY

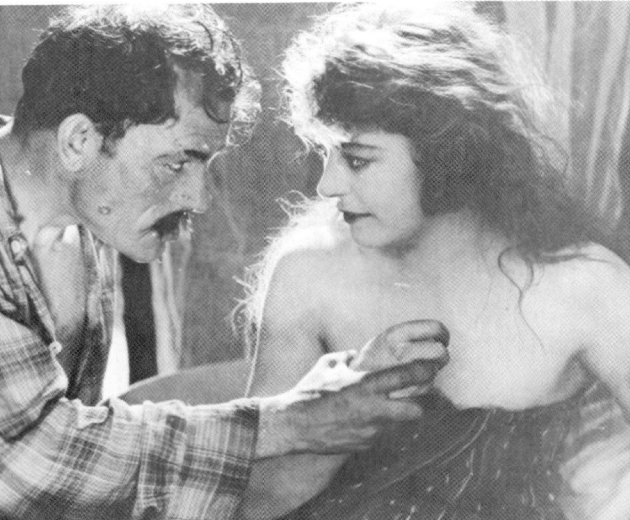

THE PENALTY

1920
TREASURE ISLAND

1921
OUTSIDE THE LAW

ACE OF HEARTS

1922
THE TRAP

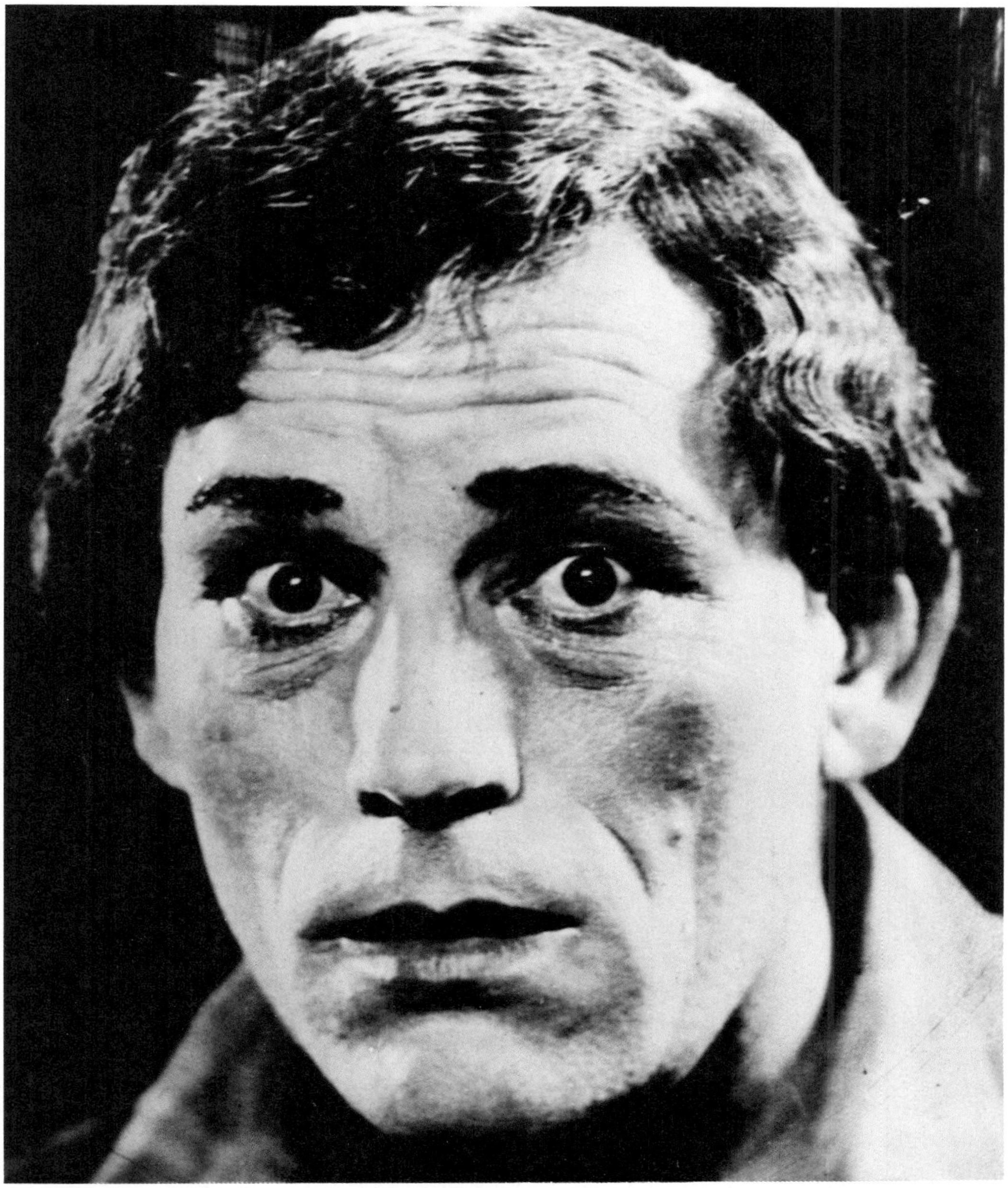

THE TRAP (1922)

VOICES OF THE CITY (aka NIGHT ROSE)

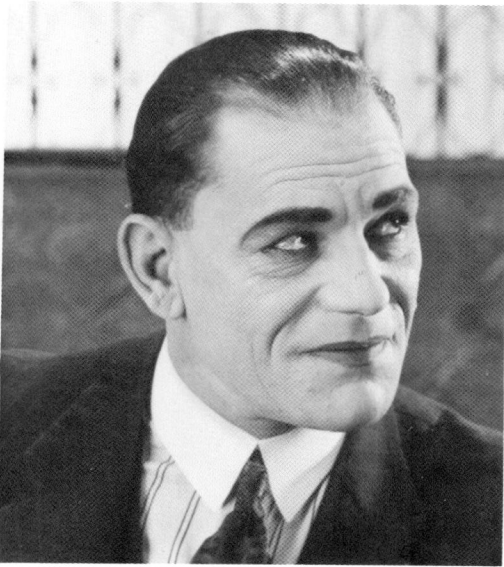

VOICES OF THE CITY
(aka NIGHT ROSE)

VOICES OF THE CITY (aka NIGHT ROSE)

THE LIGHT IN THE DARK

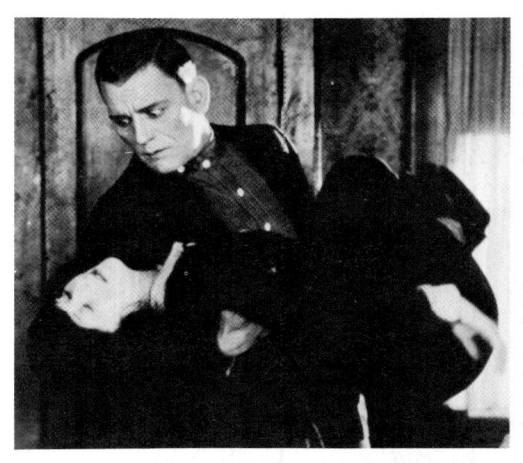

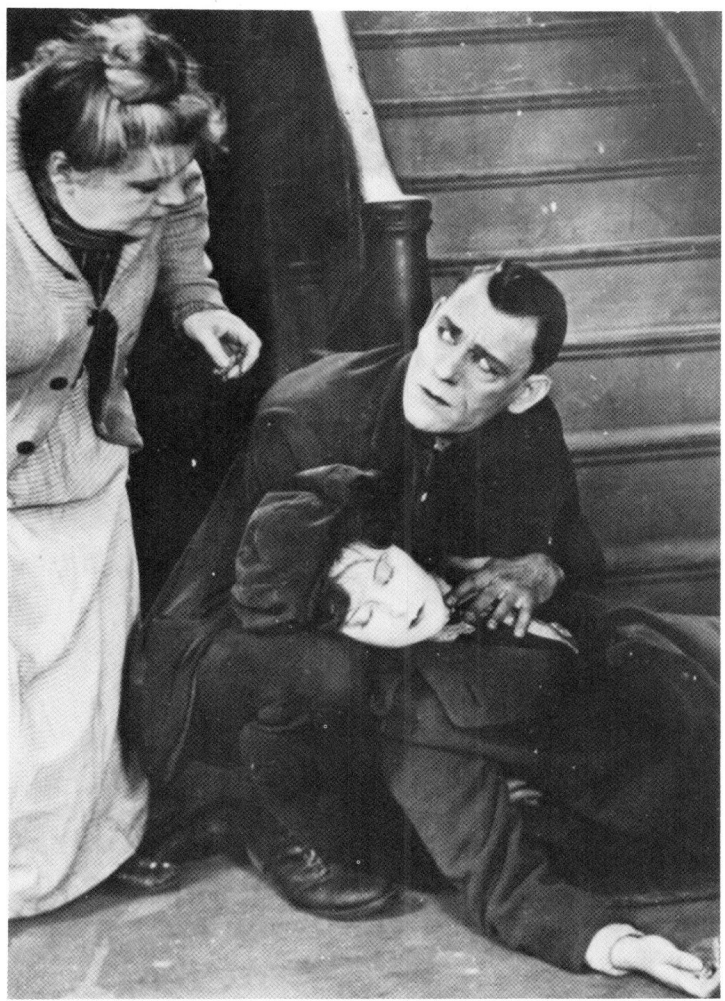

THE LIGHT IN THE DARK

OLIVER TWIST

OLIVER TWIST

OLIVER TWIST

OLIVER TWIST

QUINCY ADAMS SAWYER   THE SHOCK (1923)

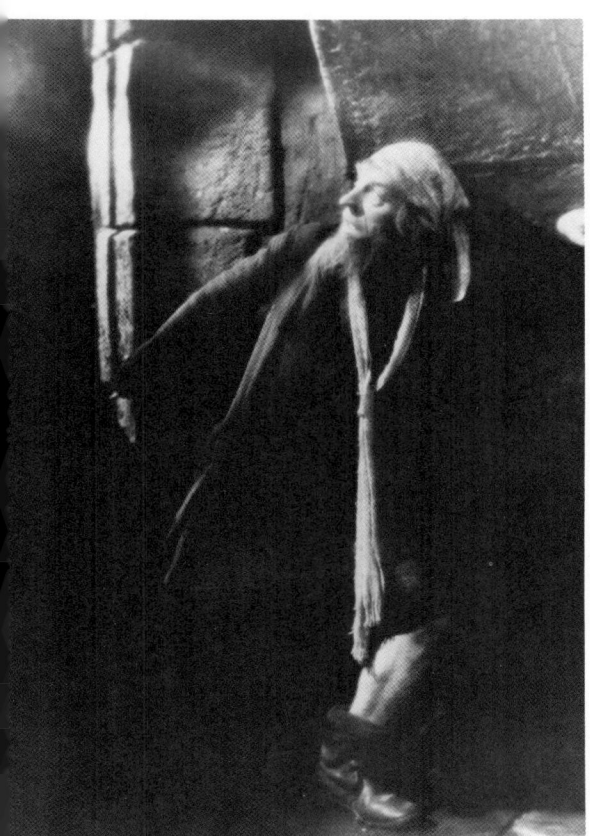

THE SHOCK (1923)

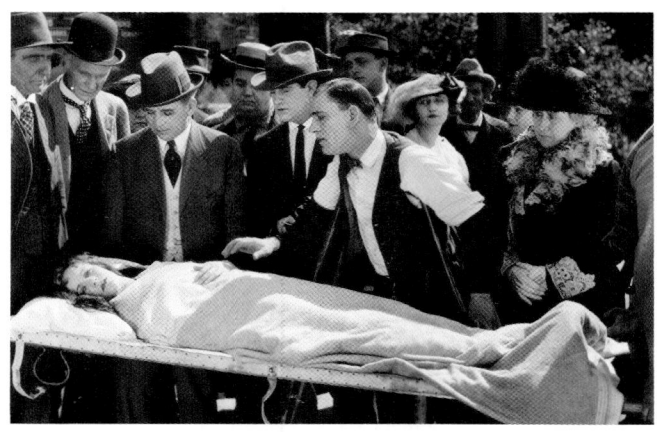

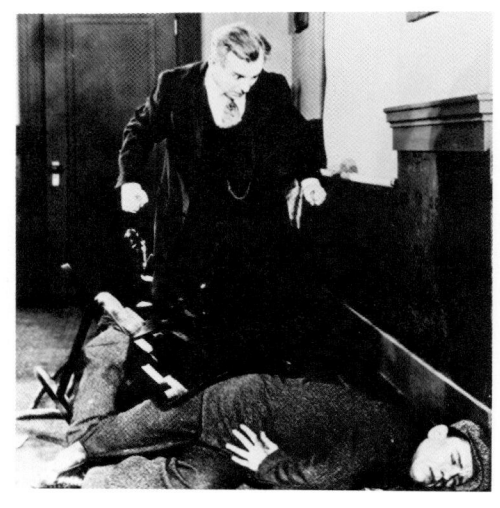
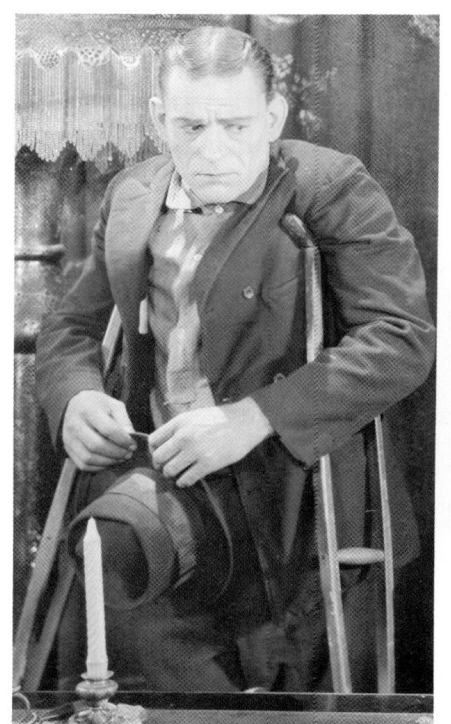

THE SHOCK (1923)

▲ THE NEXT CORNER ▶

A BLIND BARGAIN
(aka THE OCTAVE OF CLAUDIUS)
1922

DR. LAMB AND THE APEMAN: Lon Chaney. Angela, Jacqueline Logan. Robert, Raymond McKee. Scenario by J.G. Hawks from the book *The Octave of Claudius* by Barry Pain. Directed by Wallace Worsley.

A BLIND BARGAIN (1922)

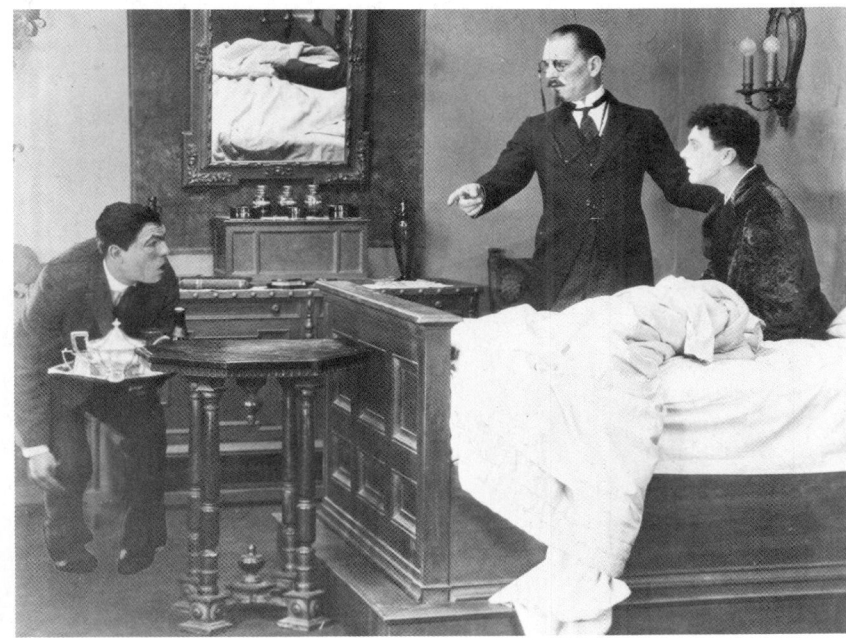

A BLIND BARGAIN (1922)

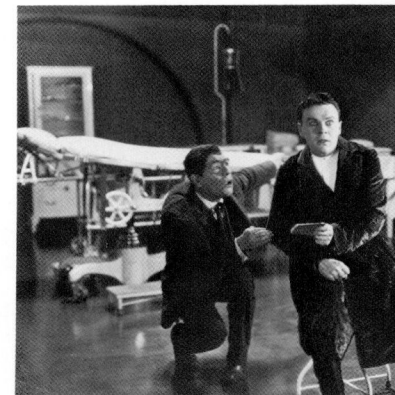

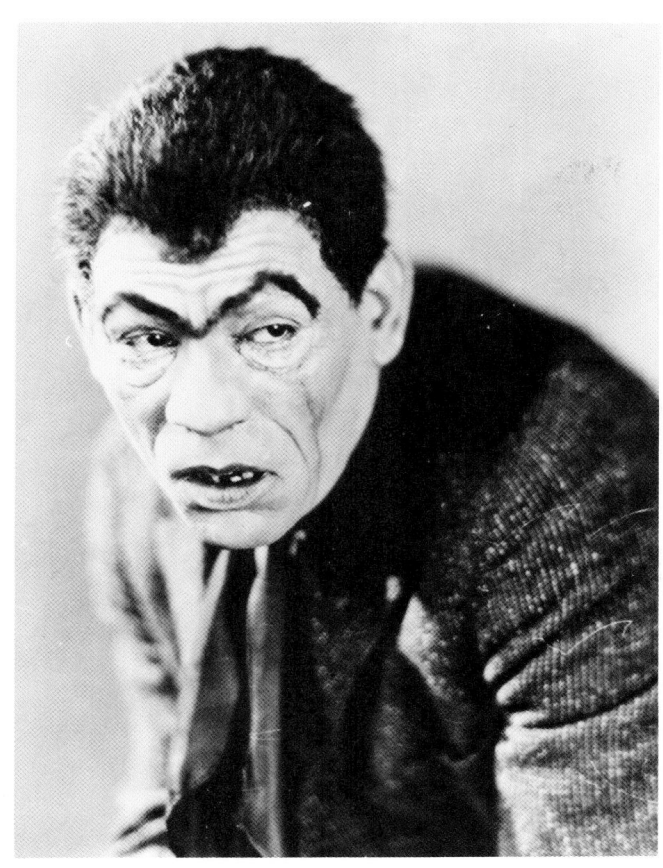

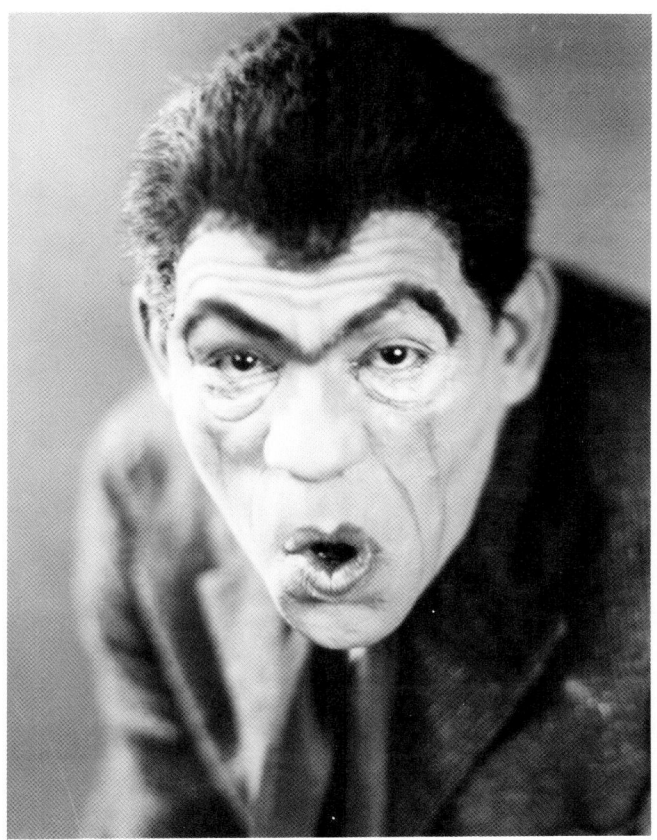

Peekaboo—I see you!

Pay or die!

Aw, g'wan!

MAN OF MANY MOODS

ONE GLORIOUS DAY an unidentified stillman got Lon Chaney to stand still long enough during the making of THE BIG CITY to take this great set of "10s"—ten photos of the master mime displaying as many emotions.

Have I got a bargain for you!

You sure know how to hurt a guy.

I won?!

Oops!

ORIENTAL INTERPRETATIONS...

I wouldn't hurt a fly!

Huh?

I'll play this hand.

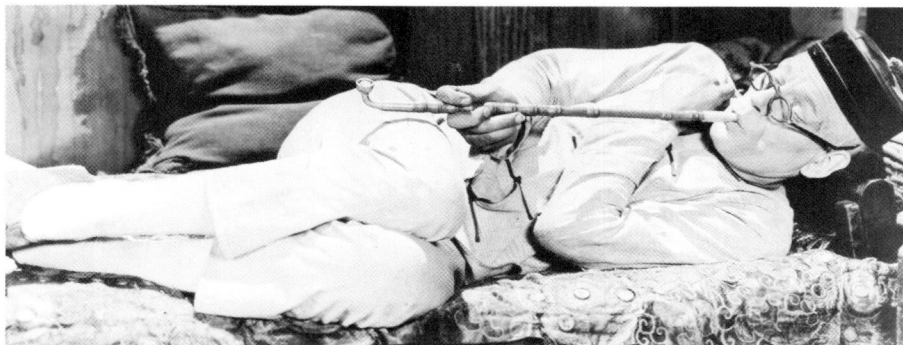
SHADOWS (Yen Sin)

OUTSIDE THE LAW (Joe Wang)

BITS OF LIFE

  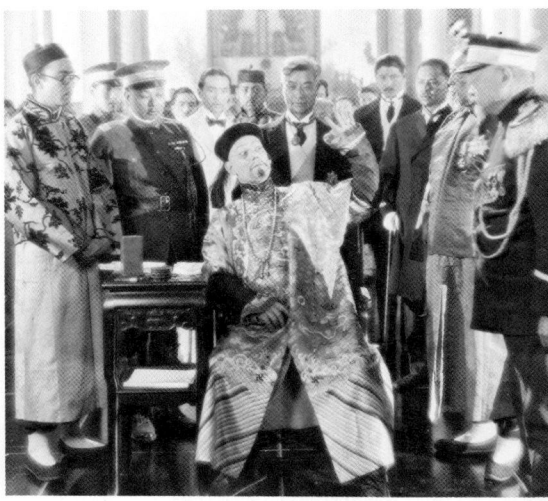

MR. WU

 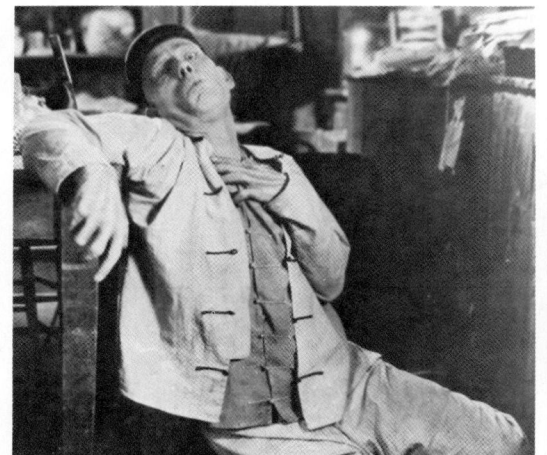 

BITS OF LIFE

  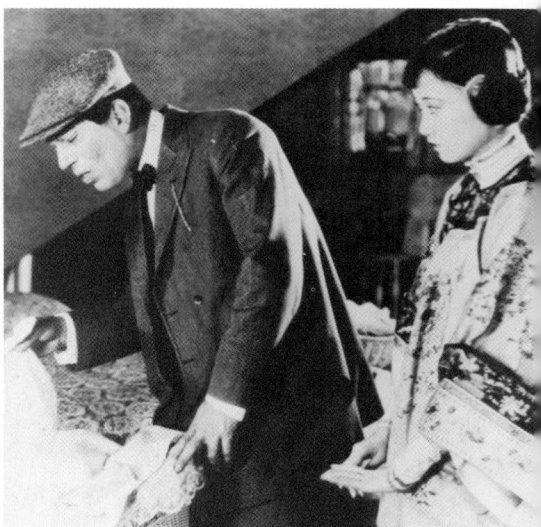

BITS OF LIFE

OUTSIDE THE LAW

MR. WU

CRIPPLED (But Not Handicapped!)...

THE SHOCK

THE PENALTY

FLESH AND BLOOD (1922)

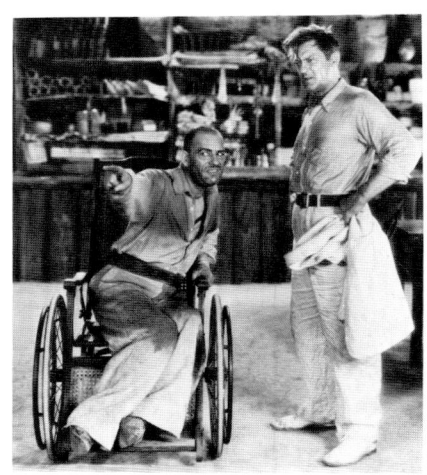

WEST OF ZANZIBAR

THE SHOCK

WEST OF ZANZIBAR

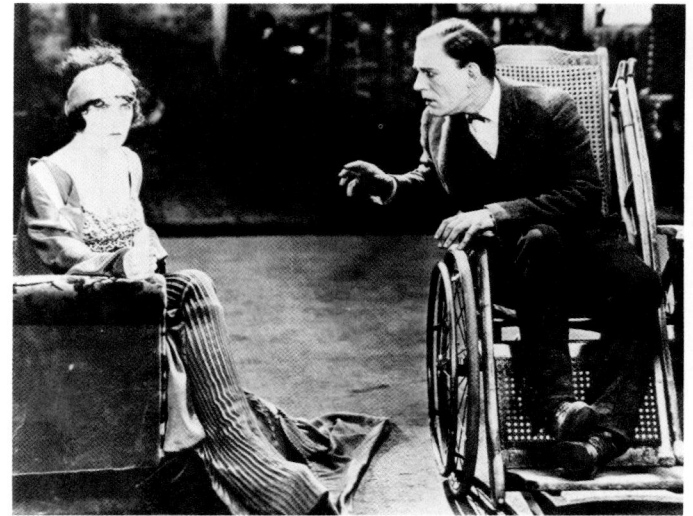

THE SHOCK

WEST OF ZANZIBAR

WEST OF ZANZIBAR

THE UNKNOWN

LON GLAD...

LAUGH, CLOWN, LAUGH

LAUGH, CLOWN, LAUGH

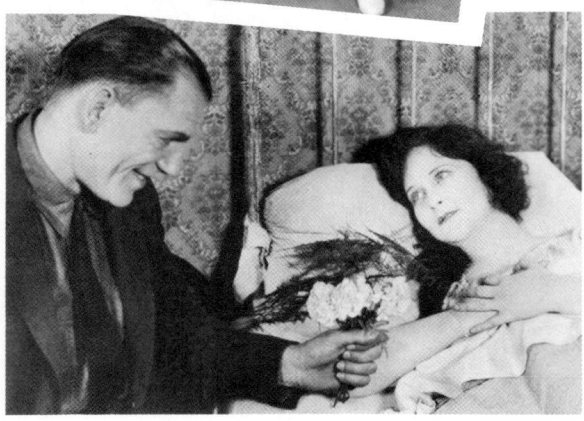
THE LIGHT IN THE DARK

OUTSIDE THE LAW

THE UNHOLY THREE (talkie)

ACE OF HEARTS

WHERE EAST IS EAST

WHERE EAST IS EAST

ALL THE BROTHERS WERE VALIANT

ALL THE BROTHERS WERE VALIANT

ACE OF HEARTS

ALL THE BROTHERS WERE VALIANT

THE UNKNOWN

LON SAD...

LAUGH, CLOWN, LAUGH (with Loretta Young —when she was *really* young)

LAUGH, CLOWN, LAUGH

LAUGH, CLOWN, LAUGH (but for Lon this role was no laughing matter)

Unidentified

THE LIGHT IN THE DARK (with Hope Hampton)

Unidentified

LON MAD...

MOCKERY

THE UNHOLY THREE (sound)

WHERE EAST IS EAST

THE SHOCK

THE UNHOLY THREE (sound)

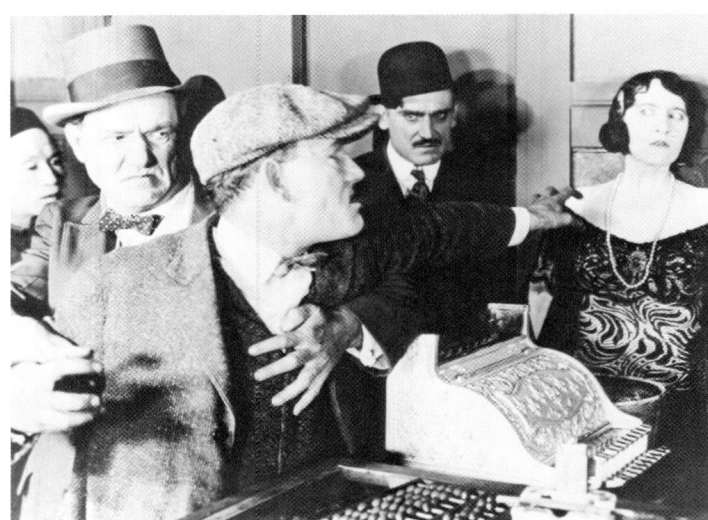

THE BIG CITY

THE TRAP

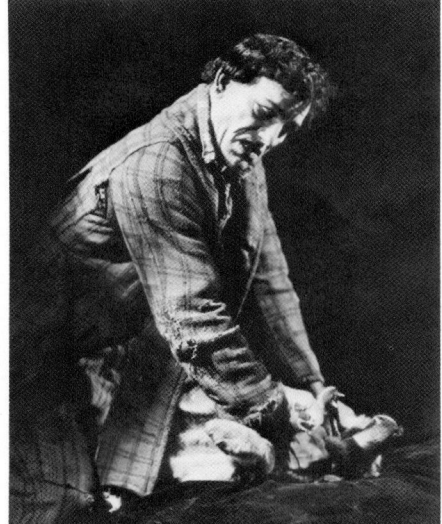

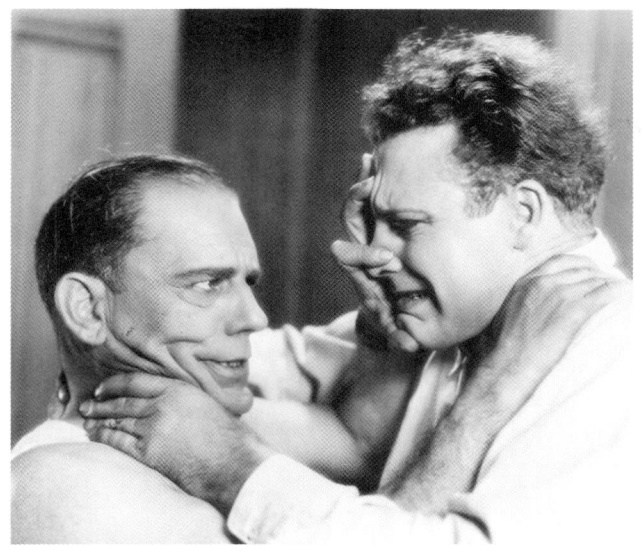
THE BIG CITY

THE PENALTY

ACE OF HEARTS

THE LIGHT IN THE DARK

LAUGH, CLOWN, LAUGH

THE BIG CITY

LON CRAZED... Lon Trods the Psycho Path

OUTSIDE THE LAW

LAUGH, CLOWN, LAUGH

MR. WU (with Ralph Forbes)

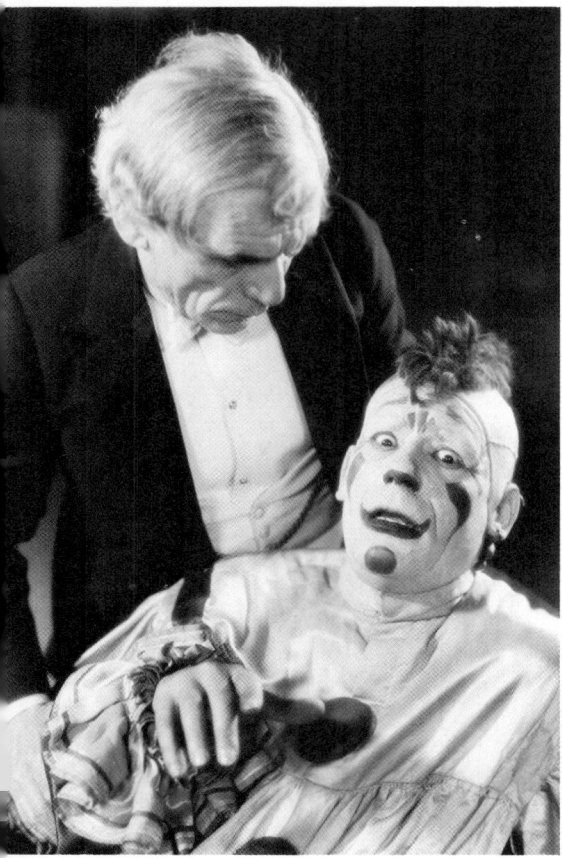

LAUGH, CLOWN, LAUGH (with Benard Seigel)

BITS OF LIFE (with Anna May Wong)

THE PENALTY

THE ROAD TO MANDALAY
(with Ower. Moore and Lois Moran)

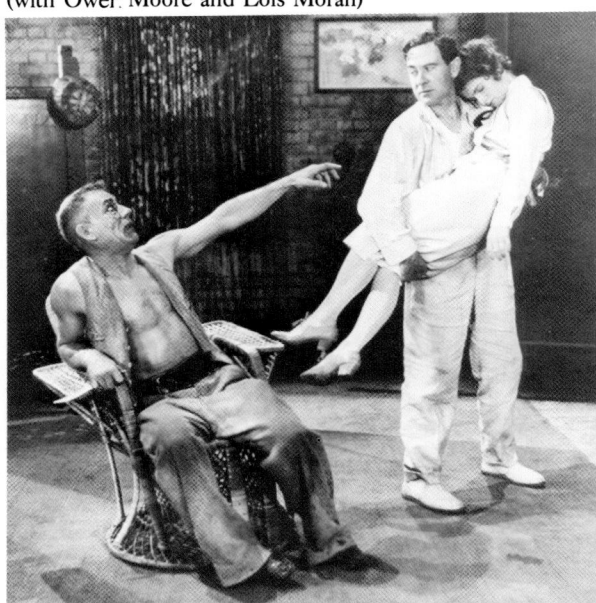

WEST OF ZANZIBAR
(with Lionel Barrymore)

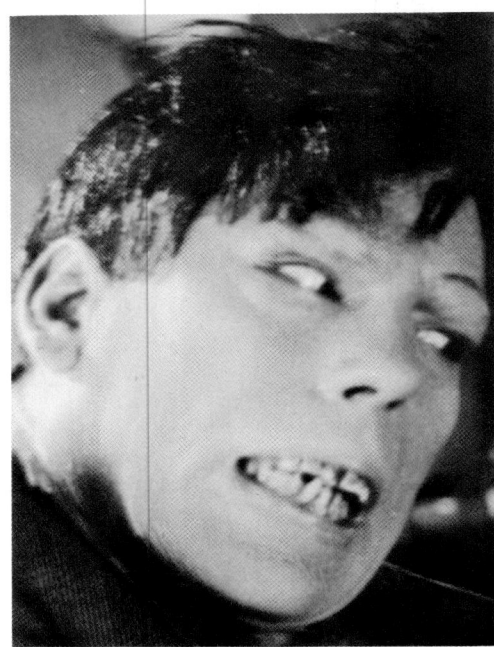

BITS OF LIFE

MR. WU

MOCKERY TOWER OF LIES TOWER OF LIES

OUTSIDE THE LAW THE UNHOLY THREE (sound)

TOWER OF LIES LAUGH, CLOWN, LAUGH MOCKERY
(with Loretta Young at 16, "You're not a boy!"

HE WHO GETS SLAPPED

WEST OF ZANZIBAR (excised dream sequence)

WEST OF ZANZIBAR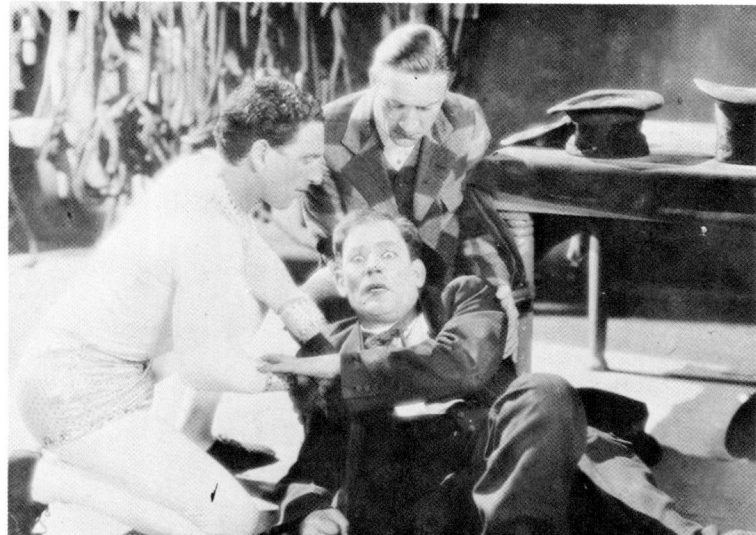

WEST OF ZANZIBAR

WEST OF ZANZIBAR

HE WHO GETS SLAPPED

MOCKERY

THE UNHOLY THREE (talkie)

THE HUNCHBACK OF NOTRE DAME 1923

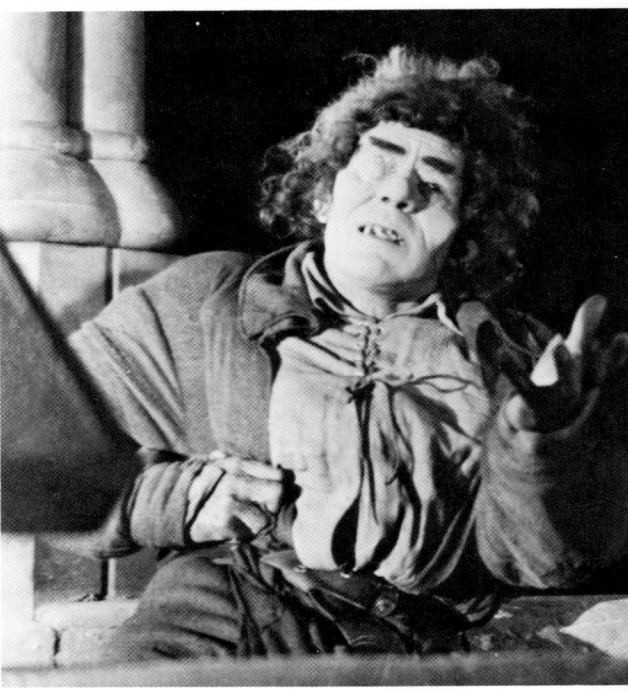

ALTHOUGH CHANEY was memorable as the quasi-cripple Frog in THE MIRACLE MAN (1919) he would make 22 more films over a period of four years before his quantum jump to fame as Quasimodo in THE HUNCHBACK OF NOTRE DAME (1923).

NOTRE DAME DE PARIS had been filmed at least three times before Lon's version (and several times since) but never with such impact. "If Lon Chaney were to be remembered by only one screen portrayal," said Robert G. Anderson in his Barnes book *Faces, Forms, Films (The Artistry of Lon Chaney)*, "it would be as Quasimodo in THE HUNCHBACK OF NOTRE DAME, for it embodied all the elements of characterization, facial as well as psychological and emotional."

The original novel, of course, was by the classic French author Victor Hugo but the screen adaptation was by one Perley Poore Sheehan, of which more should be heard. In the introduction to Sheehan's posthumously published limited edition novel *The Abyss of Wonders* (defunct Polaris Press, 1953), the late beloved book reviewer P. Schuyler Miller introduced Sheehan as "The Shadow Master", saying: "For as long as I have been reading fantasy, Perley Poore Sheehan has been one of the 'greats' of the great old days when Bob Davis was creating a new literature of the imagination in the pages of the Munsey magazines". He was persistently ranked, Miller told us, with the legendary lore-makers, A. Merritt, Austin Hall, Homer Eon Flint, Francis Stevens. He was around 45 when he adapted HUNCHBACK and supervised its screening. Lon Chaney was about 40 when he played —correction: *became*—Quasimodo.

In the 28 surviving stills which constitute this section it is almost possible to recreate, fumetti-wise, the famous film, from its seminal scenes of Quasimodo being crowned King of the Beggers in the Court of Miracles...to his discovery of Esmeralda, the dancing Gypsy girl who dances away with his twisted heart...to his sad, hang-dog reaction to the realization she loves the handsome Captain of the Royal Guard...to the trial where he is betrayed, falsely accused of a kidnapping engineered by the evil Jehan...to the torturous hours on the whipping wheel ("I thirst!")...till, stabbed by the dagger of the treacherous Jehan, he crawls away to die, to the bells, his beloved bells, and he tolls his own death-knell, telling the world that poor deaf crippled Quasimodo the ugly, the unwanted, the unloved and hate-haunted, is leaving the life that so cruelly mistreated him...

Esmeralda was played by Patsy Ruth Miller; Phoebus, her lover, Norman Kerry; the priest Dom Claude, Nigel de Brulier.

Somewhere some nonsense has been printed concerning Chaney's makeup as Quasimodo and/or Erik, to the effect that celluloid discs were inserted in his mouth and pushed up beside his cheekbones to give the accentuated effect you see in the stills. You can also discern this was so much persiflage and poofery (I don't know if there is such a word as poofery; if not, there should be) as it is plain to be seen in both cases that lumps of something or other—clay, rubber—were simply affixed to his face.

I say this not unkindly: to me his blind eye has always resembled a fried egg.

From Victor Hugo's description you can judge for yourself how well he succeeded in transforming himself:

Horseshoe mouth...irregular teeth, jagged in parts like the battlements of a fortress...horny lip over which one of the terrible teeth protruded like the tusk of an elephant...forked chin...tetrahedron nose...small left eye stubbled up with an eyebrow of carroty bristles...right eye completely overwhelmed and buried by an enormous wen...prodigious head covered with red bristles...between his shoulder an enormous hump, conterbalanced by a frontal protuberance...thighs and legs so strangely formed they touched at no point save the knees, when seen in front seeming to resemble two sickles joined at the handles...feet immense...hands monstrous...But: with all his deformity there was a formidable air of strength, agility and courage. "He looked like a giant who had been broken to pieces and ill soldered together."

Humpty Dumpty of Notre Dame.

* * * * *

AT THE TIME (1923), the Chaney classic was the most expensive motion picture ever made, costing $1,250,000 (a fortune in the days of the penny postcard, when kids under 12 could get into a Saturday matinee for nine cents). Pre-production consumed six months, actual production a year. Total personnel: 4000. In the days before the Makeup Artists Union, Chaney created and applied his own makeup—a three-and-a-half hour task daily.

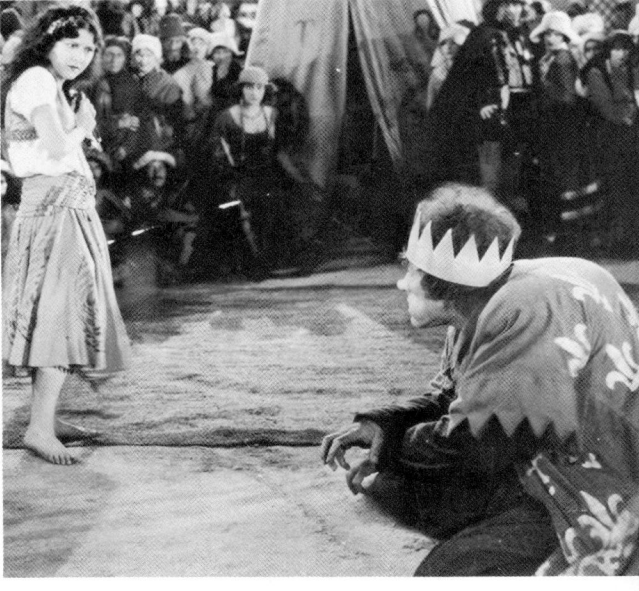

THE HUNCHBACK OF NOTRE DAME (1923)

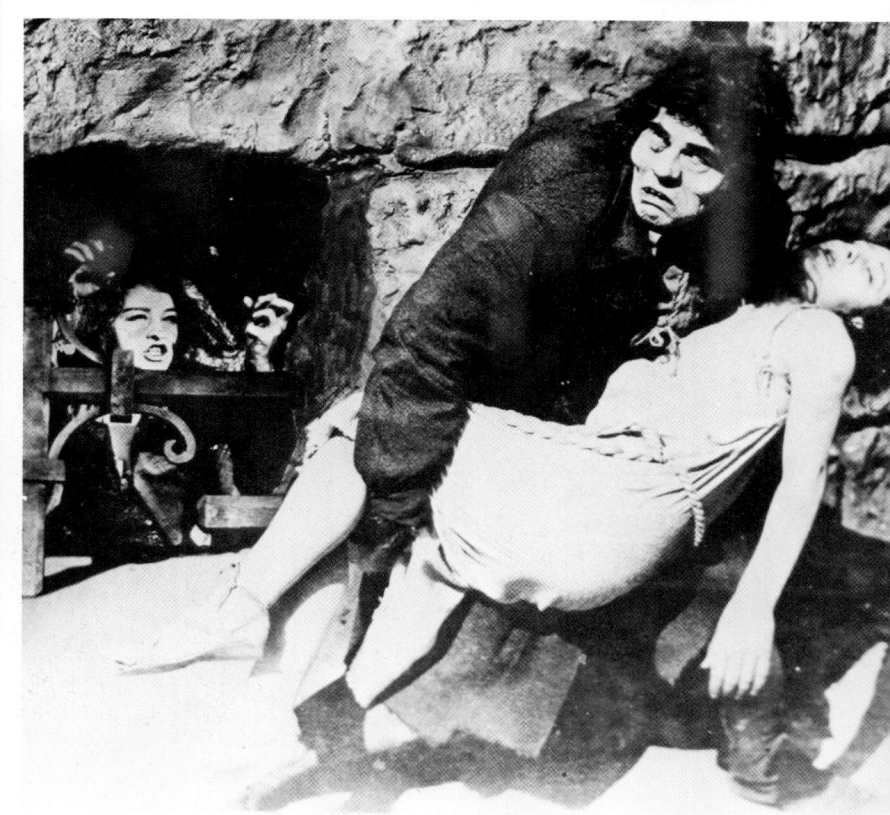

THE HUNCHBACK OF NOTRE DAME (1923)

THE HUNCHBACK OF NOTRE DAME (1923)

From internal evidence, this would be the director, Wallace Worsley, studying a portion of the script while Patsy Ruth Miller and Lon Chaney look on.

105

Left to right: Director (?), unidentified gentleman, Carl Laemmle Sr. (President of Universal Studios) and ...Quasimodo.

Nine Lon Lookalikes for quasi-Quasimodo contest held at the time.

Billy Davis attracts (or repels—note frowning lady) pedestrians as he appears on the sidewalk as the Hunchback at Oklahoma City premiere in 1923.

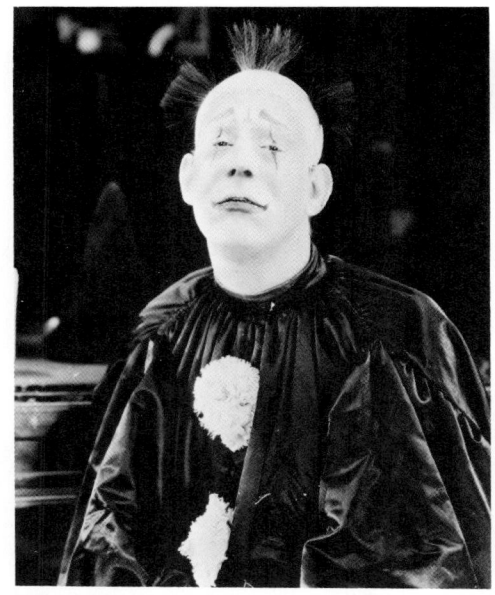

HE WHO GETS SLAPPED
1924

"HE": LON. Consuelo, Norma Shearer. Bezano, John Gilbert. Count Mancini, Tully Marshall (seen stabbing Chaney). (In the 30s Norma Shearer made a film with Clark Gable called IDOT'S DELIGHT in which quite a bit of the artificial language Esperanto was spoken. She signed a photo for me in the universalanguage at the time. She has been in retirement for many years and several years ago when asked for an autograph through the mail by an admirer, her secretary responded that Ms. Shearer no longer gives autographs. As is reported elsewhere in this volume, Gilbert was feuding with Chaney at the time this film was made. Chaney was later to have starred in CHERI-BIBI, ironically made with—John Gilbert in the lead. The film was also released as THE PHANTOM OF PARIS. By—guess who?—Gaston Leroux! He, directed by Victor Seastrom, Garbo's original mentor.

HE WHO GETS SLAPPED (1924)

1924
HE WHO GETS SLAPPED

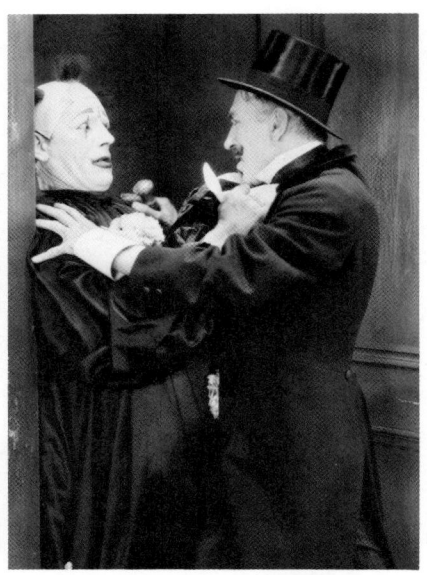

1924
HE WHO GETS SLAPPED

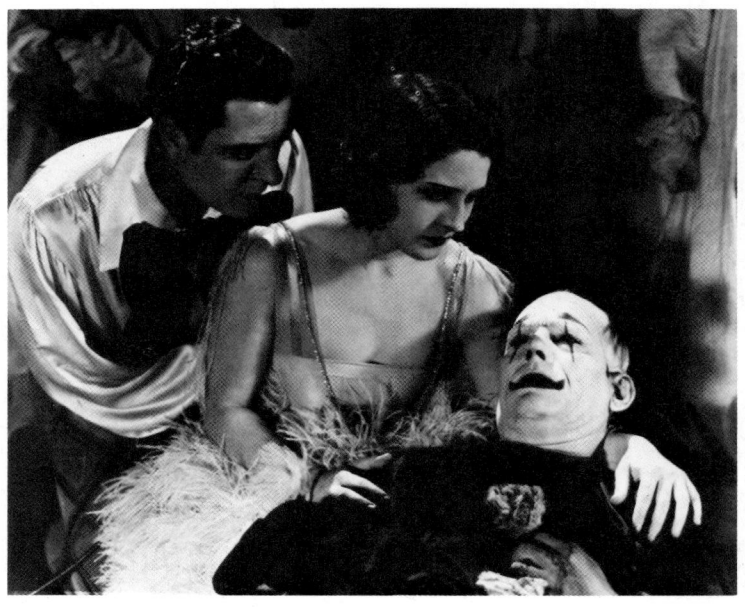

TOWER OF LIES
1925

JAN: Lon. Goldie: Norma Shearer. Lars: Ian Keith. Katrina: Claire McDowell. August: William Haines. Erik: David Torrence. Based on *The Emperor of Portugallia* by Selma Lagerlof. Directed by Victor Seastrom.

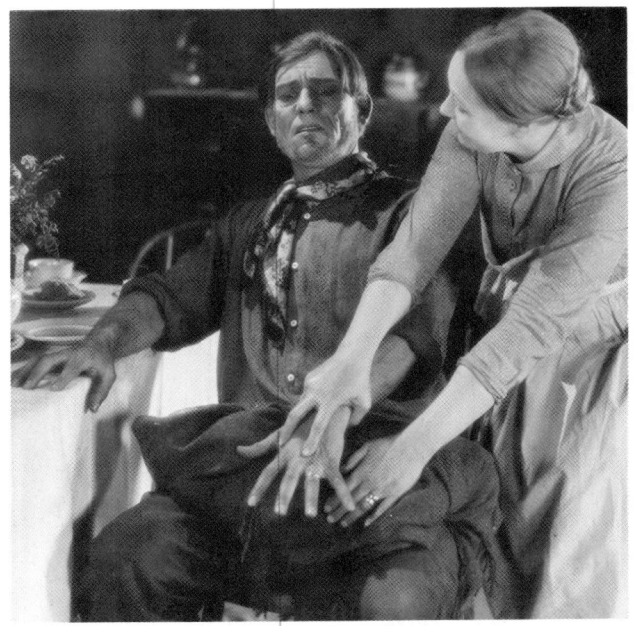

1925
THE TOWER OF LIES

THE TOWER OF LIES (1925)

THE TOWER OF LIES (1925)

THE TOWER OF LIES (1925)

THE MONSTER 1925

DR. ZISKA: Lon Chaney. Directed by Roland West. From a play by Crane Wilbur. Photographed by Hal Mohr.

I don't know which film was crazier—sillier: SEVEN FOOTPRINTS TO SATAN (a Non-Chaney fanta-farce of 1929) or THE MONSTER. Both were ludicrous to say the least: to say the most, they were ridiculous. One thing chilled me in THE MONSTER, though, and stuck in my memory from age eight: the opening, where Chaney had lowered a huge mirror across a road and caused a car to careen off when it mistook its own headlights for an approaching car collision-bound.

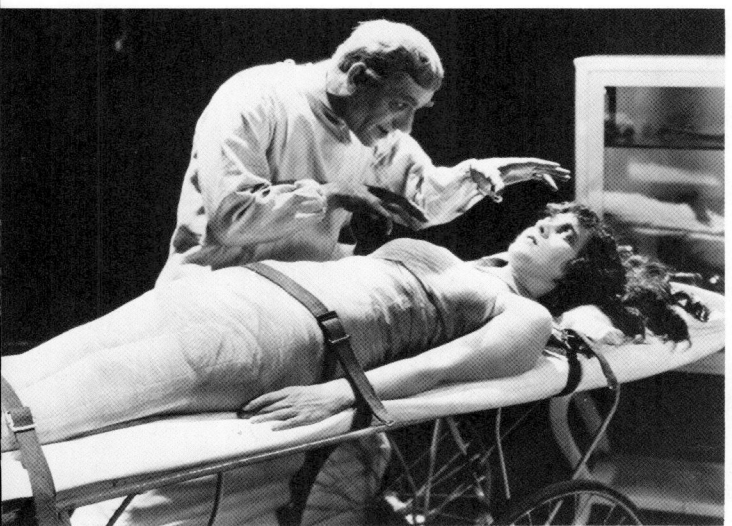

121

THE MONSTER (1925)

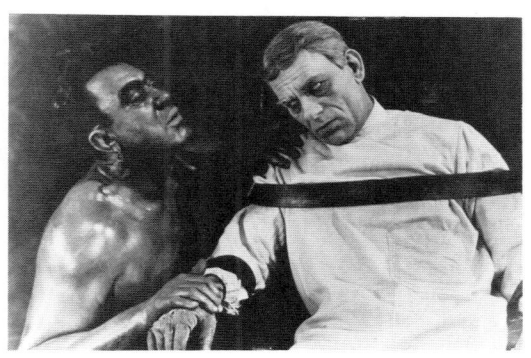

THE MONSTER (1925)

1925
THE MONSTER

TOD BROWNING, director. Chaney as Singapore Joe. H.B. Walthall, priest. Owen Moore, the Admiral. Lois Moran, Singapore's daughter. Photographed by Merritt Gerstad. The notorious "collodion cataract" film.

THE ROAD TO MANDALAY
1926

GRANDPAS (AND MA'S) OF THE 80's
MAY REMEMBER THESE OF THE 20'S

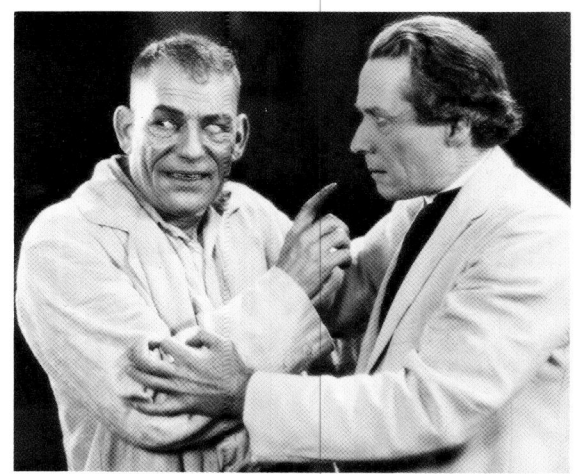

THE ROAD TO MANDALAY (1926)

THE ROAD TO MANDALAY (1926)

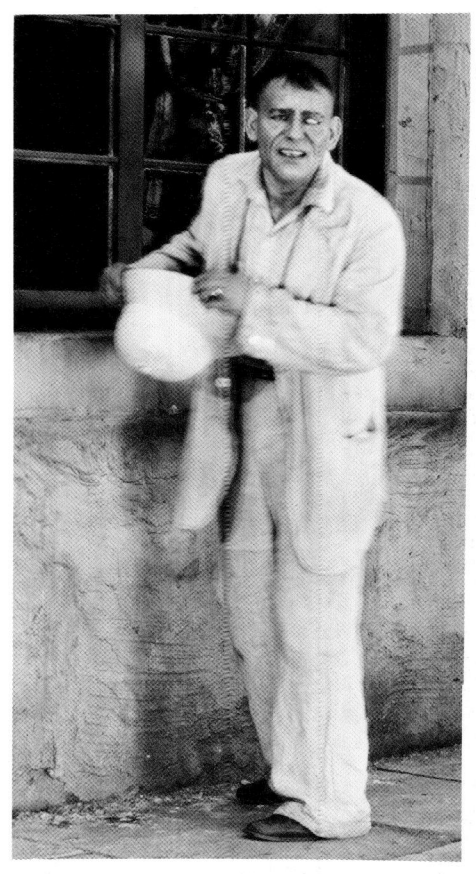

128

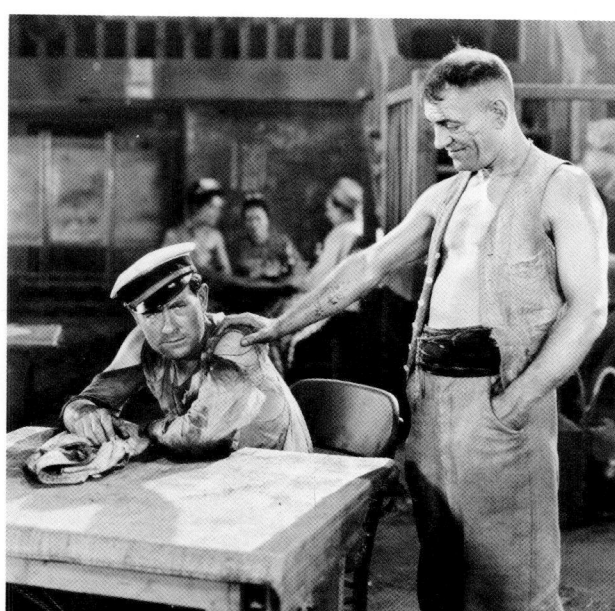

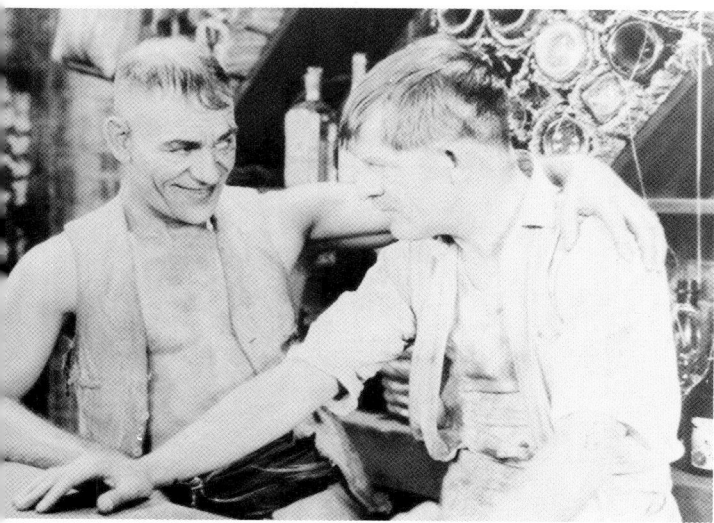

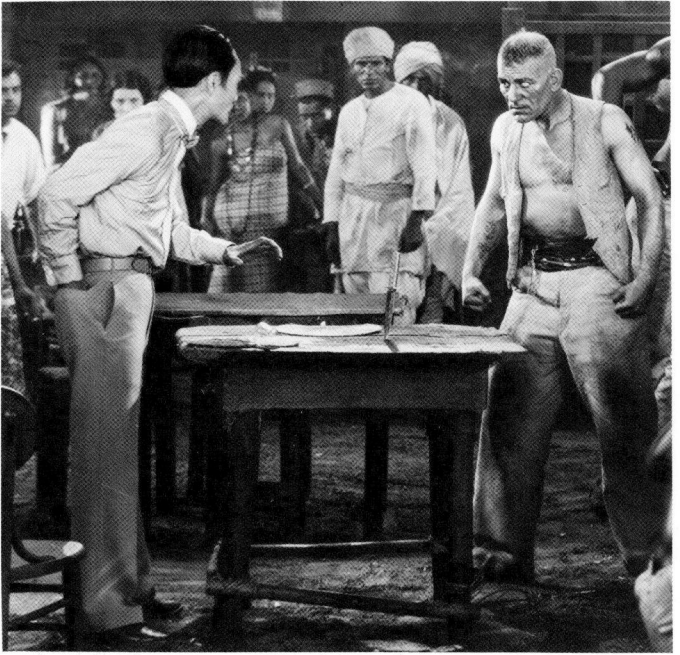

1926
THE ROAD TO MANDALAY

131

THE ROAD TO MANDALAY (1926)

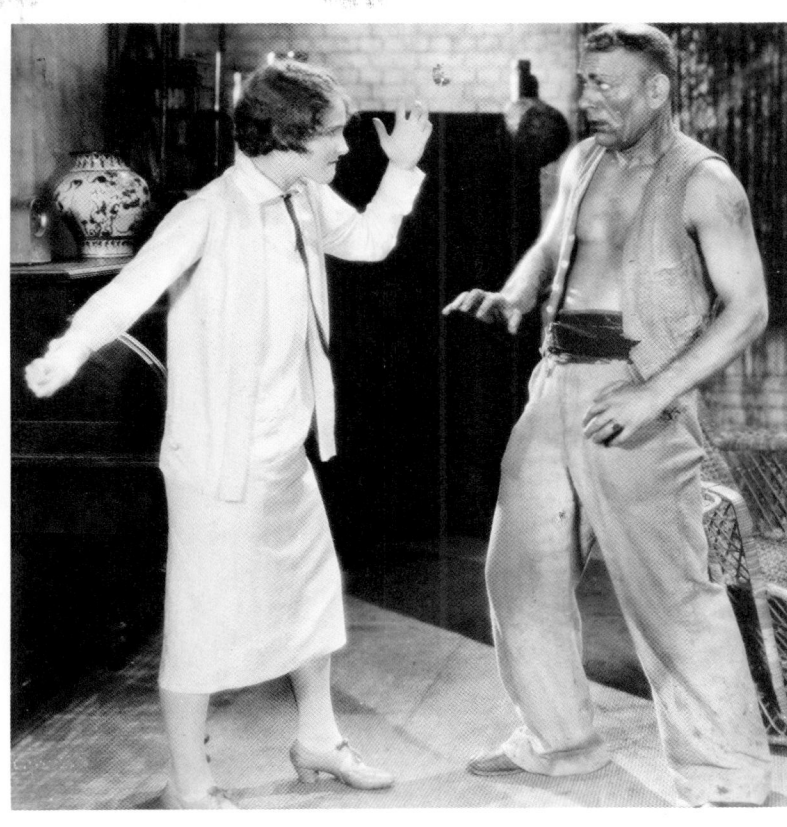

ANOTHER BROWNING (from his own story). Lon as Alonzo. (Alonzo was Chaney's real first name.) Norman Kerry (hero of both HUCHBACK and PHANTOM) as Malabar. Joan Crawford (!) as Estrellita. In the beginning of the film Lon has 2 thumbs on one hand. Later he has his arms amputated. However, even armless he is far from harmless. A nice print of this exists in the Cinematheque in Bruxelle, Belgique (translation: Brussels, Belgium). At a revival in Los Angeles in 1980, the local faithfuls were to be seen revelling in Chaney's artistry: Ray Bradbury, Robert Block, Dale Winogura, Tim Wohlgemuth, Bill Warren, Bill Nolan, George Turner, DeWitt Bodeen, Brian Forbes and, inevitably, Yours Chaneyly, FJA.

THE UNKNOWN 1927

THE UNKNOWN (1927)

MOCKERY 1927

SERGEI: Chaney. Dimitri, Ricardo Cortez. Tatiana, Barbara Bedford. Mr. Gaidaroff, Mark Swain. Director, Benjamin Christensen. Photographer, Merritt Gerstad.

MOCKERY (1927)

MOCKERY (1927)

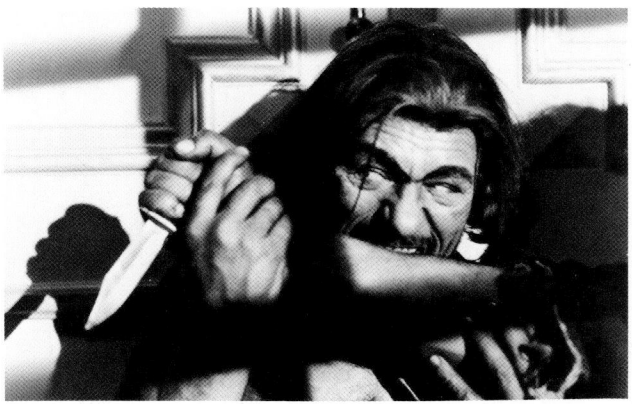

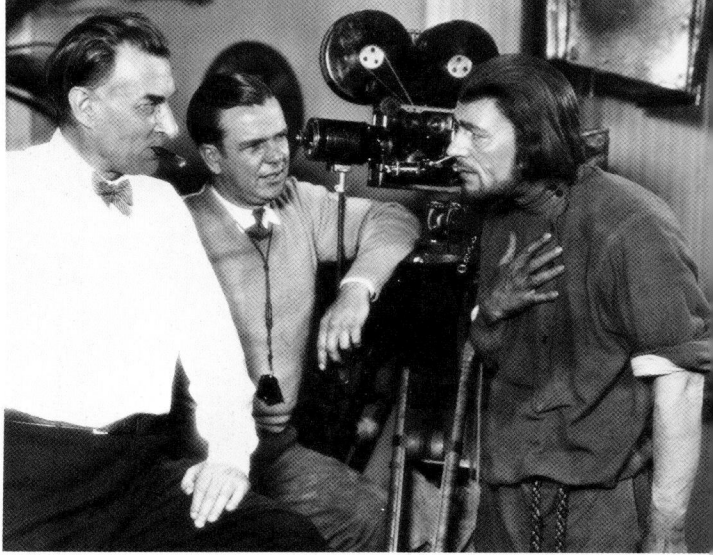

MOCKERY (1927)

TELL IT TO THE MARINES 1926

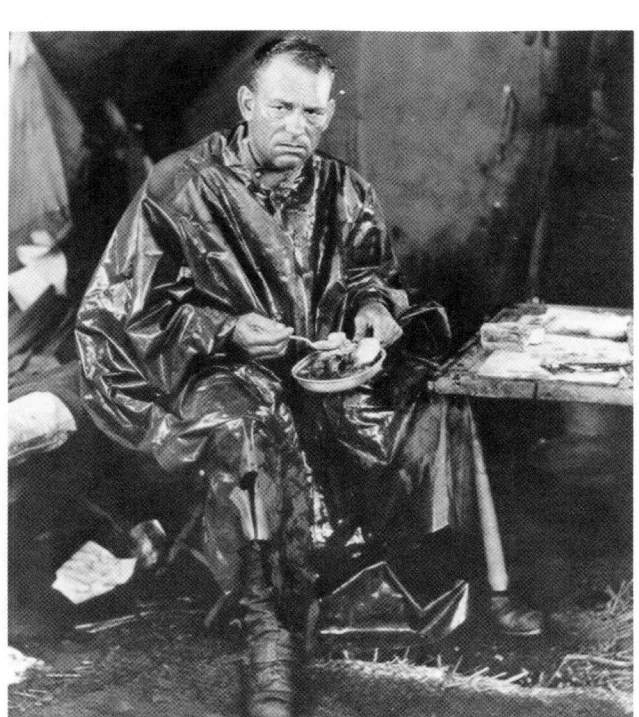

SGT. O'HARA: Lon chaney. Pvt. Skeet Burns, William Haines. Norma Hale, Eleanor Boardman. Cpl. Madden, Eddie Gribbon. Zaya, Carmel Myers. Chinese Bandit Leader (!)—Warner Oland, of Fu Manchu fame, Charlie Chan and the Tibetan lycanthrope in WEREWOLF OF LONDON. Director, George Hill.

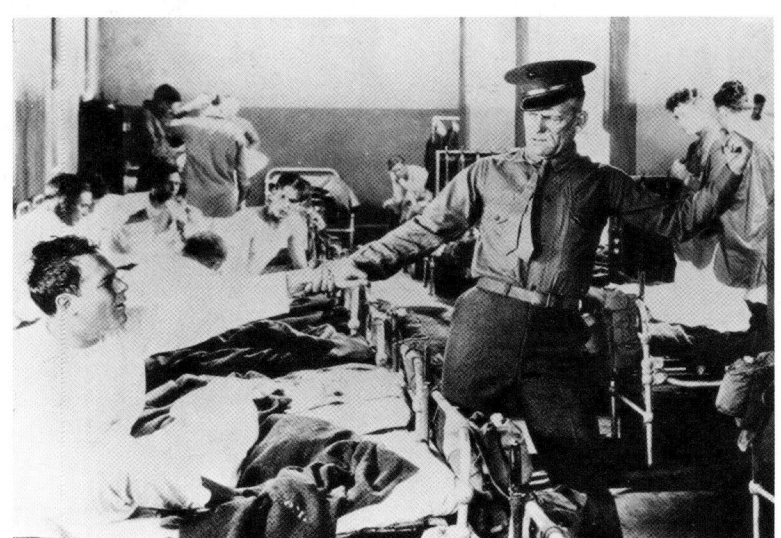

1926
TELL IT TO THE MARINES

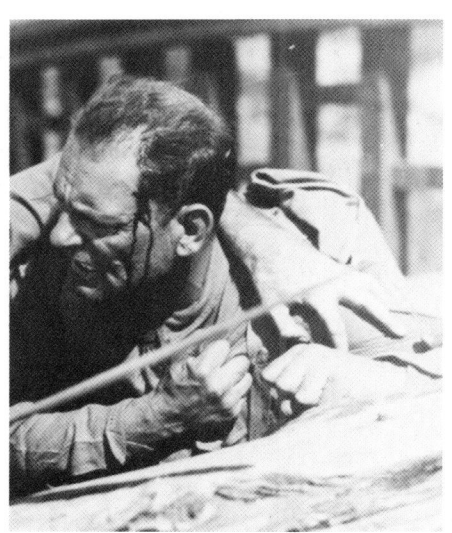
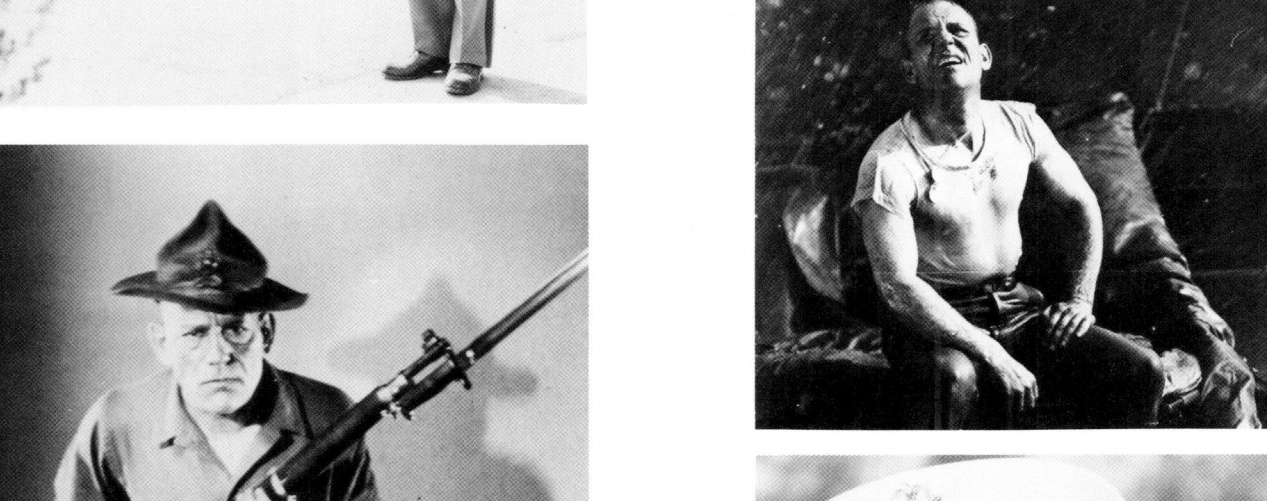

LAUGH, CLOWN, LAUGH 1928

TITO: Chaney. Simonetta, Loretta Young. Simon, Bernard Seigel. Luigi, Nils (THE MAN IN HALF-MOON STREET) Asther. From the play by David Belasco and Tom Cushing, based on the Italian play *Ridi, Pagliacci*. Director, Herbert Brenon. Photographer, James Wong Howe.

LAUGH, CLOWN, LAUGH (1928)

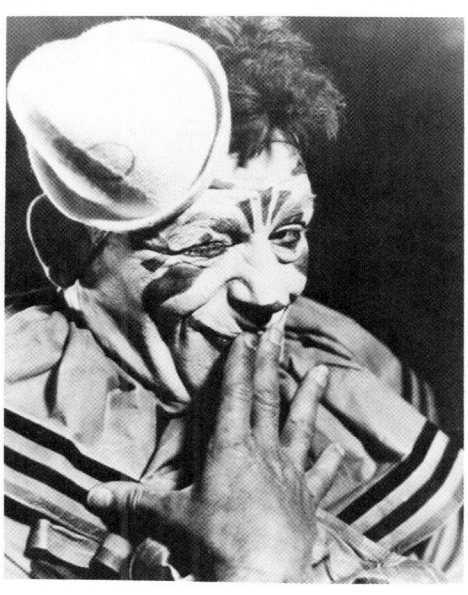
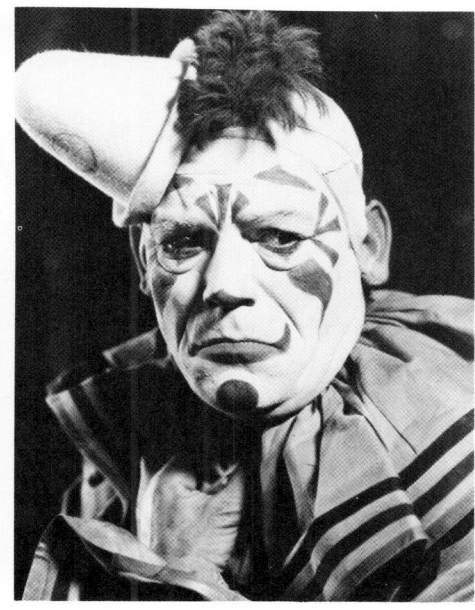

1928
LAUGH, CLOWN, LAUGH

LAUGH, CLOWN, LAUGH

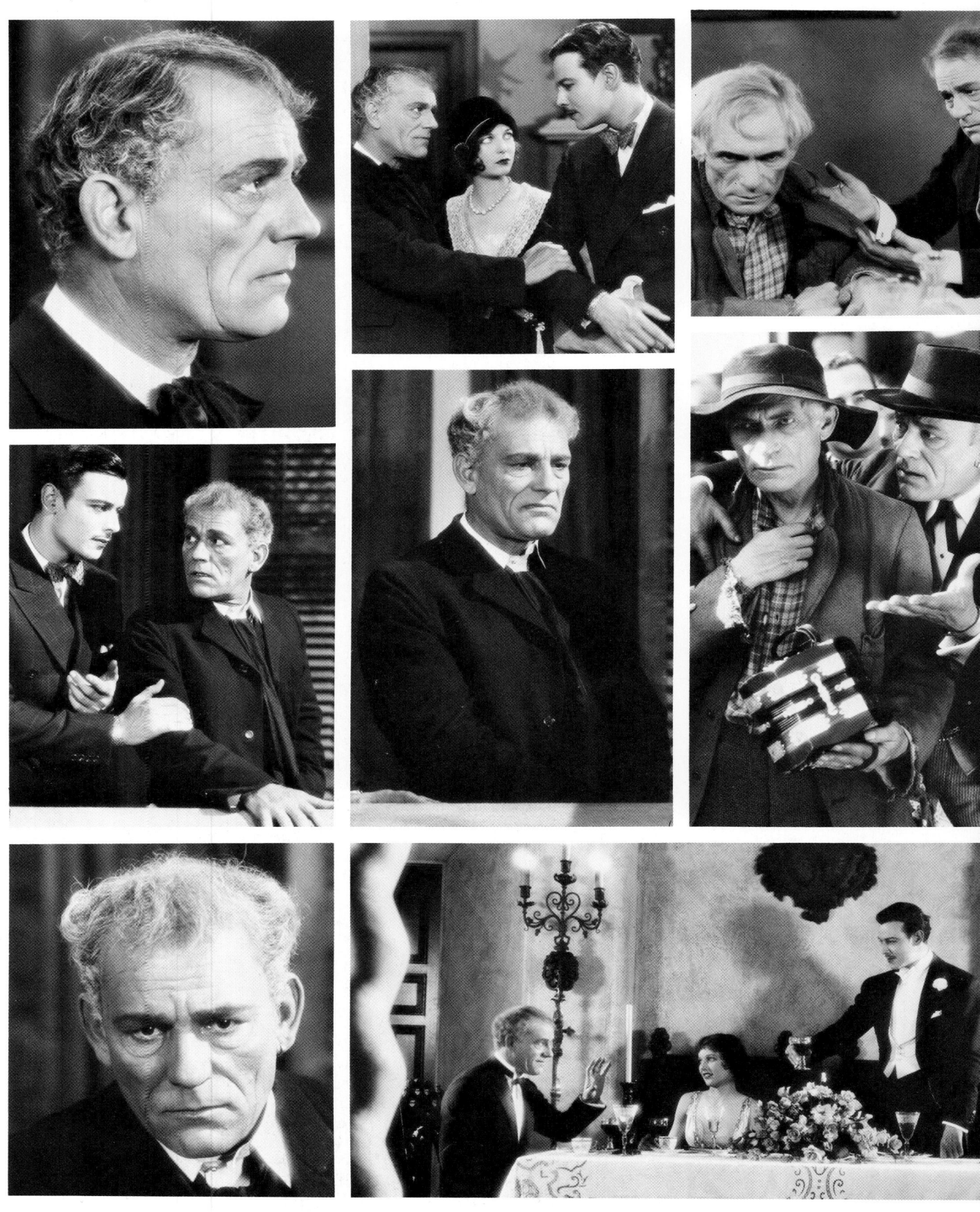

LAUGH, CLOWN, LAUGH

LAUGH, CLOWN, LAUGH

AS I REMEMBER IT, when I was 12 or 13 years old, in 1928 or '29, my parents and maternal grandparents, brother Alden and I, went to a (no longer existent) place called Tent City, Coronado, Calif., near San Diego, for summer vacations, and nightly at eight or nine there was a man who would repeat Lon Chaney's performance in LAUGH, CLOWN, LAUGH of sliding upsidedown on his head down about a 45° wire. He didn't actually slide directly on his head but, as I recall, a small wooden circle, say like a coaster for drinks, with a groove in it which fit on the wire. I looked forward to the nightly "slide for life". I wonder, now, if he perhaps doubled for Chaney in the picture?

WHILE THE CITY SLEEPS 1928

DAN: LON. Myrtle, Anita (BROADWAY MELODY) Page. Marty, Carroll Nye. Skeeter, Wheeler Oakman. Bessie, Mae Busch. Mrs. McGinnis, Polly (LONDON AFTER MIDNIGHT) Moran.

WHILE THE CITY SLEEPS (1928)

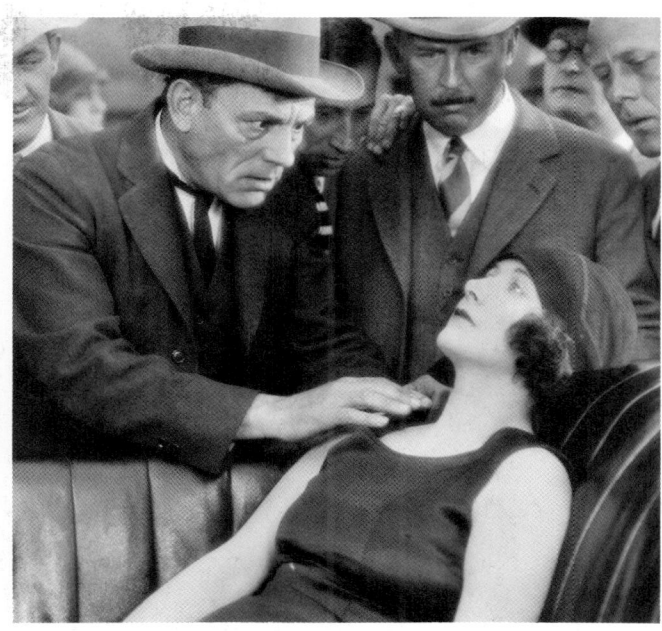

WHILE THE CITY SLEEPS (1928)

161

WHILE THE CITY SLEEPS (1928)

WHILE THE CITY SLEEPS (1928)

CHUCK COLLINS: Lon Chaney. Sunshine, Marcelline Day (brunet). Curl, James Murray. Helen, Betty Compson (blond). Directed by Tod Browning from a story by Tod Browning, scenario by Waldemar Young.

THE BIG CITY 1928

1928
THE BIG CITY

THE BIG CITY (1928

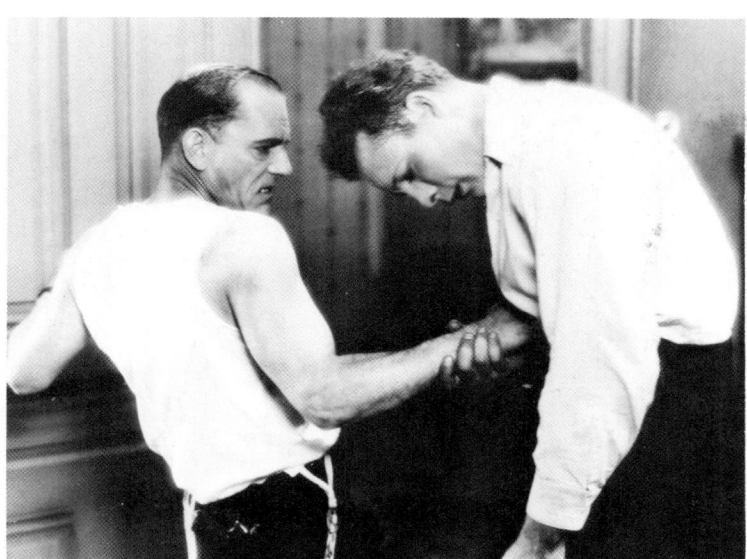

THE BIG CITY (1928)

KONGO was the name of the play from which it was adapted. Chaney played Phroso. Browning directed. Lionel Barrymore was Crane, Lon's nemesis. Warner (SIX HOURS TO LIVE) Baxter was featured. Mary Nolan as Maizie gave an *excellent* performance.

WEST OF ZANZIBAR 1928

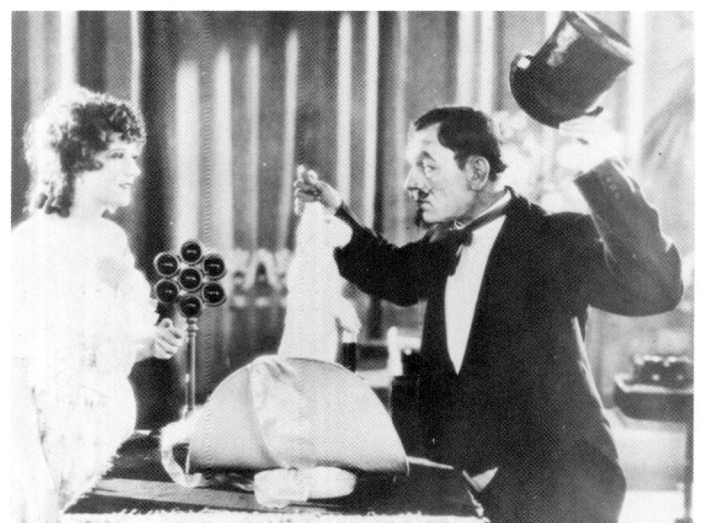

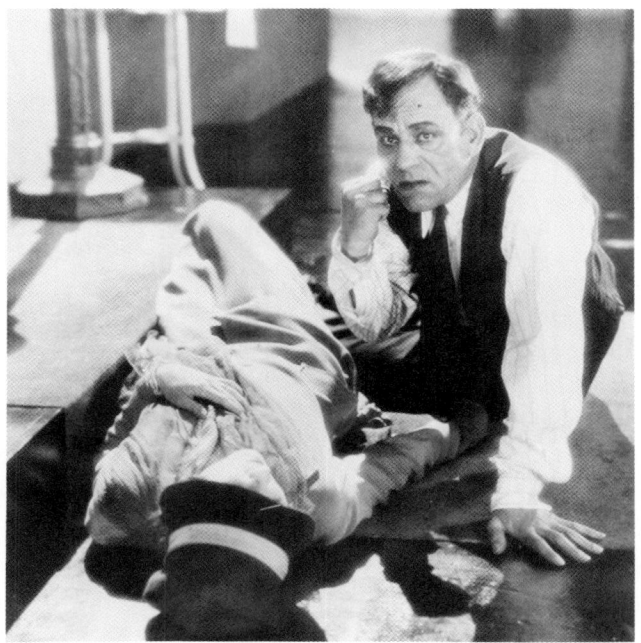

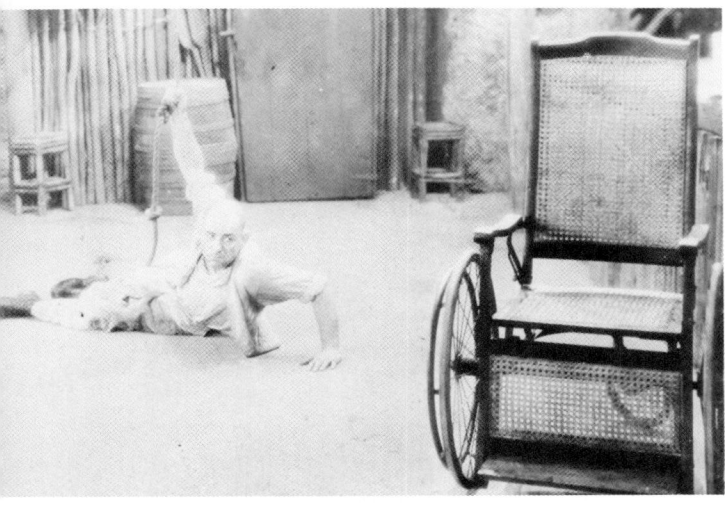

WEST OF ZANZIBAR (1928)

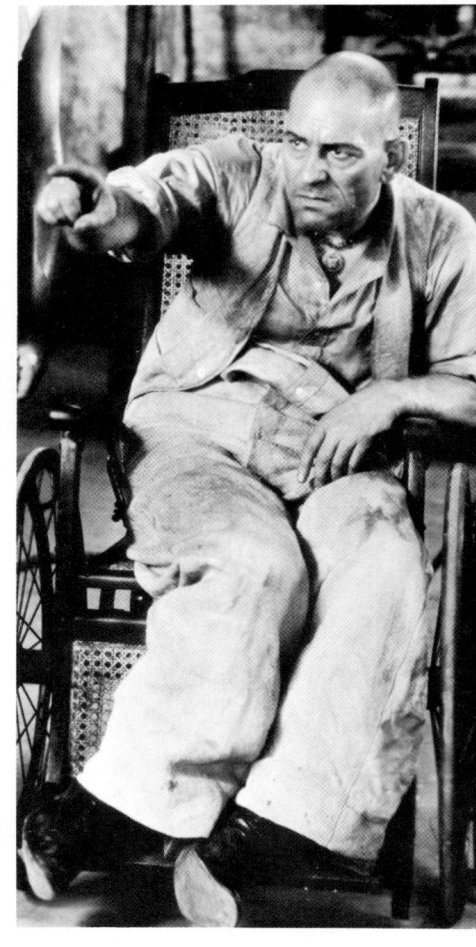

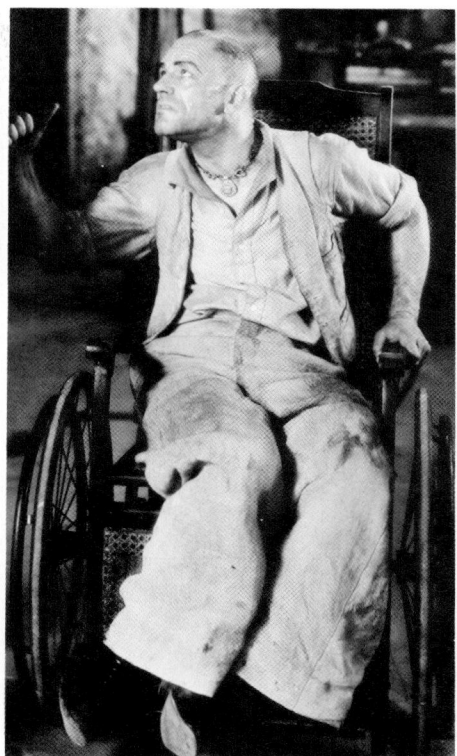
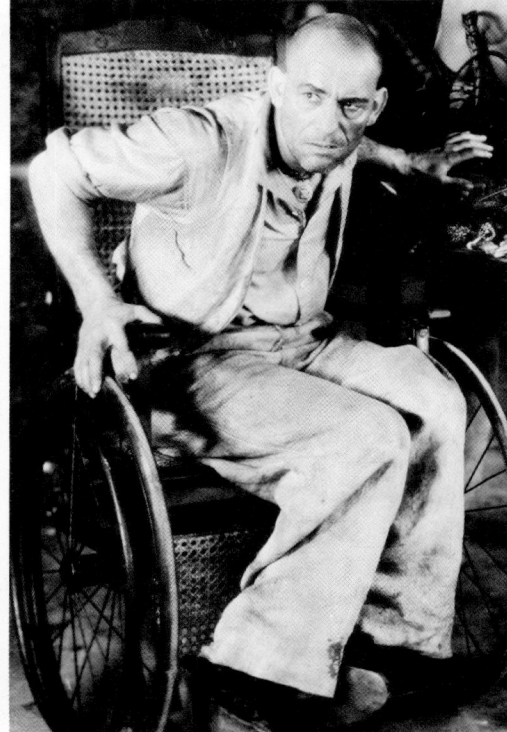

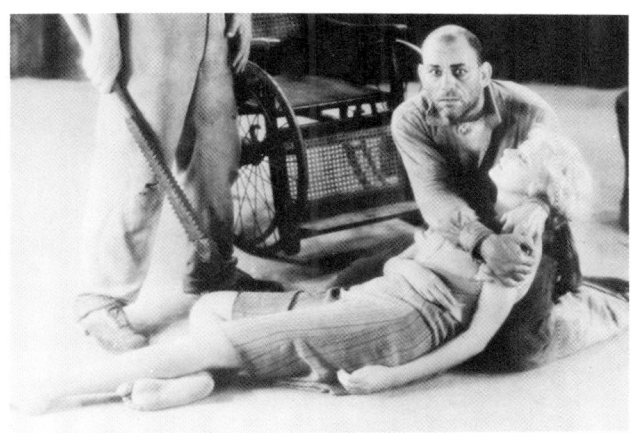

175

WEST OF ZANZIBAR (1928)

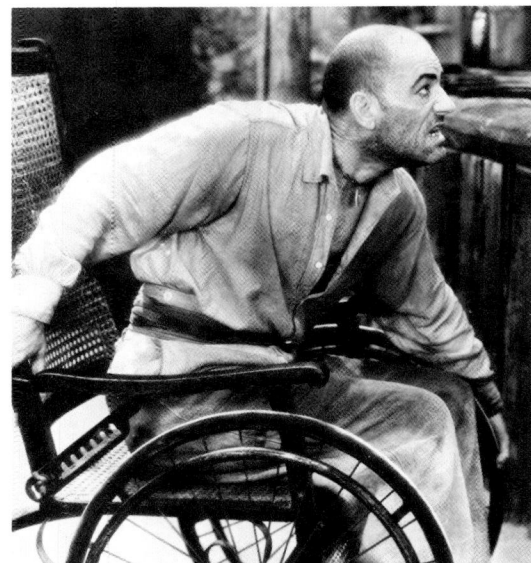
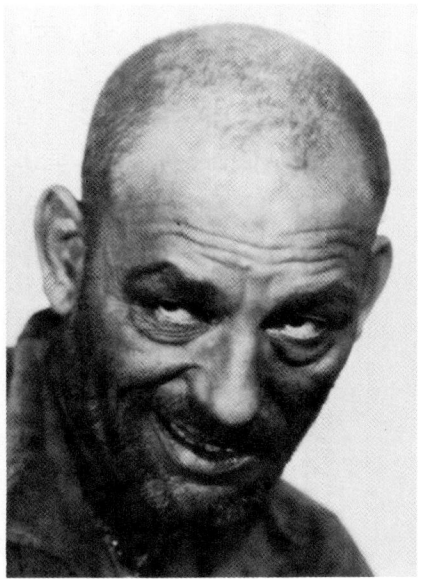

WEST OF ZANZIBAR (1928)

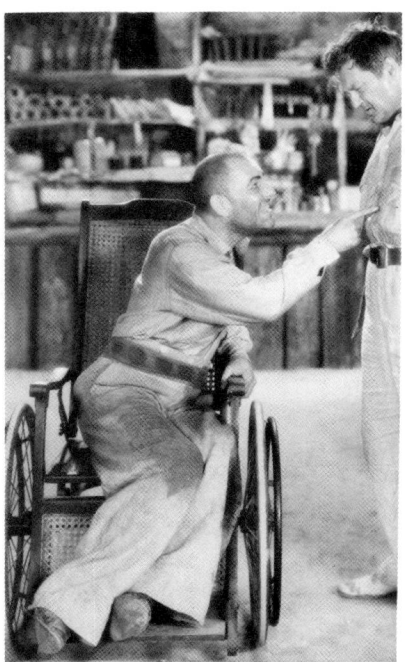
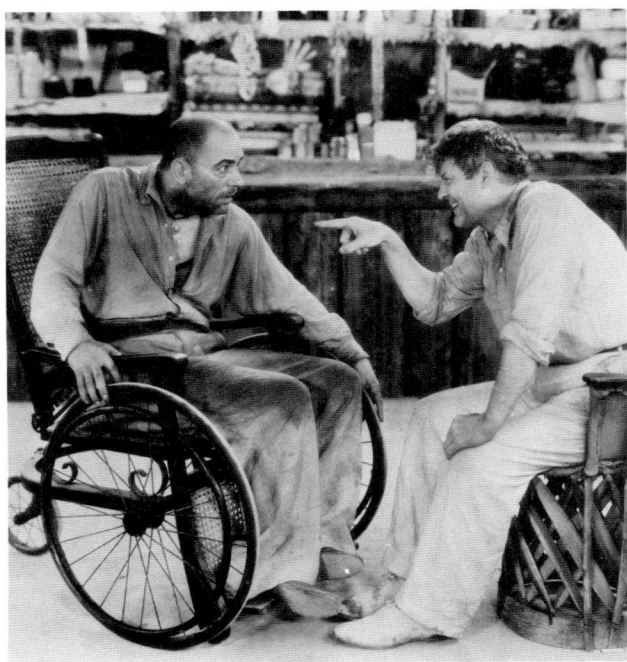

WEST OF ZANZIBAR (1928)

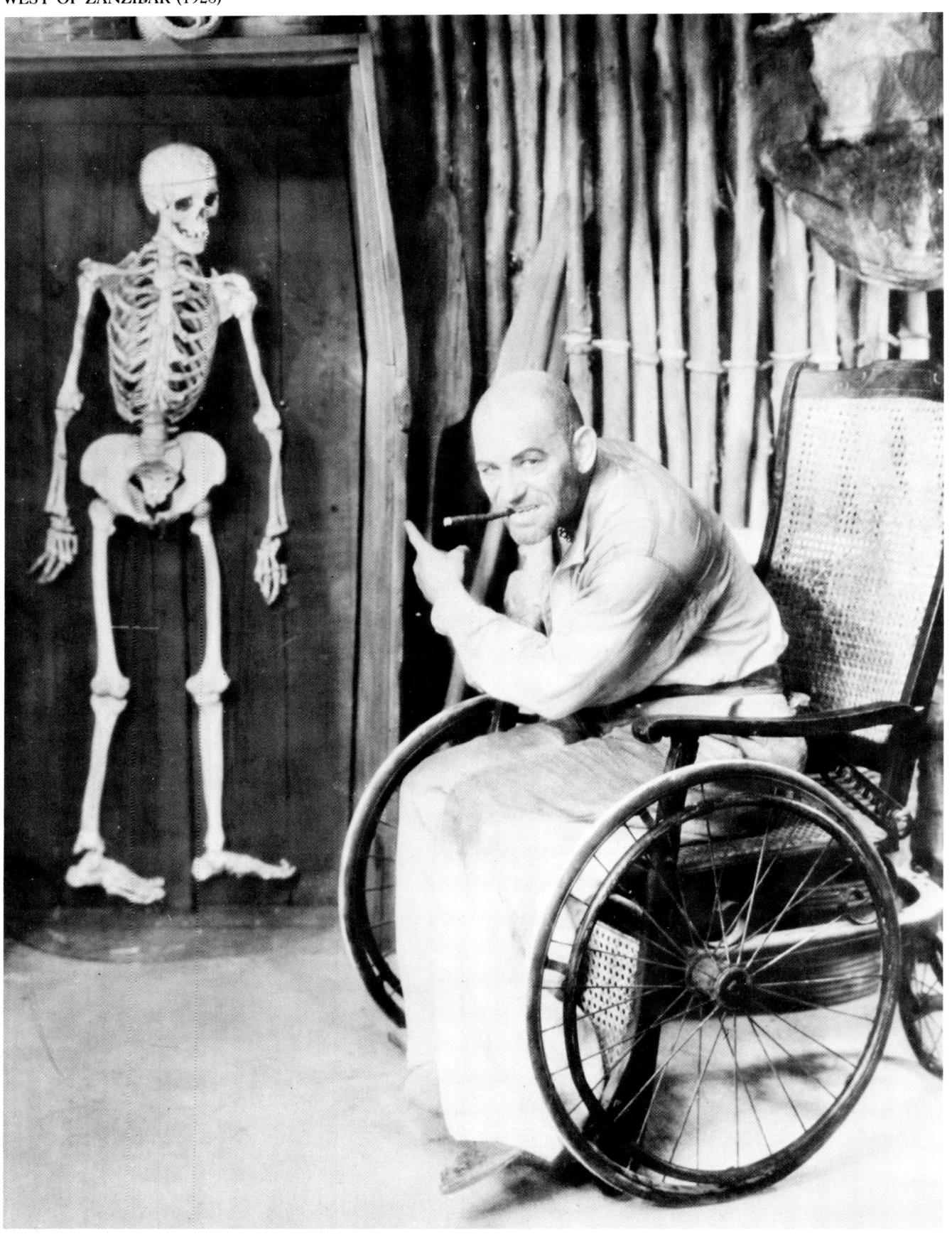

GRUMPY ANDERSON Lon Chaney. Zella, Phyllis Haver. Tommy, James Murray. Director, William Nigh.

THUNDER 1929

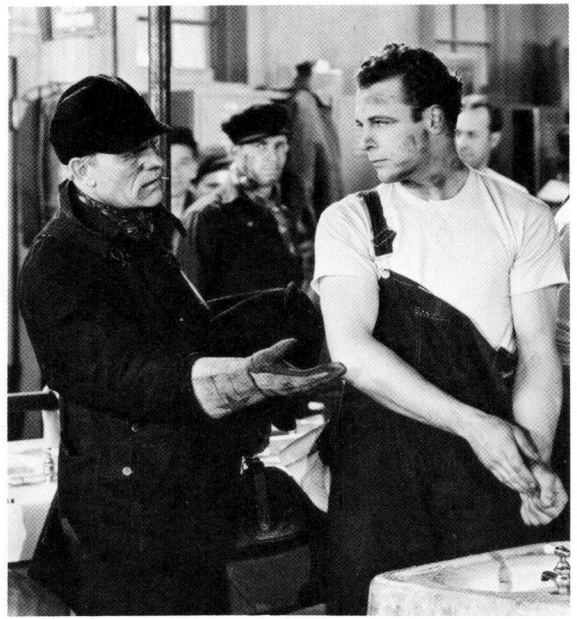

THUNDER (1929)

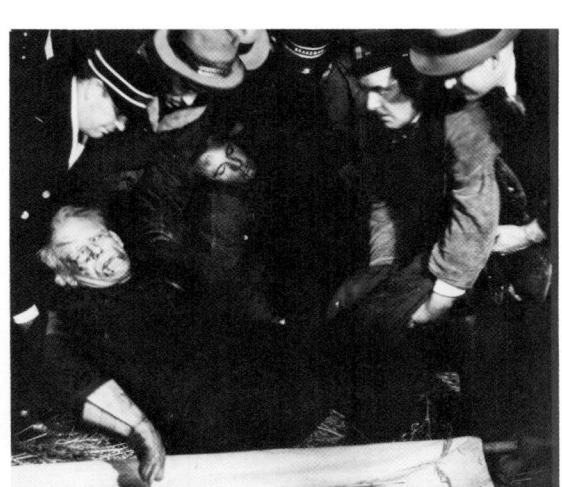

THUNDER (1929)

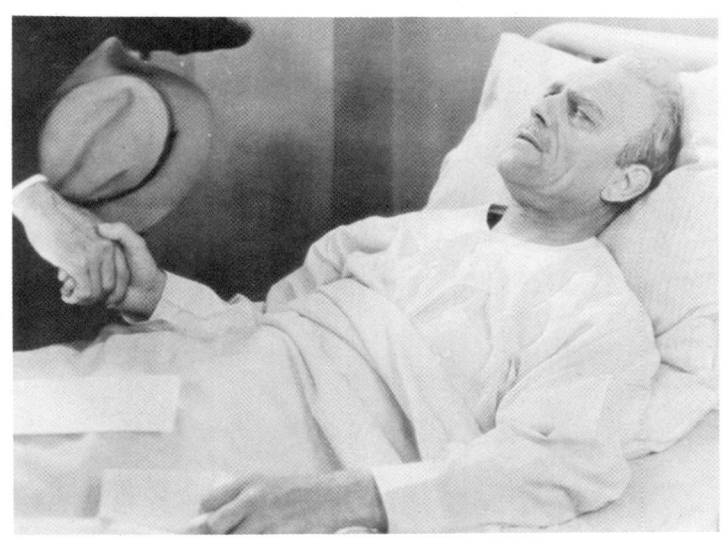

1929

WHERE EAST IS EAST

TIGER HAYNES: Lon Chaney. Toyo, Lupe Velez (seen in the majority of female scenes with Lon. Her sobriquet was "Mexican Spitfire". Once married to Johnny "Tarzan" Weissmuller. Voluntarily ended her life.) Mme. De Silva, Estelle Taylor (the Eurasian). Bobby Bailey, Lloyd (THE LOST WORLD) Hughes. Story by Tod Browning and Harry Sinclair Drago. Directed by Browning.

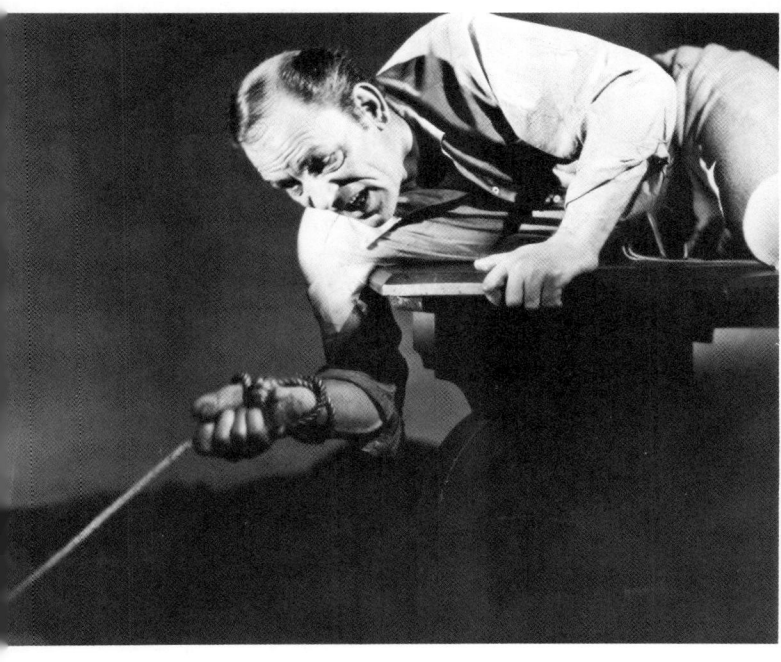

1929
WHERE EAST IS EAST

187

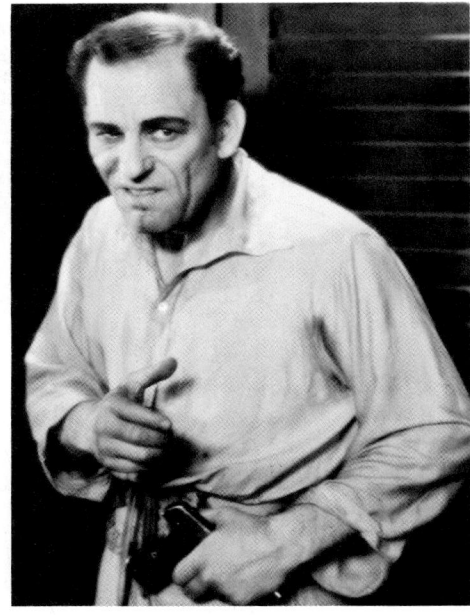

WHERE EAST IS EAST (1929)

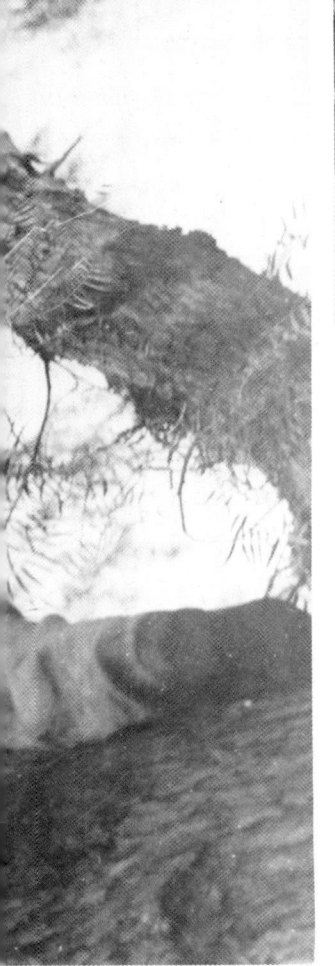
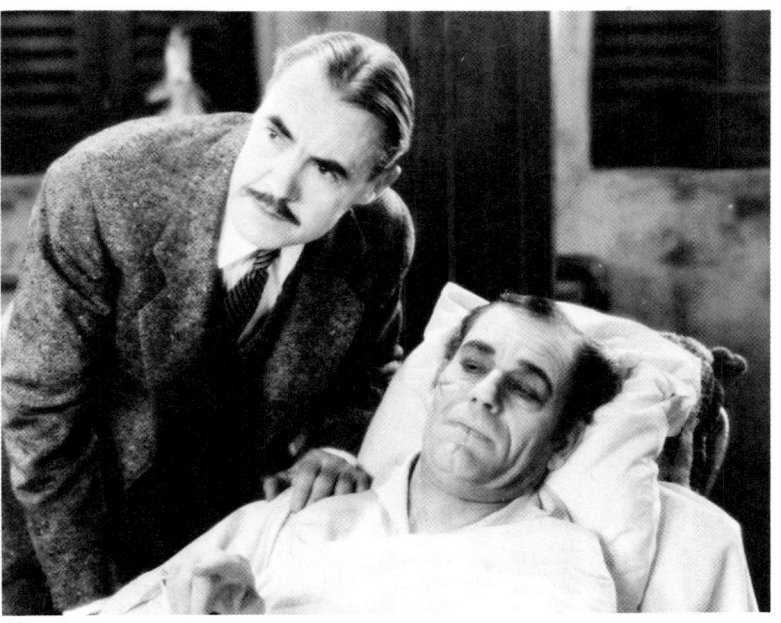

THE UNHOLY THREE (Silent & Sound)

ODD: TOD Robbins wrote it, TOD Browning directed the screenplay adapted from the original work. If that sounds like an echo, consider this: Lon Chaney played Echo in the film, a sideshow ventriloquist who connived with the circus strong man (Victor McLaglen as Hercules) and a circus midget (Harry Earles as Tweedledee) to steal jewels in a unique fashion calling for Chaney to disguise himself as an elderly lady and Earles to be a baby of buggy age. The giant and the mite commit a murder in the course of robbing a house...the midge makes the mistake of goading the goliath, much as Fritz did with the Frankenstein monster, and gets killed for hectoring Hercules, who in turn dies at the hairy paws of Echo's trained gorilla. Echo loves Rosie O'Grady (Mae Busch), who loves another, as was usually Lon's lot, and the boyfriend (Hector McDonald, played by Matt Moore) is falsely accused of the murder. Lon turns good guy in the end and, through an act of ventriloquism in an unusual court scene, established his rival's innocence.

In the following 21 scenes you see the picture almost recreated before your eyes.
THEN FOLLOWS the remake.

Lila Lee is the heroine this time, Harry Earles reprises his role, Hercules becomes Ivan Linow and Hector is Elliott Nugent. The plotline remains the same. Only the dummy has changed from a brunet to a blond. Queried as to the change, he explained, "Blonds have more fun".

THE UNHOLY THREE
(Silent and Sound)

THE UNHOLY THREE
(Silent and Sound)

THE UNHOLY THREE (Silent and Sound)

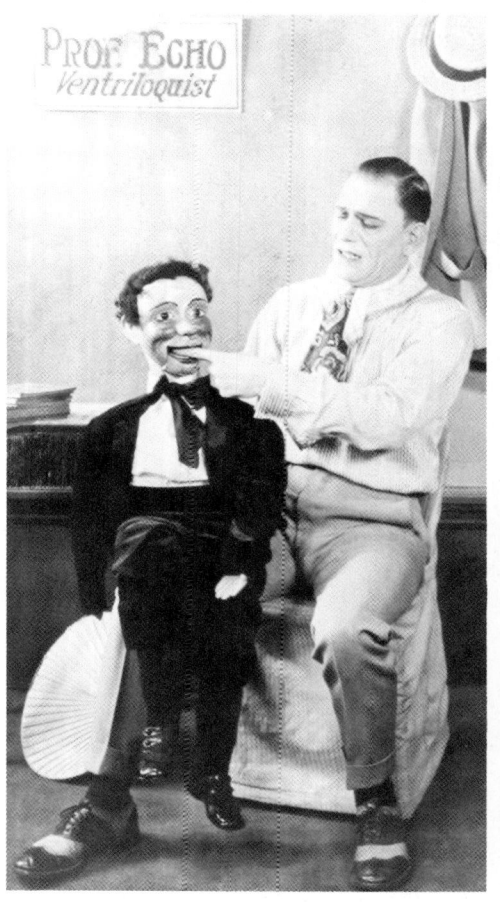

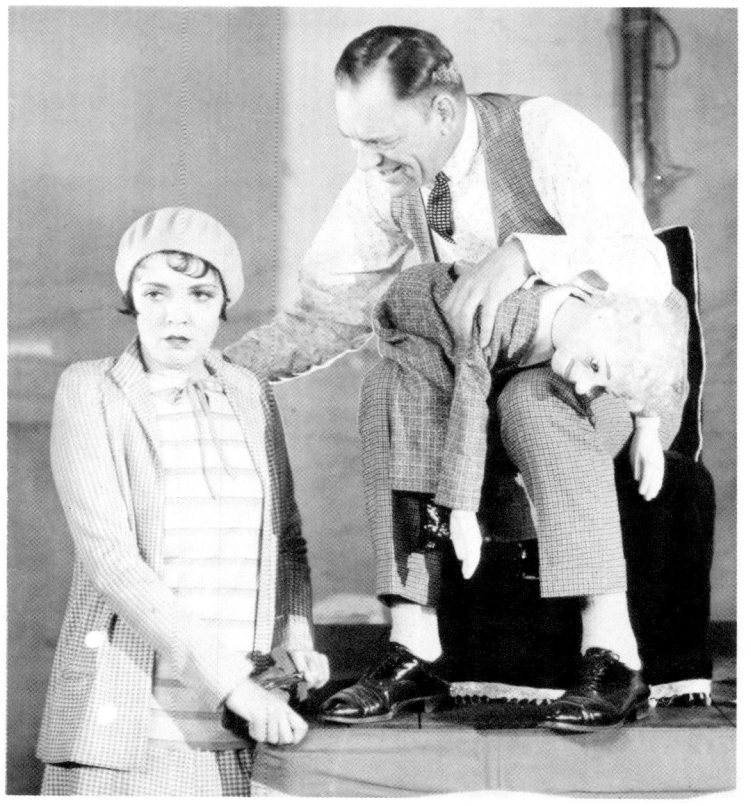

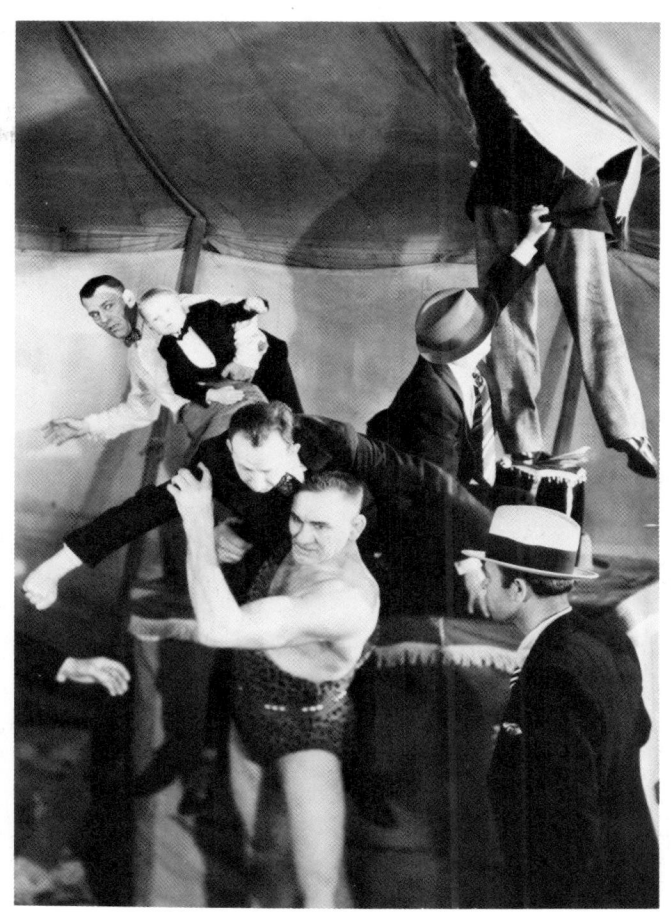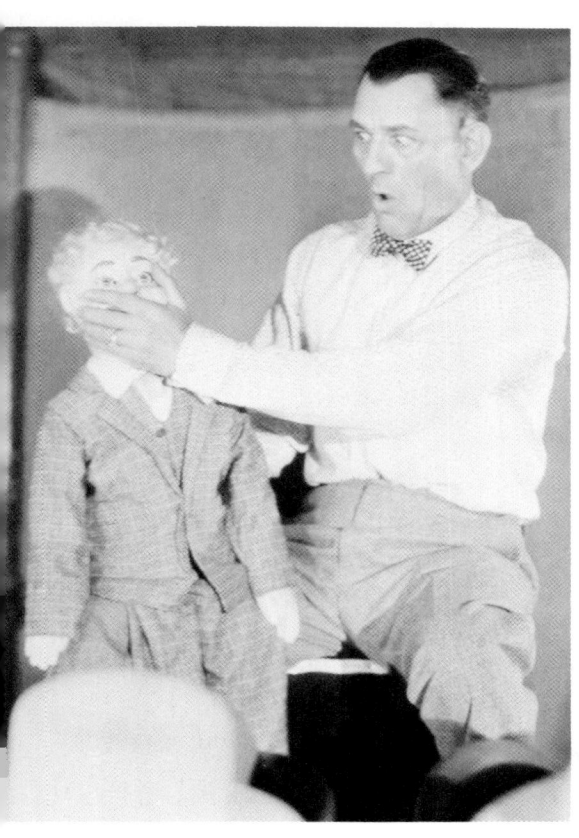

THE UNHOLY THREE (Silent and Sound)

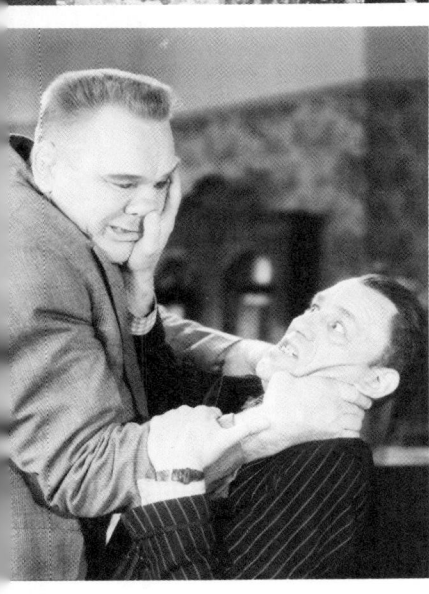

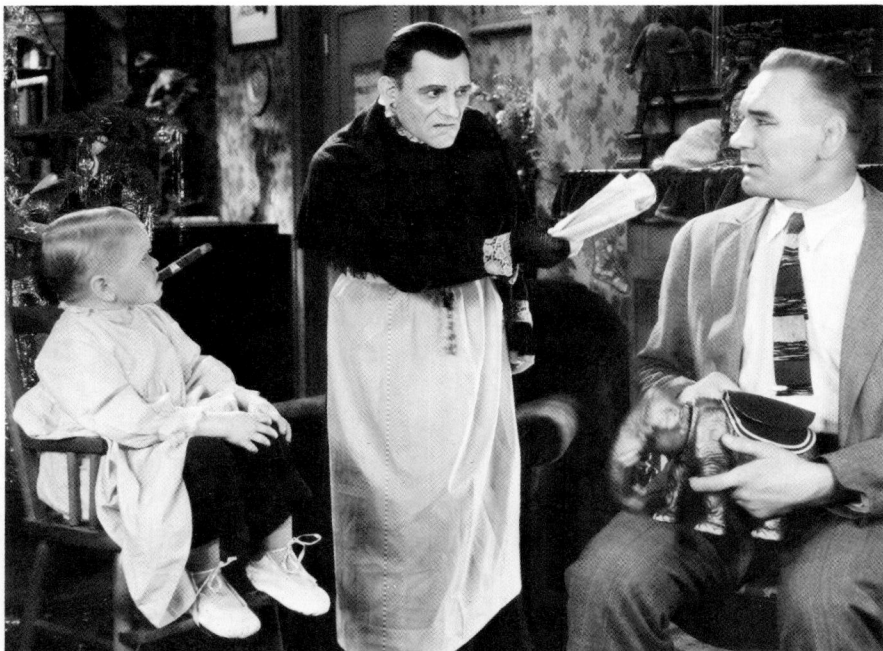

THE UNHOLY THREE
(Silent and Sound)

THE UNHOLY THREE (Silent and Sound)

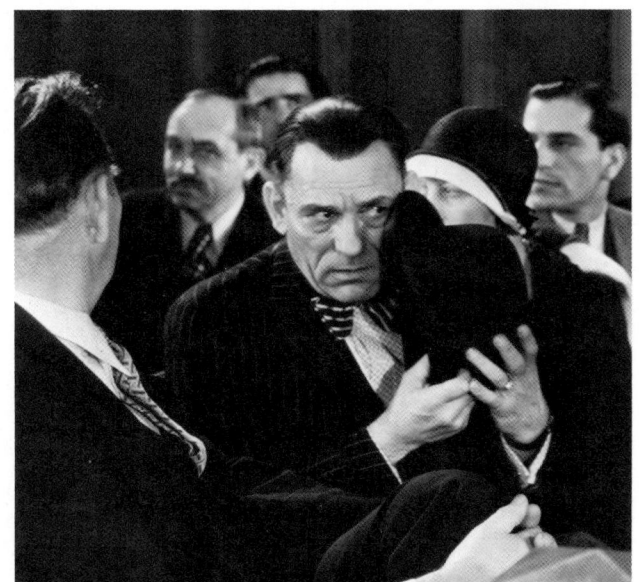

HERE ARE 22 poses of a be-hatted Lon. (Elsewhere in the book is one picture of him besotted). The shots are from THE UNKNOWN, TELL IT TO THE MARINES, THE BIG CITY, WHERE EAST IS EAST, THE ROAD TO MANDALAY and some others which you will recognize by familiarizing yourself with his faces in this book. LAUGH, CLOWN, LAUGH, for instance. The photo of him looking mean in a cocked sailor hat may not be from TELL IT TO THE MARINES, however: on the reverse side of the still the carbon-typed title has been crossed out and some unidentified individual has printed ALL THE BROTHERS WERE VALIANT, in which case he is portraying Mark Store.

MAD HATTER

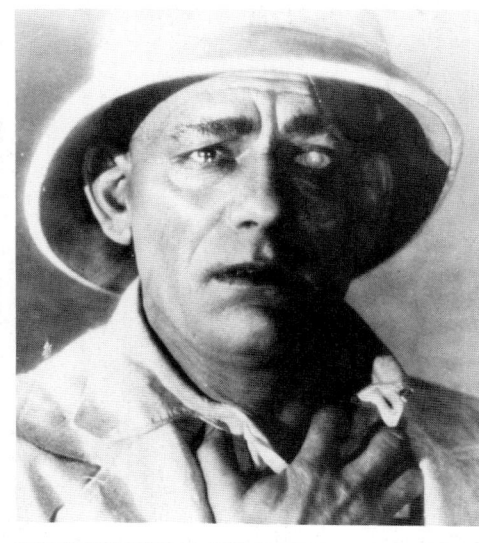

And with a tip of his hat, Lon Chaney waves you on to the next section!

By Elza Schallert

BEHIND LON CHANEY'S

EVERY DAY a new chapter of history is being made for the films. But not until tomorrow can we tell whether the events of today will have value permanent enough to leave their impress.

Talent which radiates a roseate coloring one day is often a faded memory the next. A brilliant new star or director may loom on the horizon and not even in the afterglow of that day's setting sun will the outlines of his achievements be traceable.

Personalities and events rush by with terrific momentum in the film world, and while the interested observer stands on the side lines watching the strange, fascinating group that is Hollywood create history before his very eyes, he may often wonder who among its people are writing records which will survive the test of time.

Lon Chaney, I believe, is writing his signature on the page whose ink is not yet dry. And I believe it will be in years to come a bold, vigorous impression, easy to read and remember.

Chaney is an actor who, once seen, is never forgotten. He may not win your unqualified approval, with his extreme characterizations. He may annoy you more than inspire, with his hideous makeups of clouded eyes, twisted limbs or dangling teeth in a formless head. But you *remember* him!

His masks may be to some a nightmare but the force of his acting is strong enough to make itself felt through a disguise of putty and false hair and iron clamps that would annihilate the most potent of actors.

And in the end, no matter how repulsive the character he plays, no matter how implacably villainous, he always becomes a hero—a tragic one, perhaps—who gains your sympathy and touches the heart.

I have never before known an actor who deliberately invited trouble, discomfort, and physical hardship, as Chaney does, for the purposes of his work. There is no one conparable to him except an East Indian dervish, who, fired with an overwhelming passion for his faith, inflicts corporal punishment upon himself to prove his complete devotion.

To be sure, we all have known actors and authors and other artists who have now and again invited trouble for themselves. But not from choice. They just haven't known any better. But with Chaney it is quite a different story. Of him it may truly be said, here is an actor who verily suffers for his art.

In THE HUNCHBACK OF NORTE DAME he wore a pack of steel on his back, for the purpose of creating a deformity, and a steel vise which distorted his legs, not to mention a heavy mask to emphasize facial grotesqueries, all of which doubtless caused him great discomfort.

In THE PENALTY, one of his first conspicuous pictures following THE MIRACLE MAN, he had his legs below the knee strapped upward and back to give the appearance of being legless.

A medical solution was used in one of his eyes in THE ROAD TO MANDALAY to achieve the realistic effect of a cataract. A painful process and certainly dangerous.

As the aged mandarin in MR. WU, he wore clamps on his cheeks to pull them tightly back, and thus give his face the sunken, withered aspect of senility. And, now, in his latest picture, THE UNKNOWN, he has his arms clamped down over his stomach, to dispose of them altogether.

No device Chaney uses to simulate physical deformity is easy to wear. But the more painful it is to endure, the better he likes it.

And that's the real actor in Chaney. He has an intense fervor for his work. He isn't abnormal nor mad, as some people say. Not any more than any other fine artist. He just loves greasepaint and the rest of the props, or symbols, of the show business.

He is a thorough trouper. He has traveled the long, hazardous road, beginning as a green stagehand shifting scenery for Richard Mansfield and Madam Modjeska, the famed tragedienne, and ending as a buck-and-wing dancer in vaudeville and obscure musical comedies.

He knows what the show business is about. The same with pictures, too. He started where nearly all the big ones did. Right at the bottom—as an extra, riding a horse for Universal in two-reel Westerns. Which probably means, without casting any direct aspersions on Chaney's early horsemanship, that he learned the moving picture business from the ground up.

Those who know Chaney—and there aren't many—have often told me that he is an excellent business man. I don't doubt it; and since all good business men are mainly concerned with protecting and building up the interests of their investments, Chaney well deserves the description. Because his big investment in moving pictures is talent, technique and the concentration of all his faculties and forces on just one thing—his work.

He has a wonderful business partner, however, in his wife. A woman who is the mother of his 21-year-old son, Creighton, a woman who thoroughly understands Lon, and since she herself was of the stage, a woman able to view the world of make-believe through wise and experienced eyes. Her working hand in hand with Chaney has not only been a stimulus, but a big factor in strengthening him in the courage of his convictions.

Mrs. Chaney sang and danced in a musical comedy with Lon many years ago at the old Belasco Theater in Los Angeles. Robert Z. Leonard, the director, and Fatty Arbuckle were members of the same troupe.

One of Chaney's strong convictions is that the public should never know who he is, and that he should rarely appear at premieres or large public functions where he will be recognized. Preserving the illusion has ever been his watchword. Not one person in a thousand would know him on the street, anyway, but notwithstanding this, he has isolated himself from the glamorous side of Hollywood for many years.

And on the nights when he and Mrs. Chaney go to the theater, it is toward the close of the run of a play or picture, and not even the wide-awake ushers and managers are aware of their presence. At parties they almost never appear, and if they happened to be present at a dinner dance at the Mayfair Club, I am quite sure some one would drop dead from shock.

Probably the most satisfying compliment ever paid Chaney's wizardry in makeup came from a man at the Los Angeles opening of TELL IT TO THE MARINES, in which Lon plays a top sergeant minus disguise or any makeup at all. On this occasion, for the firsttime in his career, Chaney made a personal appearance at the theater. He broke his steadfast rule, not because of studio exhortation, but because he thought this was the one occasion and hour to let down the bars.

When he came out on the stage and bowed and smiled, he received a tremendous ovation. The aforesaid man clapped vociferously and then said, "I sure would like to see what that guy Chaney looks like without makeup some time."

I have already alluded to Chaney's business ability, which in his case is another way of acknowledging his judgment and vision. A particularly striking example of his farsightedness was evidenced years ago when he was still with Universal and decided to strike out and make character roles his forte.

"I had been playing everything from heroes to heavies in those early days," he said. "But I wasn't getting anywhere. Salary, yes, but no personal satisfaction out of my work. I'm one of those people who have to love an awful lot what they're doing, or else they're unhappy. So I decided to make the break and change my heavies into characters. I dressed them up with makeup that was different from what anybody had ever used.

"I had decided that any actor of ability could express emotion and thought with his eyes, a muscle of his face, a gesture of the hand or body. But that it would take a very good one to act through a heavy makeup, with a couple of pounds of putty on his face, his eyes out of gear and his mouth pulled around to meet one of his ears.

"THE MIRACLE MAN brought me fame. Fame is a very strange lady. I had done things every bit as good as THE MIRACLE MAN years before but they had passed unnoticed."

Chaney is an almost bitterly sincere man. He lives the philosophy of "to thine own self be true". He despises pretense. Therefore, he is never guilty of it. Where some men would choose diplomacy as the most graceful way out of an awkward or irritating situation, he right then and there calls the spade by its name, and the matter is settled definitely for all time.

He is extremely instinctive and intuitive. If he likes you, you immediately know it. He may even tell you so. If he doesn't like you, or hasn't any interest in what you have to say, you will have evidence of that too—promptly.

On the rare occasions when some visitor gets on the set where he is working, if the matter proceeds as far as an introduction, he takes exactly one minute to determine whether the person is to his liking. If he is, he remains. If not, through some mysterious signal code, Chaney is called back to work at once by a messenger from the director.

"I loathe curiosity seekers," he has told me. "The people who are so darn anxious to get a look at what is behind the scenes. What does it mean to them? Nothing, except possible disillusionment.

"Why should I tell the whole world what my private life is? That belongs to me. Why should I share sacred hours, which are all too rare anyway, with the world in general? Why should any but just a few friends know that Mrs. Chaney and I love our home, and enjoy sharing it with congenial souls who drop in now and then for dinner, and that later we all talk, and listen to music and cut up like human beings?

"Who, except ourselves, should care that when the weekends roll around, or when work gets to heavy, Mrs. Chaney and I love to go up to our shack in the mountains and hang across rocks for days at a time, catching beautiful fish in the cool mountain streams?

"Who should care that I like to find a congenial pal every Tuesday and Friday to go to the fights? And just why should it matter to any one but ourselves that every now and then we run into friends of the old days in vaudeville, and go on tour with them to a few honkatonk towns, just for the fun of trying to call back some of the spirit of yesterday?"

A man who has known Chaney for years once said to me, "I love Lon Chaney. He is a great human being.

"Lon has befriended more people in need, and to this day does more for people who have no idea who their benefactor is, than any person I have ever known. And it is likely he will hate me for the rest of my life for telling this."

There is an expression in the eyes of Lon Chaney which conveys more than words ever could his compassion, understanding, and feeling for the man whose life is lived under a shadow. His eyes are such a deep brown that they are almost black. They are so deeply set that you have to look far down into them to be really sure they are there. That is why people either know him well, or not at all. There are lines gashed from his nose to his chin which resemble cuts that took a long time to heal. Yet his laugh is hearty and seems to roll and surge before it gets a good start. It comes back to you sometimes but its echo is far different. It is like a sad song.

Out of the misty shadows of the past there must at times hover about Chaney tender memories of his childhood—a mother and father, both deaf mutes—a little boy at Christmastime, peering hopelessly into a rich shop window—and many more unforgettable memories.

Whether Lon Chaney is the clown who does not want to laugh but must, as in HE WHO GETS SLAPPED, or the armless freak who desperately loves the beautiful lady, or a vengeful, relentless Oriental who demands "an eye for an eye and a tooth for a tooth", he remains the great tragedian of the screen. He arouses keen interest, he evokes warm sympathy. On the screen he is a lone figure, as truly great as we can imagine, contributing handsomely to the history of the profession he loves. ∎

MY DARKEST HOUR

By Lon Chaney

As Told to Maude Cheatham

"WHEN I saw my first picture on the screen, a comedy I *wept!*" and Lon Chaney grinned cheerfully, now that it was all safely in the past.

"I had been playing in musical comedy and naturally supposed I could get over in pictures. In fact, I recall thinking how I would knock Ford Sterling—*cold*. As I considered Sterling a great artist, you see, I was aiming high.

"Instead of dealing him a blow, I gave it to myself, I was crushed, mortified, discouraged—oh, desperately discouraged. I thought if this is screen comedy I'll go back to Kolb and Dill, for at least my humor was welcomed on the stage.

"Positively, I did the most *unfunny* things imaginable before that camera, and for the life of me I couldn't get the idea. Well, I made three attempts, each worse than the last. Then, one day, disgusted with my failure, I gritted my teeth and determined I'd win or die in the attempt.

"That very afternoon I ran into Jack O'Brian out on the lot: He was directing Jeanie MacPherson who wrote the scenarios and was being featured. Harry Van Meter was the lead. O'Brian told me he was looking for a *heavy*. I felt so discouraged with my comedy, however, that I thought I might as well take a chance, so went at it.

"Well, I made good, and Jeanie then wrote two stories expressly for me, one had a weird hunchback role—great! This was when I began the study of makeup. In musical comedies you can paste green whiskers on your chin, do a funny little dance along with your song and get away with it, so I knew nothing about makeup, but having embarked as a *heavy* in motion pictures I went at it heart and soul.

"I brought home greasepaints, putty and whiskers of every kind and spent long hours trying out character parts before my mirror. I used to be something of a sketch artist and this helped me understand light and shade, while the clay modeling I studied at school taught me how to use the putty for nose and eyebrow transformations. I'm a little proud of the fact that no one ever taught me a single thing about makeup, that I worked it out by myself.

"Perhaps some may think I dropped into my particular niche with ease when I started in on character parts, but believe me, I say I made it through hard work, study and experimenting, always urged on by a definite ambition.

"Here's a secret," he added, his eyes twinkling. "Sometime I would like to try an old fashioned slapstick comedy, just to see if I could do it." ■

One of his personal favorite poses.

At baseball game in 1921. Wonder if the lucky kid knew who he was being photographed with?

JUST PLAIN LON
The Face Behind the Mask

Early days.

Being greeted at the train depot in L.A. Young man to the left with cap in hand is Lon Chaney Jr.

Union Station (railway depot), 14 June 1928.

L.A. train terminal, 1930.

And here is how Lon Chaney looks when he is all dressed up for stepping out. This is the only picture of its kind in existence, because Mr. and Mrs. Chaney have hitherto refused to pose for informal photographs together

From a movie magazine, complete with the publication's own caption.

Just Lon.

Alonzo.

Intense.

Before James Bond and his gadgets—polaroids in pens, a movie camera in a contact lense, a railroad train in a ring, a zeppelin in a zippo cigaret lighter—there was Lon Chaney with this *mini-makeup kit!*

Chaney speaks!

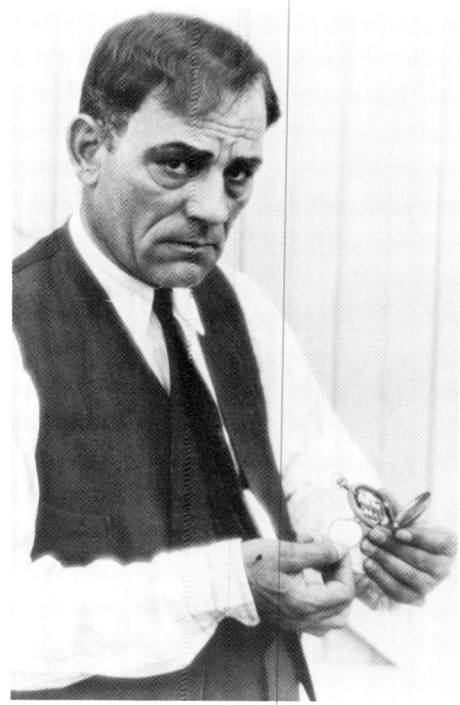

If you still have that autograph, soldier, you're a rich man! And even if you don't you have a rich memory that every owner of this book envies you for!

I PANICKED THE PARIS OPERA HOUSE AS ERIK

By Kenneth Strickfaden

KENNETH STRICKFADEN *at 86 is a Living Legend. "Edison Medicine" (electricity) has kept him young.*

He has had a lifelong love affair with that mysterious man-made lightning and has shared his fervor (and his genius) with the world via a myriad of motion pictures stretching back into the silent era from the Oscar-winning WINGS (for the version augmented with sound he created the eerie whining never-to-be-forgotten death-moan of dying warplanes as, their bodies riddled with machinegun bullets, ofttimes their fuselages aflame and trailing smoke, they plunged from the heavens to the hell waiting below)—from WINGS to the same sound effects for RAIDERS OF THE LOST ARK!

When the-body-that-had-never-lived, that exhibited only the simulucrum of life, was elevated for the birth of animation from the floor of Frankenstein's laboratory to its roof, Strickfaden dazzled the eye with his electrical marvels in Colin Clive's cauldron of creation. And repeated—with improvements—in BRIDE OF FRANKENSTEIN. And reprised his wizardry in SON OF FRANKENSTEIN.

It was his tribute to Edison and Marconi and Tesla that, in 1930, made the 1980 laboratory of JUST IMAGINE a sense-of-wonder studio set; his machinery that brought Warner Baxter back to life with SIX HOURS TO LIVE; his "electrickery" that melted the sword that would have unleashed the Mongol horde upon the world in THE MASK OF FU MANCHU; and he has survived into modern times with his elaborate electrical effects (and electrifying sounds) in such hits as YOUNG FRANKENSTEIN and STAR WARS.

A modest man, with an amazing memory, it was only by a miracle that at the penultimate moment as this book was going to press I learned from Strickfaden that he had actually known Chaney! *Here are his recollections:*

IN THE 20s I was working at Universal Studios in the electrical department. The president, Carl Laemmle Sr., personally showed me the ropes. I had the run of the lot and my work brought me on every set at some point or other.

I remember THE PHANTOM OF THE OPERA. Everything was manufactured for the sets right there on the Universal lot. For the opera house sets, everything was white on white. I worked on the mechanical end of the picture, on call all the time for the high intensity side-arc lamps that were used in the stages. I wasn't too much interested in actors or directors but all of the equipment and teamwork that went into THE PHANTOM—I remember marveling at the HUNCHBACK OF NOTRE DAME sets too. And gruesome films with sets that had bodies hanging from ropes, stretching their spines.

Us electricians had meals at midnight after days and nights of work. We all worked overtime. "The show had to go on". New lighting equipment came in from Germany—that's where they made METROPOLIS, you know—and these new babies were great big ten kilowatt brutes that took 150 amps direct current to get them started! Then we settled back to 50 amps for steady burns...if they didn't explode! those incandescents ate a lot of current and required big portable generators. The head electrician had to cool the generator cables off, they were so hot, by throwing wet rags on top of the hot cables. It was hazardous but they *had* to have all that juice.

About Lon Chaney. I didn't know the man very well personally but I used to bump into him when he'd come out of his dressingroom on his way to the sets. He was a *huge* man, really tall; but he was a nice man. He just went about his business, sort of like Boris Karloff later on. Tall as he was, they built up Chaney even taller sometimes by his shoes. Again, same as Karloff.

They reproduced the interior of the Paris Opera house exactly on the inside. They had balconies and a packed audience—hundreds of extras. I used to spend as much time as possible on the opera set, just lost in admiration.

You remember when Erik caused the great chandelier to fall and crush people beneath it? I guess you could say I became Erik for that sequence because it was my job to make the chandelier crash without actually injuring people.

[I wondered at this point how I would have handled the responsibility if it would have been mine—Brian Forbes. Had the chandelier made of balsa wood perhaps? But "ElecStrick" came up with a cleverer solution.]

It was a huge thing and it had to fall all the way down from the top of the ceiling. At first I couldn't imagine how it could be handled. But I huddled with some of the "boys" and we came up with a trick that worked: we rigged the chandelier so that it was lifted from the floor to the ceiling *and photographed the sequence in reverse!* There were no mangled bodies, no blood spilled, and I thought it was believable when I saw the result on the screen.

In THE PHANTOM Chaney lived in the catacombs near to the sewer and I remember there were all kinds of rats used for some of the underground scenes. They used real rats and had a rat wrangler on the set. They lost a few rats because they'd wander off into the sewers and have to be replaced.

I remember the filming of THE HUNCHBACK OF NOTRE DAME there on the backlot too.

I saw quite a lot of Chaney in various makeups while we both were working at Universal.

There never was another like him. ■

THE PHANTOM AND I *By Ray Bradbury*

IT IS NIGHT in a small Midwest town. Autumn and a good wind and the city-hall clock edging toward 12. Along the dark and empty Main Street comes a man, myself, walking with a brisk cloud of autumn leaves rustling at my heels. Before a deserted theater, I glance up at the broken marquee bulbs that read:

LON CHANEY IN "THE PHANTOM OF THE OPERA"

Even as I watch, the bulbs begin to flicker on and off. I peer at the dusty foyer. The ticket booth is empty. A spider web covers the round glass hole where you chat through at the ticket seller. As I approach, a spider hung at the web's center skims down to the brass cashier plate. A ticket jumps with a cough of dust into my hand. All to itself, the theater door hushes open.

I hesitate. The autumn wind blows a scuttle of those dark leaves about my knees. I enter the dim and totally deserted theater. My feet are soundless in the heavy carpeting.

I survey the Gothic interior, the uninhabited seats, the opera boxes, the chandelier like a vast constellation of tears above, the dust-throttled Wurlitzer organ below.

"You're late," a voice calls, softly.

The town clock strikes midnight.

"No. Just on time."

I move down the aisle.

"Are we all here?"

A second whisper makes me glance up at the right-hand box. The Phantom of the Opera, pale-masked, is there. We nod. I sit.

"Please to begin." ■

New role for Chaney: cameraman. Director Jack Conway, seated.

BEHIND THE SCENES

"Mom" Chaney shakes hands with man who appears to be Tod Browning's twin! (THE UNHOLY THREE).

Chaney greets Oriental visitor during making of WHILE THE CITY SLEEPS.

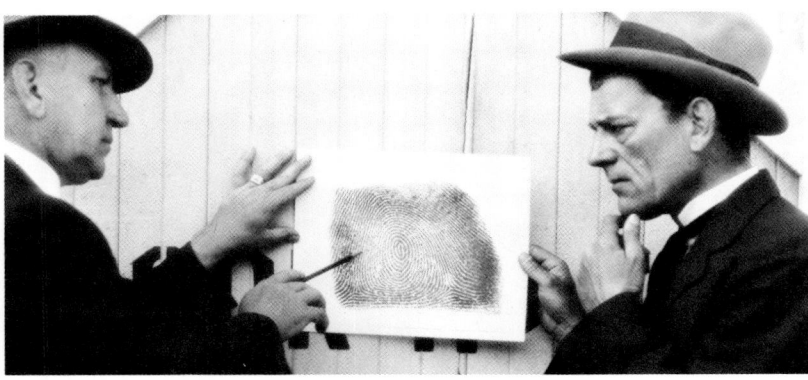

Chaney's head is in a whorl as expert explains to him inside info on fingerprints.

On the set of TREASURE ISLAND.

The shirtsleeves man to Chaney's right turns up time again in his candids. A producer? Director?

CANDIDS

Surrounded by cast and crew of ALL THE BROTHERS WERE VALIANT.

There are enough shots of Chaney's various wardrobes in this book to present a challenge: identify what picture he was filming when the candid was taken by studying the suit he's wearing!

Meeting Rhiba Crawford, "The Angel of Broadway", during the filming of WHERE EAST IS EAST.

There's that man again.

Somebody's birthday? Anyway, Chaney takes the cake...and shares it with director Victor Seastrom.

In addition to the ubiquitous man, someone new had been added: a calow youth on the left who hasn't left us yet (in 1983) and when he goes will leave a legacy of music such as Lon left to motion pictures. It's Irving Berlin.

With "Mr. Everywhere" and Lew Cody, the latter known by the sobriquet of "The Butterfly Man".

With his leading ladies of THE BIG CITY: Marcelline Day, brunet; Betty Compson, blond.

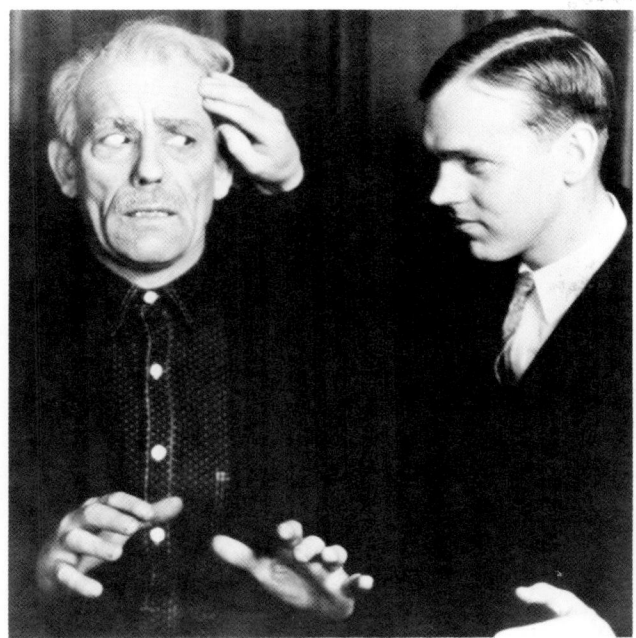

Looks like Lon could use a bandaid. But where's the band to aid him?

Onlooker has the look of a studio executive about him.

Identifiable: Lon, Norma Shearer, Victor Seastrom, John Gilbert. Left of Chaney, noted European circus clown George Davis.

What's his line? Chaney's Dancing Dolls, of chorus!

Now that took *acting* on Lon's part—to look glum with those glamor girls as background.

Clowning around with his makeup kit.

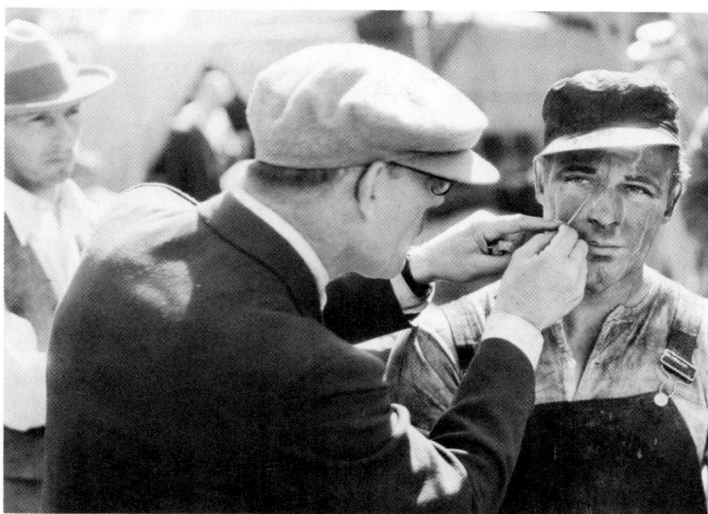

Here's a switch: Chaney making up *another* actor!

Browning checks his costume in THE UNKNOWN.

With Tod Browning, his director on THE ROAD TO MANDALAY.

With Browning on the excised scene from WEST OF ZANZIBAR.

Sans parole. Chaney died of cancer of the throat.

Autographing a baseball for visiting Chinese. Civilian smiling at him (his knobby chin was usually adorned by a villainous beard—he would have made a splendid Ming the Merciless) was the famous actor Sojin (of THE THIEF OF BAGDAD, SEVEN FOOTPRINTS TO SATAN and the famous knife fight in THE ROAD TO MANDALAY).

Donating to charity at HUNCHBACK premiere. Little girl, are you a grandmother now?—and do you remember the occasion?

Even in 1914 it's not difficult to recognize Lon (top left).

Whaddya hear from the mop? Or, Going to pot. (With Wallace Beery, once considered to carry on when Lon was gone but the roles never materialized for him).

LAFF, LON, LAFF
or, Lon Hammy

You always bite the one you love (that's what drove Oscar Wilde); or, Love At First Bite. (With Lupe Velez in WHERE EAST IS EAST.)

Ya wanna tip, kid? Funny Face in the third.

Hoop, hoop, hurray!

How about a game of Russian roulette? (With Barbara Bedford in MOCKERY.)

The day Whistler's Mother went off her rocker. (THE UNHOLY THREE).

Have you seen the price of gas lately?

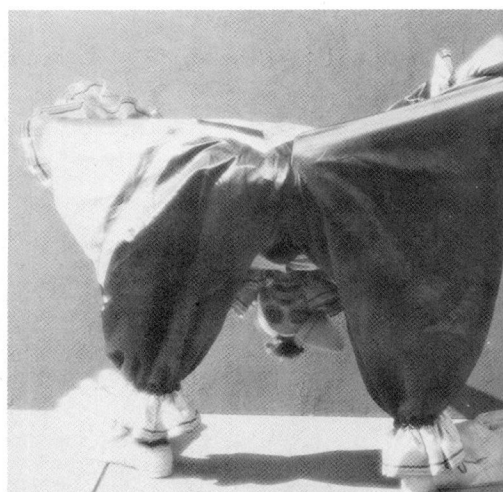
Posing upside clown!

Lon Chaney is eary in THE UNHOLY THREE (all-squawking version).

He thinks it's a polaroid—and they haven't even been invented yet!

Eat yer heart out, Superman!

The Twinkletoes Quartet. (They killed vaudeville).

He took nose lessons from Jimmy Durante and now Loretta Young sez "Powder there, pal!" (LAUGH, CLOWN, LAUGH).

Here no evil but if you do—TELL IT TO THE MARINES. (Via William Haines).

227

Even without makeup he's Clown Chaney.

Let's play Kick-the-Bucket.

Whaddya mean, it's not your cuppa tea?

Dummy up! (THE UNHOLY THREE, talking).

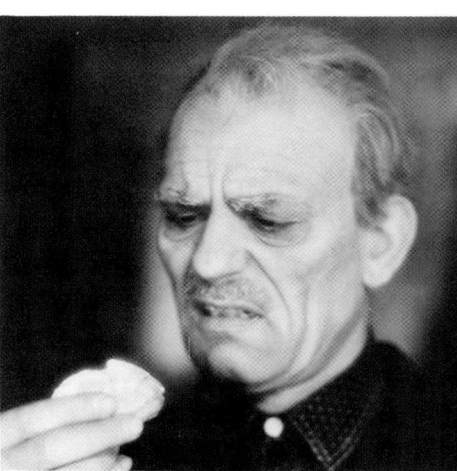
Whadda they think I am, a creampuff?

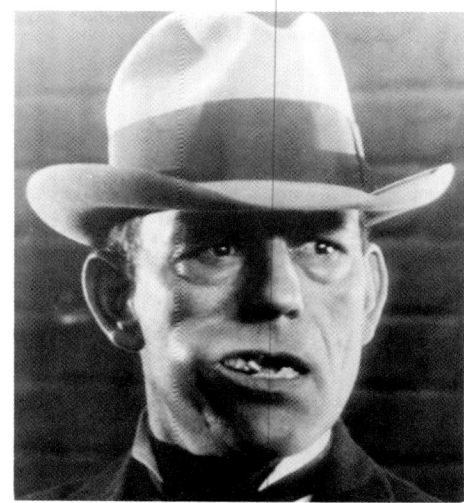
You said a mouthful.

I didn't know Pagliacci's first name was Ridi.

Leatrice Joy enjoying Lon's impromptu performance as "Bulldog" Drummond.

I shot an arrow into the air,
It fell to the earth, I know not where.
I lose more darn arrows that way!

You sure that thing doesn't bite? (The first talkie for the man who eventually would also have been known as The Man of A Thousand Voices).

A burp in the hand is worth two in the bush. (Ford Sterling, left).

The Man of A Thousand Languages! (The "distaff" member of THE *HOLY* THREE clowns around in Hebrew!)

CURIOSITIES & RARABILIA

An autographed photo like this of Chaney sells today (in 1983) for $1500 or more.

Out of a thousand photos this the only one I found of Chan kissing! (He Who Gets Smacked

Lon! What was in that candy WEST OF ZANZIBAR? I nev knew an Abazaba to have *that* fect! You've gone wild, wilder th the wild man of Borneo! Wait the tom-toms start telling t natives about this, they'll *really* restless: "The Fun-Tom Strik Again!"

A home in which "he" once live

Out of a thousand photos this is the only one I found of Chaney sleeping! From MOCKERY.

The only reason I have not included a major selection of stills on LONDON AFTER MIDNIGHT is that the entire film is covered in intimate detail with every possible picture from it in a volume by Philip J. Riley and myself, reconstructing this lost motion picture. These two photos are simply to whet your appetite and also to invite Edna Tichenor, the Bat Woman, if she is alive, to contact me.

From a French cinemagazine "wy back when".

Two of the five fabulous onesheets from the original PHANTOM OF THE OPERA, displayed by Robert block (right) and myself. Boy seated (now a grown man) is one of the two grandsons of...the Frankenscience Monster, Boris Karloff! The posters are prize possession of film historian, director, instructor and collector David Bradley.

Cortlandt Hull's award-winning re-creation of Chaney's Red Death (THE PHANTOM OF THE OPERA) at *Famous Monsters* Fantasy Film Convention in New York in the 70s. (Photo: Walt Daugherty.)

I wonder if this bench still exists?

Tell me, is it my imagination or do you see the same suggestive similarities in these scenes that I do? Chaney with the little girl is from LAUGH, CLOWN, LAUGH. Karloff with "The Daisy That Didn't Float" is, of course, from FRANKENSTEIN. Then there are the three shots of Paul Wegener in action in THE GOLEM. If I had actual frame blowups from all three films I feel I could show an even more striking relationship between the scenes.

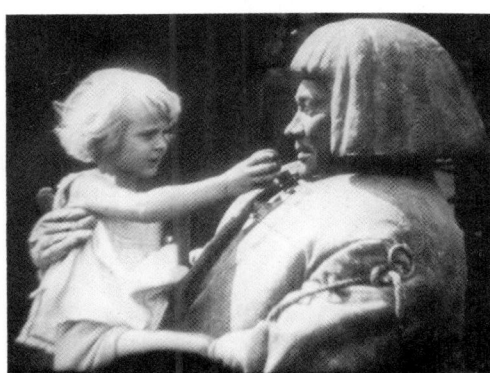

It seems to me this is a postcard I bought in a Ten Cent Store on Market Street in San Francisco about 1929.

"This devil doll is going to put the voodoo hoodoo on you!" Tod Browning kids Lon Chaney as Betty Compson looks on amused.

Unidentified drawing that turned up in my files. I *think* it's from a *long* time ago. ▶

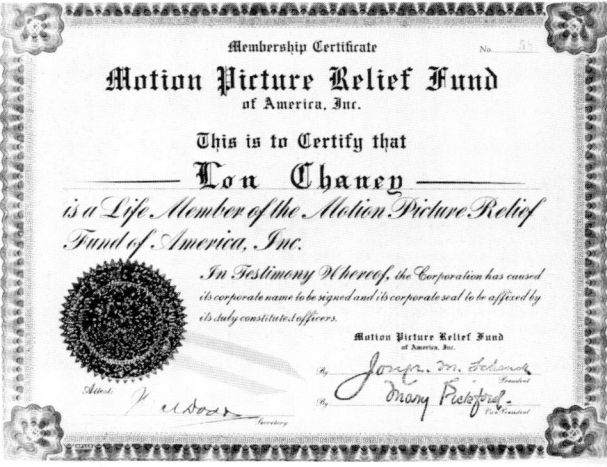

The famous musical number "Lon Chaney's Going To Get You If You Don't Watch Out!" in MGM's HOLLYWOOD REVUE OF 1929. Chaney did not appear in it but only masks suggesting his 1000 faces. ▼

234

In April 1973 I wrote on the back of this still: *Said to be Lon Chaney's favorite foto from his favorite film. (From his personal collection).* the Film: LAUGH, CLOWN, LAUGH. ▲

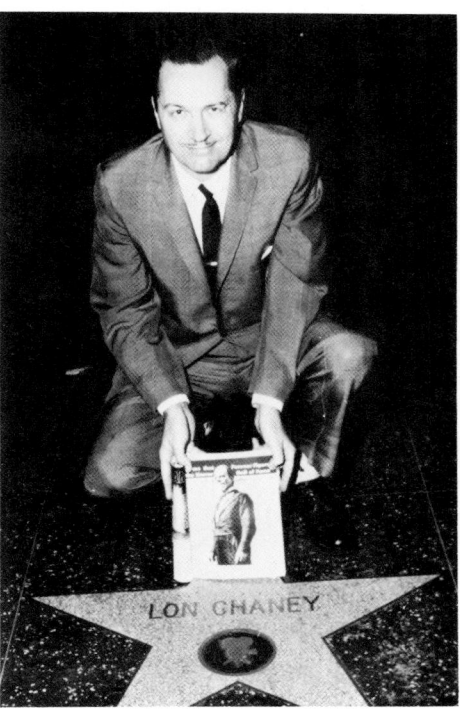

In the summer of 1963, accompanied by Wendayne "Rocket to the rue Morgue" Wahrman (my wife, Mrs. Ackerman), I took an 8700 mile drive back and forth across the USA over a period of five weeks to meet as many as possible of 1300 filmmonster fans who had expressed a desire to see the "Ackermonster" in person. This was the photo I autographed for fans on the occasion. Lon Chaney's star still graces the sidewalk on Hollywood Blvd. (Photo: Walt Daugherty.)

Myself posed beside framed photo of Lon in the salon of the hotel in northern California run by his brother John in the 60s. (Photo: Wendayne Ackerman.)

Signing an autograph with his foot on the set of THE UNKNOWN. (I was tempted to caption this "A fotograph of a footograph" but uncommonsense prevailed.) Whoever is in possession of Lon Chaney's most illegible signature, this is probably the reason for it!

◀ Rick Baker—Monster Maker—with his remarkable sculpture of Chaney in his LONDON AFTER MIDNIGHT characterization.

▲ Mystery Photo. Can *you* identify it? Contemplating the still in my hand, for some reason I get a "psychometric" feeling that it's from ACE OF HEARTS.

The showbiz motto is "Always leave 'em laffing" so Lon completes this section by doing his strongarm act. He calls this one "Testing My Metal". The Man of Iron!

MY FATHER LON CHANEY

By Lon Chaney Jr.

IT ISN'T easy to write about your father who is dead. Especially when that father happened once to personify all the fiendish attributes in the world to several millions of his countrymen. But so many of his friends have spoken to me since his death, those friends he never knew, asking what he was really like. Only the other day I received a letter from a lady in Mobile, Alabama, who had seen every Lon Chaney picture and wanted to know whether I was related to him.

Strangely enough these friends remember him not as the unspeakable Phantom of the Opera, nor even as the deformed but heroic little man who poured boiling oil on the attackers of Notre Dame, but rather as a superbly gifted and incomparably versitile player who could be all things in all pictures. I can't blame them for their curiosity. And I feel that it is only fair to his memory to tell what the man of a thousand faces looked like to his son. My father was a kind man. Perhaps through overuse that word has lost something of its pristine strength. We have come to think of a kind man as one who helps elderly ladies across the street and gives coins to beggars.

My father was kind in a deeper sense than that. He loved people and he knew how to please them. Nothing gave him greater joy than helping other people along, whether they were lifelong friends or chance acquaintances. And I don't mean merely assisting them financially or getting jobs for them, though heaven knows he was generosity itself in those respects. He gave unflaggingly of the far more precious gifts of sympathy and understanding.

Even at the height of his fame, he still preserved his sincere and democratic attitude towards all persons with whom he came in contact. Success failed to destroy his standard of values. There was no time when he felt that he was too great to listen to the troubles of the lowest stage-hand, or give a kind word and a helping hand to a struggling extra.

At the same time, with his utter lack of affectation, he had the same kindly interest in the less poignant troubles of the greatest stars, and was constantly the confidante of Hollywood's biggest names.

In later years, when the whole world knew him and wondered what he was like, he would spend hours talking to some beggar who had approached him for a handout and who frequently found himself, to his own immeasurable surprise, the recipient of a staggeringly munificent sum. And the friends of his trouping days! How he enjoyed chatting with them when they came to see him. No former fellow players were ever turned away from the lot on which Lon Chaney was working. He saw them all, and talked to them all, and somehow found means to help many of them on their way to belated success.

As for my own view of him, that is a matter of which I could never write calmly or dispassionately. Lon Chaney was always for me the greatest of all heroes, the personification of all that was fine and true. He was my father.

HIS LIFE FOR HIS ART?

By Dorothy Donnell

LON CHANEY is dead at 47. He was a strong man, of sturdy build. He should have lived a long life.

He was the most popular star in motion pictures, the greatest box-office attraction of them all, making one of the largest salaries in the business. He should have lived to convert his labor and suffering and fame into terms of ease and luxury and freedom.

One of the last things he said to a friend at the studio was—with a deep breath, "Now I've got my mountain cabin built, boy—at last, I'm going to have some *fun!*" But Lon Chaney was never to have his "fun".

He lived a cruelly hard life as a boy, brought up in a sad, strangely silent home, with deaf and dumb parents. His first wife deserted the struggling young actor when their son was two months old, and for two years the father took care of his baby himself, with clumsy man-tenderness. He heated the nursing bottles over the spirit lamp where he melted his greasepaints, in draughty dressingrooms in country theaters. He tucked the baby awkwardly asleep in his open trunk to rush up onto the stage to do a song and dance. He hurried back to wash small clothes and string them on an untidy line among his costumes.

When Chaney died, he and his family were still living in a humble neighborhood. The beautiful Beverly Hills home he was building was not yet quite finished.

Lon Chaney was not ready for Death. He was full of plans for his next picture, for the future that was to make up for the dinginess of the past. *He did not dream that he was dying.* His family and friends and everyone at the studio had known for three months that he was doomed from cancer but the dread word was kept from him. He thought, happily, that the trouble in his throat was caused by a tonsil operation that was slow in healing.

When his last week came, the newspaper men were summoned to the office of the publicity chief of Metro Studios. "Boys". he told them, simply, "Lon Chaney is dying of cancer of the throat. He doesn't know it. If you print the truth, he'll read it and it will kill him immediately. You can be cruel or you can be kind. It's up to you."

They all joined in the conspiracy of mercy and Lon Chaney drew his last breath believing that in a week or two he would be putting on his beloved makeup for CHERI BIBI.

There are probably few actors on the screen who have as happy a prospect of a long professional life as Chaney had. The popularity that he won by his grotesque characterization of the distorted *Frog* in THE MIRACLE MAN had remained steadily his through all the changes of the business. And he had just triumphantly made his first talkie, which he dreaded, and found that his cherished mystery was not lost by speaking.

His death was unexpected, untimely. Was it also, perhaps, unnecessary?

Those who knew him well say so. They say that the roles he played, with their necessity for physical strain and suffering, actually lowered his vitality and shortened his life by a third.

They say that Chaney never spared himself; that he worked when he was a sick man, rather than hold up the picture; that he eagerly endured agonies to perfect one of his distorted and *macabre* characterizations; that he invented devices himself to cripple his strong body for his roles; and that he tried dangerous experiments in order to obtain the weird effects that made his fame.

Lon Chaney was not an old man but his face was deeply seamed with lines. Lines of pain. *He had a suffering face.* Interviewers will remember his odd trick of suddenly straining his head back on his shoulders. They put it down to a mannerism but it was not that. Ever since Lon Chaney played the part of a legless man in THE PENALTY he was in constant pain from the injury that the role had inflicted on his spine.

The usual movie method of playing a legless man—keeping the leg, from the knee joint, bent backward out of range of the camera—was not good enough for Chaney's passion for realism. With the help of a prop man—and without consulting a doctor—he had a leather harness constructed, which bound his legs tightly against his thighs, so that he walked erect upon his knees, thrust into the leather pads that mutilated beggars wear.

The studio physician was horrified at this atrocity and ordered Chaney not to wear it more than two minutes at a time. But when the two minutes were past, the actor, face glistening with the sweat of his agony, would urge the director to go on. "I can stand it a while longer. Let's get something done! We'll try another scene," and then, "Another"—

The public saw an actor toiling through the picture on the stumps of his legs and hailed Chaney as a great "makeup artist". They did not see him writhing on the studio floor while they unstrapped him and freed his cramped and bloodless legs from their unnatural position. But it was his spine that suffered most from the strain of maintaining a balance and caused that involuntary backward tug of his head that so many afterward noticed.

Having established a vogue for monstrous characterizations, Chaney next made THE HUNCHBACK OF NOTRE DAME, creating with straps, pulleys, rubber hump and face-putty a figure of such grotesque horror that critics were inclined to call it "overdone". But Lon Chaney, with the zeal for accuracy that made him great, built up the hideous figure of "The Hunchback" from an original pen-and-ink sketch by Victor Hugo himself.

First, he had a harness made that pulled his head and shoulders forward, halfway down to his waist. Utterly unable to straighten up in this, he added a 70 pound rubber hump to the back of his neck and shoulders, obscured one eye with putty, distorted his mouth with a vice hidden in false teeth, and in this condition worked for an hour at a time—until even his staunch spirit could not bear the torture another moment.

"For two years after that picture," Chaney told me once, "I could not stretch out full length in bed without groaning aloud."

Next came THE PHANTOM OF THE OPERA, in which Chaney wore a device in his nose that spread the nostrils wide and lifted the top of the nose upward and back to give a skeleton effect. The skull-like grin was gained by false teeth, with prongs at the ends forcing the lip corners back.

The UNKNOWN was another effort of self-flagellation for Chaney, though he was completely happy in adding a new kind of cripple to his movie collection. The picture told the story of the Armless Wonder in the circus. In order to make the character as realistic as possible, Chaney had a straight-jacket invented that pressed his arms so tightly against his sides and into his body that he was able to appear in silk tights in the picture, with the startling illusion of having really lost both his arms at the shoulders.

Again warned that this stopped the circulation and threatened serious injury, Chaney showed himself impatient of his own pain and time after time refused to have the jacket taken off for a rest. The result was that the blood, denied its proper circulation, flowed into his legs and burst blood vessels there. For the rest of his life, Lon Chaney bore the black scars of ruptured veins on both legs, and had the habit, also put down as a mannerism by strangers, of leaning forward and absently rubbing his knees while talking.

In LONDON AFTER MIDNIGHT and THE ROAD TO MANDALAY, Chaney transferred his experiments in self-torture to his eyes. For the former picture, in which he played a maniac with an appetite for frightening people, he used a thin wire, which went around the eye socket and—when he was ready to go before the camera—was screwed up until both eyeballs bulged horrifyingly. In THE ROAD TO MANDALAY, he obtained the effect of a cataract by filling one eye with collodion*a substance that covered the ball with a white opaque film, which gave the character the nickname of "Deadeye". For months afterward this eye troubled him. For a time, indeed, it seemed that he might never see with it again.

With THUNDER, his first sound picture, Lon Chaney stubbornly held out against talking, believing that as soon as he spoke he would be an ordinary mortal to his fans, instead of a strange creature of mystery. Just as stubbornly, he refused to return home from the location trip into frozen mountain wastes, although he was working with a high fever from a chest cold. Finally, the location finished, Chaney was taken to the hospital with pneumonia.

The knowledge that the picture was being held up by his sickness was more than his trouper spirit could stand. Before he was well, he had forced his physicians to let him return to the studio. And there he finished the picture, in a prop snowstorm in which he breathed the uncooked cornflakes that the camera's eye look exactly like whirling snow.

With lungs and throat still inflamed from his illness, might it not be that this irritant was the source of the dread disease that was to end his life several months later?

Lon Chaney, all his life as a movie star, shunned interviewers. He was one actor who never had a portrait made of himself, never answered fan mail, never invited the press or the profession into his home. He would not talk about himself.

"Between pictures," he would say in a blood-curdling whisper, *"there is no Lon Chaney."*

It was a clever catch phrase, but it was more than that. It was nearly the literal truth. Lon Chaney lived only for his work. He never learned to play. He had no hobbies. Between pictures he hardly knew how to live. His work *was* his life. If it was his death, too. Would he not have preferred it that way? ∎

---

*Egg membrane! Collodion would have blinded him!

Lon Chaney Jr. escorts bereaved widow of Lon Chaney Sr. from funeral.

DEATH OF THE IMMORTAL

D FACES TAKES BUT ONE TO GRAV
y Final Role in Drama of Death Tomorro

Cleveland Press

Late News
WEATHER: Fair, rising temperatures today.

CLEVELAND, TUESDAY, AUGUST 26, 1930 — Entered at Cleveland Postoffice as Second Class Matter Under Act of 1879 — PRICE THREE CENTS

SCREEN STAR, DIES

FADES FROM LIFE'S SCREEN

Lon Chaney's Proteanism
Became Matter for Jest in Vaudeville—Favorite Allusion a Left Hand Compliment—His Glory Belonged to Present—Griffith's "Abraham Lincoln" Opens in New York.

END COMES SUDDENLY

Transfusion of Blood Fails

Hemorrhage Cause of Death for Actor Known as Man of Thousand Faces

Career Begun as Clown in Circus Closes With Fame Won in Pictures

Lon Chaney, famous for his motion-picture characterizations, died at 12:55 a.m. today at St. Vincent's Hospital, where he had been waging a bitter fight for life for the past several days.

Chaney's death followed three blood transfusions performed to aid him in his battle against an acute attack of lobar pneumonia. The immediate cause of death was a hemorrhage suffered after what studio officials termed the most restful afternoon he experienced during his illness. With him at the time of his death were Mrs. Chaney and Creighton Hale, Metro-Goldwyn-Mayer star.

BORN IN 1883

Lon Chaney, the man of a thousand faces, started life and his career as a clown. He was born on April Fool's Day (April 1), 1883, in Colorado Springs, the son of deaf-and-dumb parents. Before he reached the fifth grade of the public schools there he quit to become a tourist guide on Pike's Peak.

His introduction to the theater was as a property boy, from which he advanced to a stage hand and carried a card from their organization until his death. From behind the scenes he studied the regular actors and got his first break in a song-and-dance act at a stage hands' benefit when he was 16 years of age, and soon became a comedian in musical comedy.

WROTE PLAY

He and his brother George, who now lives in Oakland, wrote a play and staged it on the road, but went broke and Lon drifted into Chicago, where he appeared briefly as a musical show comedian. He soon returned West, however, and appeared with the Hartmann Opera Company in San Francisco for a short time before joining up with Kolf and Dill, in the same city, as stage manager.

While with the Hartmann company he married Hazel Hastings, a member of the troupe, who was his faithful companion for twenty-two years.

n Chaney, regarded as one of the greatest actors produced by the screen, died today in a Hollywood hospital after a week's illness from anemia. The star was believed recovering over the week-end but a hemorrhage of the throat early today resulted in death.

LON CHANEY

His entry into motion pictures in Southern California was via the slapstick comedy route, but in 1912 became an extra in "westerns" at Universal City, with ambition to become a director. He did direct Warren Kerrigan, then a western star, in seven productions. He received his first screen credit in 1914 from Universal for appearance in "Hell Morgan's Girl."

By JAMES MUIR

"Don't step on it. It might be Lon Chaney."

This jesting reference to the comedian's clever proteanism would always provoke a laugh in vaudeville. The joke could be sprung when every other "bon mot" failed and it could be depended on to save the day for the most arid vaudeville act. It was reliable, so far as Dayton is concerned, as the mention of Springfield or Middletown.

But the joke will never be heard on the vaudeville stage again. Chaney now lies cold in death and there is no performer who would risk the chance of incurring the ill will of the public by making a facetious reference to him, even though the old allusion was sort of a left-handed compliment.

It would, of course, be very bad taste to refer to him, now that his earthly work is finished, except in the most respectful manner, even if he had not been a popular and talented actor. As a matter of fact he was singularly gifted and had an unexcelled knack for disguise and for facial pantomime. Without saying a word he could express any sort of emotion.

But he was at his best in expressing the terrible, the melancholy and the gruesome, as "The Frog" in "The Miracle Man," the horribly deformed hunchback in "The Hunchback of Notre Dame," the title role in "The Phantom of the Opera," etc. But sometimes he would depart from the grisly and horrific and play some sound and healthy character such as the hard-boiled sergeant in "Tell It to the Marines" and the protective father in "West of Zanzibar."

Chaney died when he was at the zenith of his popularity. He had not become a legend or tradition; his glory belonged to the present. He had made only one talking picture, a dialogue version of his famous "The Unholy Three." But he gave not only an extraordinary characterization, but he spoke in five different tones, impersonating three men and two women.

The management of Loew's theater, which has been exhibiting Lon Chaney pictures for years, found that his absence from the screen had not left him forgotten by the public or staled his infinite variety. He drew almost packed houses when he appeared there in "The Unholy Three" several weeks ago.

Manager Ernie Austgen was awaiting his new film, "The Bugle Call," with impatience, knowing full well that the theater never had to take any chances with a Lon Chaney picture. Now he is mourning deeply the passing of a great artist, knowing that no other can take his place in the

Noted Actor Succumbs to Anaemia Following Pneumonia

IN GROTESQUE ROLES

Was Little Known Off Stage Shunning Friends and Public

LON CHANEY

Will Rogers Remarks:

TAHOE TAVERN, Aug. 27.—[To the Editor of The Times:] When Lon Chaney passed away the whole amusement world lost a great asset, and our profession lost its most outstanding character actor and a man that brought the movies credit.

His art was understood the world over regardless of titles or language and to know him personally was a privilege. He was a fine fellow and would have been an honor to any profession.

ffalo Times

METROPOLITAN — WEATHER: PARTLY CLOUDY, LITTLE TEMPERATURE CHANGE.

TUESDAY EVENING, AUGUST 26, 1930 — Scripps-Howard Newspaper Alliance — PRICE TWO CENTS

LON CHANEY, FILM STAR

Dons Death Mask

Lon Chaney, Man of a Thousand Faces, has played his last role and donned his last mask—the mask of death. The famed screen star, master of makeup, died early today in St. Vincent's hospital, Los Angeles, after an illness of several weeks.

MOVIE WORLD MOURNS NOTED MYSTERY MAN

Grotesque Character of Silver Screen Was Believed on Road to Recovery

SUFFERED FROM ANAEMIA

Versatile Actor Started as Stagehand, Worked Way to Top of Ladder

Blood transfusions were resorted to in the 10-day battle to save his life. Yesterday he took his first nourishment in three days and hope was renewed as he regained some of his waning strength. At midnight a lung hemorrhage occurred so suddenly physicians failed to reach him before he passed away.

Those close to Chaney, and they were few in his 47 years of life, were with him as the curtain fell. They were his son, Creighton, and his wife, Hazel Hastings, whom he married 22 years ago.

Chaney, ironically, was born on all fool's day, in 1883, in Colorado Springs, Colo. His parents were deaf mutes. To this circumstance has been attributed much of his peculiar ability as a mimic.

By the slow steps of stage property boy, stage hand, song and dance man in a benefit show at 16, wandering "ham" actor, and then film extra, Chaney climbed into the movies as a slapstick comedian in 1921. His first screen credit was two years later when Universal Pictures gave him a leading role in "Morgan's Girls."

As "The Frog" in "The Miracle Man," Chaney's unrivalled talents in grotesque characterization brought him the recognition of the world.

Chaney is one of screendom's immortals. Carl Laemmle, his associate of years in the studio said, of his passing, "we saw him in a humble beginning, from which he reached the height of brilliancy in the roles he loved."

Recognition of his skill in portraying strange and unhuman characters, was followed by Chaney's retreat into a life of seclusion akin to that of many of his screen people. Only a few persons were welcomed to his home and on the lot he was reserved.

Among his closest friends were General Smedley Butler, noted marine officer, and Eddie Gribbon, stage and screen comedian. Funeral services will be held in a mortuary

ous Character orld, Dies Of Pneumonia

Chaney was a master at the art of make up. This artistry made him the fake cripple of "The Miracle Man," the deformed dwarf of "The Hunchback of Notre Dame," the evil brother of "The Blackbird," and the dive keeper of "The Road to Mandalay."

Each role was convincing, not alone due to the make up but because of the artistry that Chaney put into his acting.

Was True Artist

No person in his profession studied more earnestly the art of mimicry. No person knew to a greater degree the greatness of the pathetic appeal of a deformed and repulsive appearing character who could rise to heights of great sacrifice.

To Lon Chaney it was all a make believe that was most real. When he prepared himself for the role of a dumb, sodden, slow-witted peasant in "Mockery" he studied the characterization for months.

He fitted his walk and manner of thinking to the part he was to play. He would follow a person for miles who seemed to be one of those he sought to copy. He did that for all of his characterizations.

Chaney's start in the profession that brought him fame was modest. As a youth he played on the stage doing "everything," as he once put it. He was the hero, villain, chorus man, dancer and scene shifter. All the time he was experimenting with makeup.

The company he was with was stranded in Santa Ana, Cal., and Chaney sought out the motion picture studios. For some time he was one of the cowboys in the old-time western thrillers.

Hands fascinated this man who deformed his body to make live the "Hunchback of Notre Dame." It has been said that members of Chaney's family were deaf mutes and Lon was compelled to communicate with them by manual talk.

He grew to understand in an unusual degree how human thoughts and kindness and passion could be portrayed by fist and finger.

Death Unexpected

Altho it was known the noted character actor was suffering from carcanoma of the bronchial tubes and that his life was to be shortened by that ailment, his death was unexpected.

Physicians believed he could live only a few months, but they announced he was out of danger temporarily when a blood transfusion was made last Saturday.

Chaney's death was a shock to all Hollywood. He was one of the most beloved and successful of the film favorites.

News of the actor's serious illness first was generally known in the screen colony shortly after he finished work on his initial talking picture "The Unholy Three."

Planned Vacation

He had planned to take a long vacation before working again but instead hastened to New York to consult with specialists about his throat ailment.

Apparently much improved, he returned from the East three weeks ago and went to his cabin in the high Sierras.

The first of three hemorrhages forced him to enter the hospital last Wednesday. His condition was regarded then as critical but when blood transfusions were successful, optimistic reports were given out.

Lon Chaney, Famous Mimic Who Won World's Applause By Characterizations, Dies

Actor, Whose "Thousand Faces" Are Known Wherever Pictures Are Shown; Succumbs to Complications; Wife and Son at His Bedside.

LOS ANGELES, Cal., Aug. 26.—(AP)—Lon Chaney, the actor whose "thousand faces" were known wherever motion picture unfolded upon a screen, wore his last mask today —in death.

The artist whose heroic pantomime won the applause of millions in "The Miracle Man," and "The Hunchback of Notre Dame," died at a hospital here last night from complications of pneumonia, a throat affliction and anemia.

WS
LON CHANEY

FINANCIAL EDITION

PRICE TWO CENTS

1930

Times
STAR, DIES

TRIAL FREEDOM

Late News EDITION

DAILY, FIVE CENTS

NEWS
DIES

CITY EDITION

PRICE TWO CENTS

RALD
STAR, DEAD

HOME EDITION

PRICE—TWO CENTS 18 PAGES TODAY

ILLNESS RESULTS IN Death of Filmland's Noted Character Actor.

LON CHANEY

Actor With "Thousand Faces" Is Dead

Lon Chaney, the "man of a thousand faces," died early Tuesday. He had been suffering from anemia in a Hollywood hospital. Photos show Chaney off the screen, left and in various roles from some of his better known pictures.

THE WEATHER: Fair tonight, Wednesday; not much change in temperature.	**DAYTON DAILY**
	ONLY AFTERNOON PAPER IN DAYTON RECEIVING ASSOCIATED PRESS S[...]

VOL. LIV. NO. 3.   DAYTON, OHIO, TUESDAY, AUGUST 26, 1930

LON CHANEY IS DEAD FOLLOWING

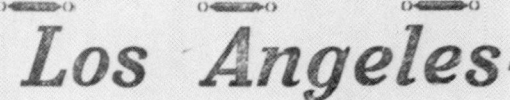

Los Angeles

WEDNESDAY, AUG. 27, 1930

HIS LAST MASK

Watching Mute Parents Inspired Chaney "Faces"

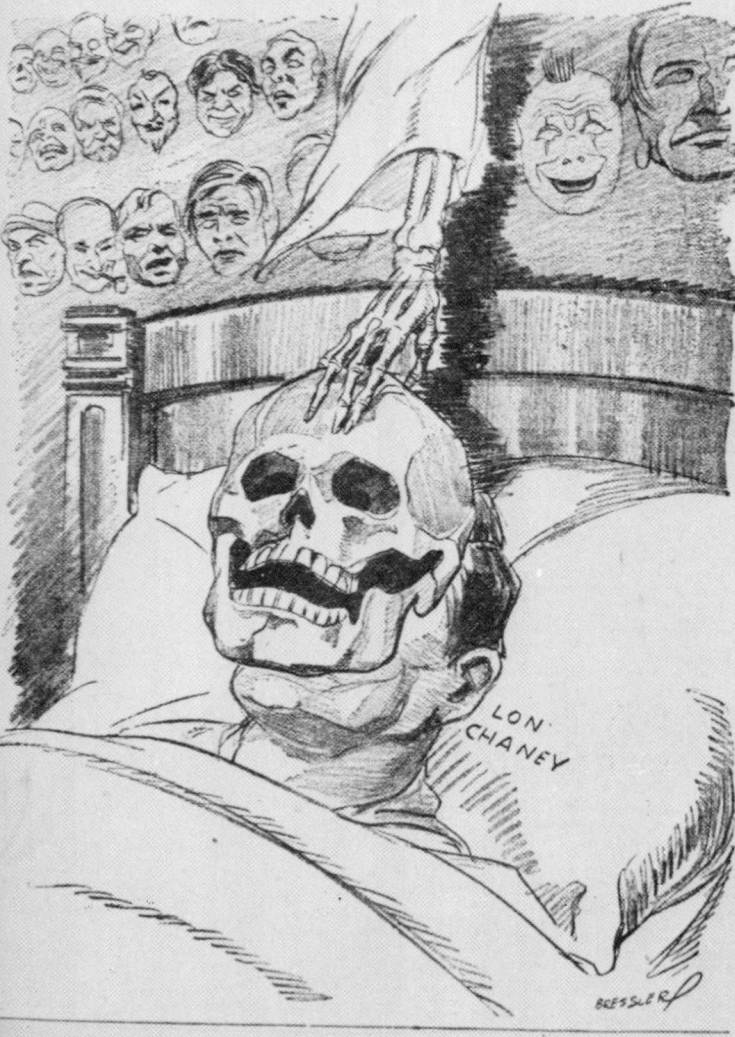

LON CHANEY

LON CHANEY

To the Editor of The News:

Regarding that most interesting editorial entitled "An Inimitable Artist," in Wednesday's News, it was the type that makes us appreciate the real genius of an artist whose life work was simply to amuse, awe, and perhaps terrorize the many people who crowded into the theaters to watch his plays.

That article, instead of describing Lon Chaney's struggle with death, simply dwelt on his wonderful ability as an actor, his skill in disguise, and the sacrifices and pain he underwent to achieve the grotesque characters which were his.

Like the writer of the editorial, I feel that Chaney's characterizations "leave as distinct an impression as one of Poe's gruesome and hair-raising tales."

DOROTHY CURTIS.
946 Ferndale Av.
Dayton, Aug. 30.

LON CHANEY

Lon Chaney was not only a good actor, but a fine fellow. After he became rich and internationally famous, his few friends were the same simple people who had been his friends when he was a stage roustabout and assistant stage manager in the days of the old Pop Fisher girl shows on Spring street. No actor ever worked harder or more faithfully to do his job.

The Bu

47TH YEAR, NO. 296 — International News Service

DEATH TAKES

Columbus Evening Dispat

OHIO'S GREATEST HOME DAILY

COMPLETE EDITION — TUESDAY, AUGUST 26, 1930. — TWENTY-EIGHT PA

Chaney In Character and Off the Screen

Lon Chaney, Fame Actor of Movie W Brief Illness of

ILLNESS IS FATAL TO "MAN OF 1000 FACES"

Famed Actor Was Recovering and Had Planned Vacation; Hollywood Is Stunned by Sudden Death

Special to The Press

HOLLYWOOD, Aug. 26—The features of the "man with a thousand faces" were reposed in death today.

Lon Chaney, greatest character actor of the flickering silver screen, died early today from a hemorrhage of the throat. He was stricken after he apparently had won a valiant fight for life.

The end came without warning. Chaney had been in St. Vincent's Hospital since last Wednesday, suffering from an acute attack of anemia. Yesterday physicians reported that the veteran actor showed great improvement and strong hope was held out that he would live.

Mrs. Chaney and her son, Creighton, who were at the death bed were too grief-stricken to give the details of Chaney's last moments. He had been in the best of spirits until a few minutes before his death.

Won Strange Popularity

Lon Chaney made and won a strange bid for the affections of America's moving picture loving public. Cast by choice in unsympathetic roles that portrayed him in grotesque characterizations, he

WILL ROGERS SAYS:

TAHOE TAVERN, Cal., Aug. 26.—When Lon Chaney passed away the whole amusement world lost a great asset, and our profession lost its most outstanding character actor, and a man that brought the movies much credit.

His art was understood the world over, regardless of titles or language, and to know him personally was a privilege. He was a fine fellow and would have been an honor to any profession.

Long before THE FLY there was Lon. This composite of him as The Human Fly epitomized the phrase that characterized him at the height of his career. Lon Chaney might be a frog, an ape, a phantom, a vampire—God knew what next! So some un sung press agent (I'd love to know his name and credit him) came up with the slogan *Don't Step on It!—It May be Lon Chaney!*

"DON'T STEP ON IT— IT MAY BE LON CHANEY!"

Front row, left to right, heroine Mary Philbin,?, Carl Laemmle Sr., LON CHANEY, Carl Laemmle Jr.,?. row behind, man with megaphone, director Rupert Julian; to his left, hero Norman Kerry.

MEMORABLE MAKEUPS
ERIK UBER ALLES

ERIK, THE PHANTOM of the Opera, is, without doubt, the crowning jewel in Chaney's diadem of diverse characterizations. In Los Angeles, Filmex 1981, for its 50-hour marathon of monstrous movies, chose Chaney's PHANTOM OF THE OPERA—accompanied by organ—to open the fantastic film festival. The theater was packed, the applause enthusiastic. Apart from the organist, I was possibly the only person in the theater who had seen the picture when it was originally released in 1925. One sad note: the heroine of the film, ironically, lives but a block or so from the theater! Had it been possible to persuade her to make an appearance. I am convinced the audience would have torn down the theater! I'll bet there would have been bouquets of flowers and asks for autographs and... After all, this is the woman who removed the mask from the Phantom of the Opera! When Carl Denham said of Ann Darrow, "Bravest girl I have ever known", because of her relationship to King Kong, he obviously had never met Mary! Their fans can be grateful that Gloria Swanson, Lillian gish, Ruby Keeler, Ginger Rogers, Mae West (to her dying day), Karloff and Lugosi (till theirs), George Burns, Fred Astaire, Fay Wray, John Carradine don't shun the limelight. But for whatever their reasons—infirmity, vanity, shyness, illness, change of interest—we must respect their desire for privacy on the parts of Brigitte Helm (Maria and the robotrix of METROPOLIS), Marlene Dietrich, Johatan Frid, David Manners, Jean Arthur *et autres*...and Mary Philbin. Arms around you, Mary—and I hope you'll accept a complimentary copy of this book in the spirit of wishing you a Happy 80th Birthday.

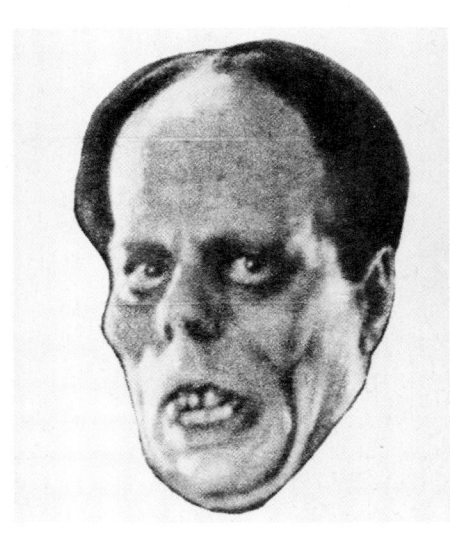

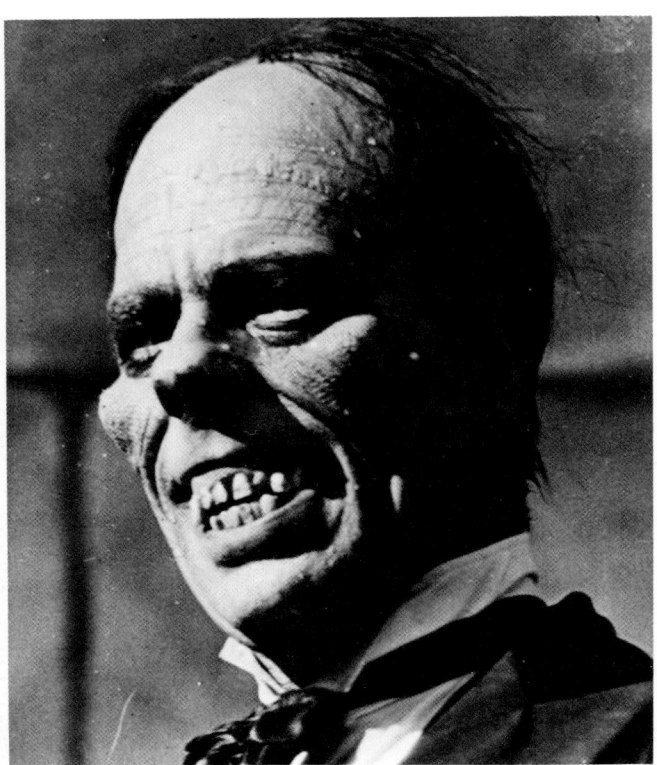

In a Parallel World it looks like the Phantom died at his organ rather than at the hands of the mad mob, beaten to death and his corpse thrown into the river.

THE ROAD TO MANDALAY

SINGAPORE JOE blind in one eye. Erroneously, in February 1958, I repeated in the first issue of *Famous Monsters of Filmland* a potentially harmful piece of misinformation which I had seen printed somewhere years before. The misinformation was that Chaney had used collodion (a mixture of guncotton, alcohol and ether) to simulate his blind orb. Wrong. Tilt. No no no. I have utilized every occasion since to correct the unwitting error. *Don't ever get collodion anywhere near your eyes!* It is now believed he achieved the effect with egg skin from the interior of the shell.

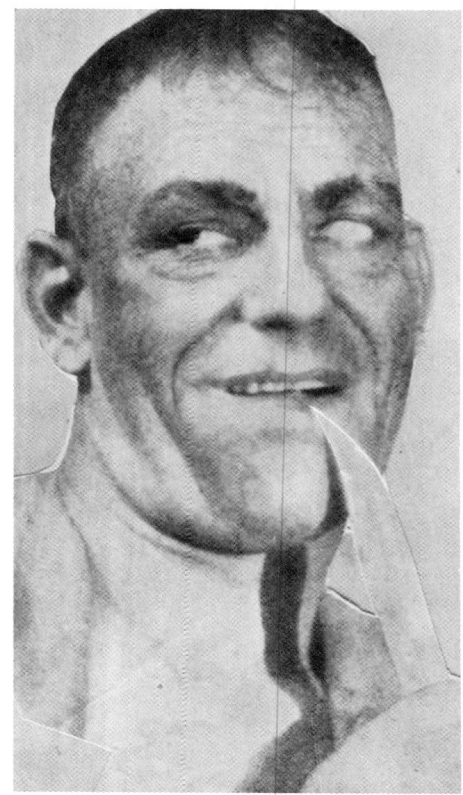

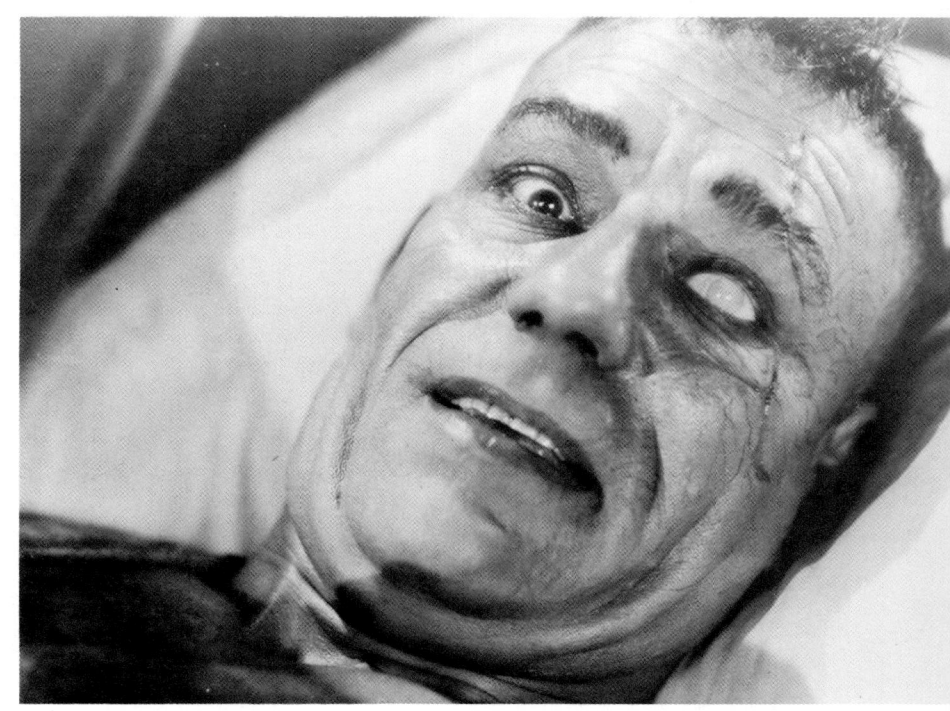

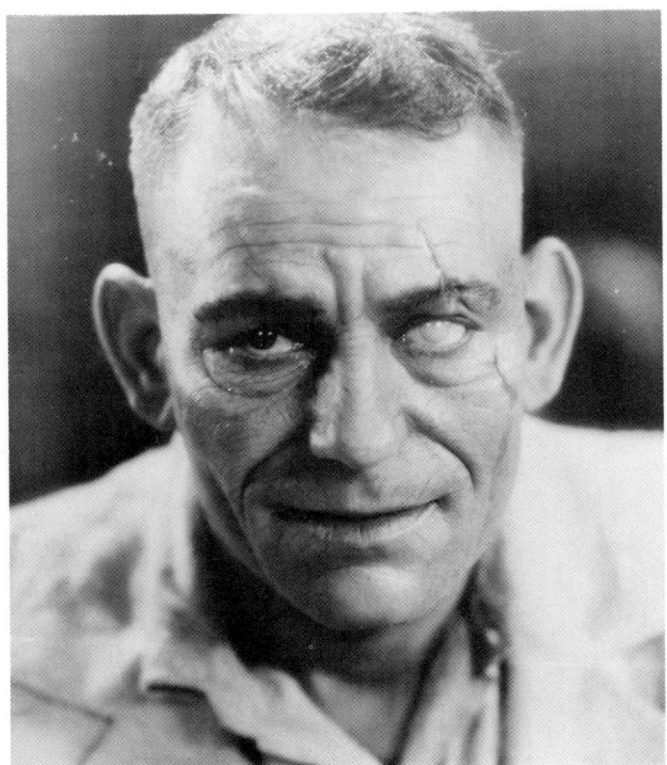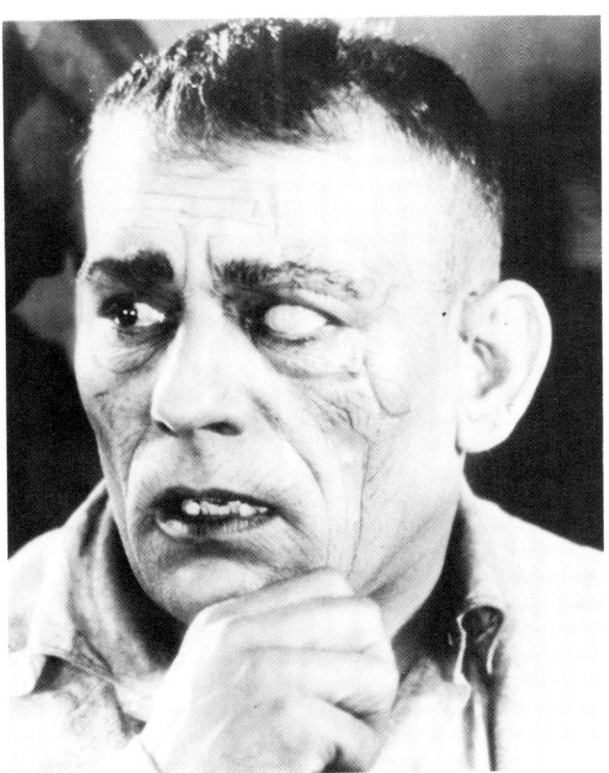

As Simon Legree

As Fagin (1922) OLIVER TWIST

As Russian peasant Sergei
MOCKERY

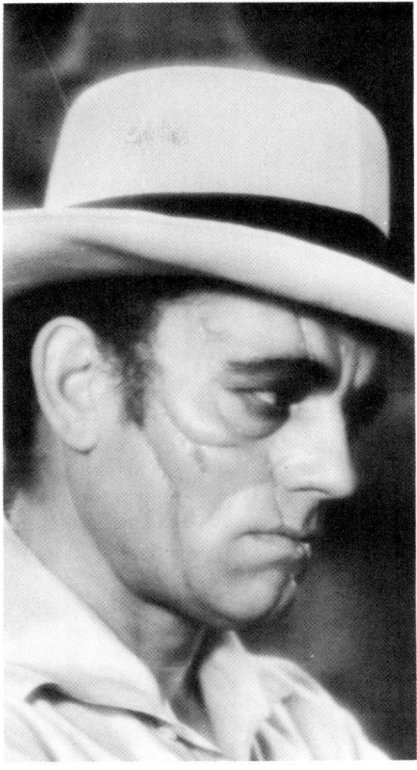

Okay, collodion *scars*...but not in the eyes.

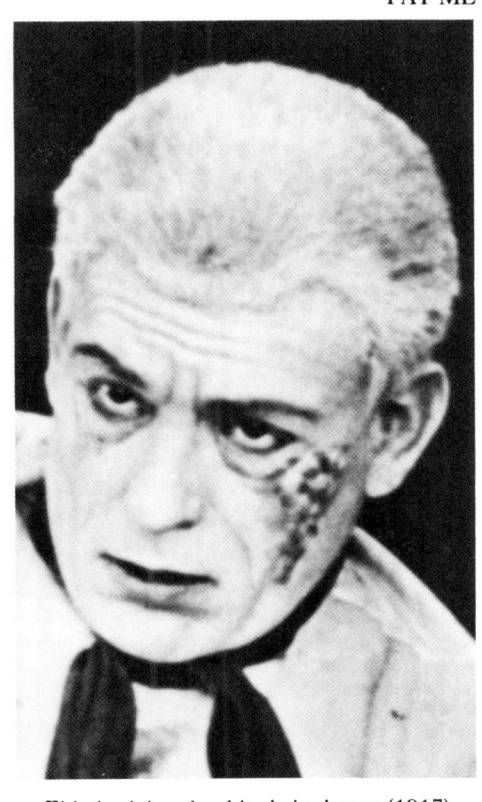

Elderly, injured, white-haired man (1917).

Mystery Photo. Your guess is as good as mine. (If better, let me know, in case there's a revised and enlarged edition). [THE *2000* FACES OF LON CHANEY?]

MR. WU
Three Orientals for the price of one! Lon Chaney as father Wu, grandfather Wu and great grandfather Wu. Wu-Wu! (Any resemblance to a pun is purely Occidental).

Quasimodo, the demented bell-ringer of the great Parisian cathedral.

Lon as an elderly peasant with the delusion that he is the Emperor of Portugallia.

THE HUNCHBACK OF NOTRE DAME

THE TOWER OF LIES

In the *persona* of a pirate. Better be prepared to give up your pieces of eight or walk the plank! (Possibly "Merry" in TREASURE ISLAND, 1920).

Looking for all the world like Walter Huston would about 20 years later in THE DEVIL AND DANIEL WEBSTER, 1940

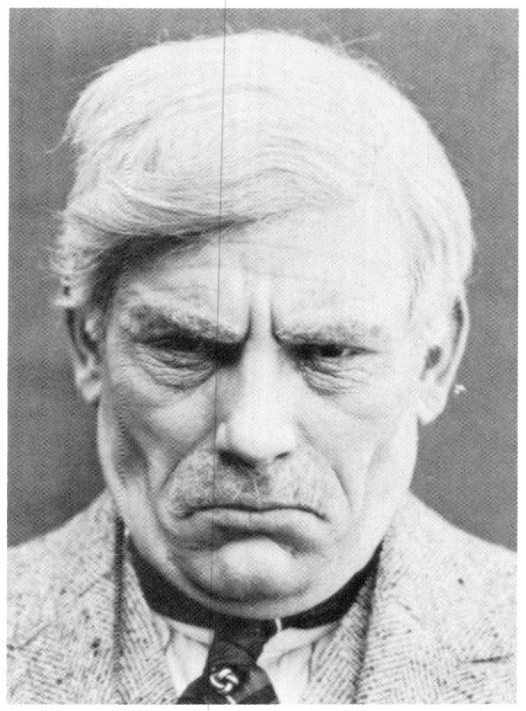

A young Chaney, through the marvel of his makeup looking older than when he died.

As the Inspector and as the ghoul in his dual role in the legendary lost one.
LONDON AFTER MIDNIGHT

Mad Dr. Ziska.
THE MONSTER

REINCARNATIONS...

HAD CHANEY LIVED there seems little doubt he would have played the "motherly" role essayed by Lionel Barrymore in THE DEVIL-DOLL, 1936.

And why shouldn't he have been Count Mora in the semi-remake of LONDON AFTER MIDNIGHT, MARK OF THE VAMPIRE?

THE MIRACLE MAN was remade.

WEST OF ZANZIBAR saw the light of the silver screen again as KONGO.

Following is a handful of photos showing interesting similarities between the pictures in this "Don't Step on It!" section and other films.

◀ Bela Lugosi in the Undead role in MARK OF THE VAMPIRE similar to the one created by Chaney in LONDON AFTER MIDNIGHT. (Similar in plot gimmick, totally different in characterization). Carroll Borland played the Edna Tichenor role of the Vampire Woman. It was veteran makeup artist William Tuttle's first film.

Compare this picture of Walter Huston as Mr. Scratch in ALL THAT MONEY CAN BUY (aka THE DEVIL AND DANIEL WEBSTER) with sly Chaney pose just before LONDON stills.

Looking like his sister Ethel is Lionel Barrymore in the female impersonation role in MARK OF THE VAMPIRE, which was shot under the title of THE WITCH OF TIMBUKTU. Mustached individual with the beret is Lon Chaney's legendary director, Tod Browning. Compare picture of Barrymore with shot of Chaney on the witness stand in the talking version of THE UNHOLY THREE; note similarity in flowered hats.

They once thought of grooming Humanitarian Award namesake Jean Hersholt as a replacement for Lon Chaney but didn't get very far. He did play weird Dr. Patterson, however, in THE CAT CREEPS, the 1930 version of THE CAT AND THE CANARY.

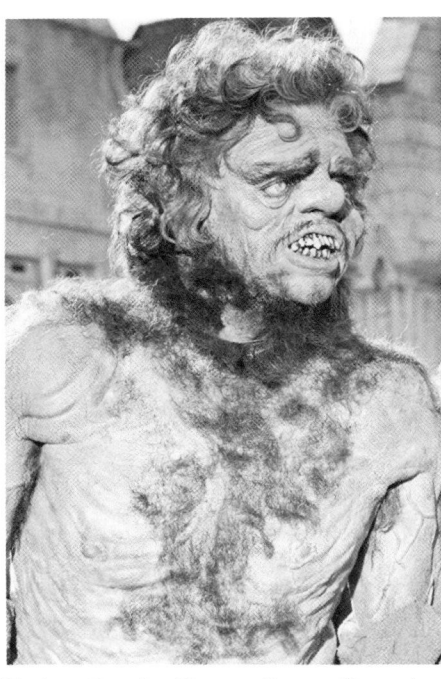

Yankee Doodle Chaney (James Cagney) as Quasimodo in the biofilm MAN OF A THOUSAND FACES.

SHADOWS? BITS OF LIFE? OUTSIDE THE LAW? Can't say. Can only say the unidentified acotr portraying the Oriental is the individual who played one of Lon's roles in a *Spanish* version of the film.

John Wray as Frog the cripple-faker in the remake of THE MIRACLE MAN.

Boris Karloff as he appeared in the remake of THE MIRACLE MAN. But—miracle of madness—Karloff did *not* play the role of Frog, the phoney cripple!

Reincarnation? Well, if Lon Chaney Jr. wasn't a flesh-and-blood chip off the old block, who was? I'm not devoting a large segment to LC jr because after all this book is about his dad; however, following is a sampling of seven real life and reel life photos of "the son of the Phantom of the Opera", including his Quasimodo makeup from TV's *Route 66* Special with Karloff and Lorre, and his studio makeup (gray-haired) vs. his personal makeup (dark-haired) for ONE MILLION B.C. Photo *(bottom page)* recreating 'Lenny' and receiving his Radcliff (Gothic) Award from the Count Dracula Society.

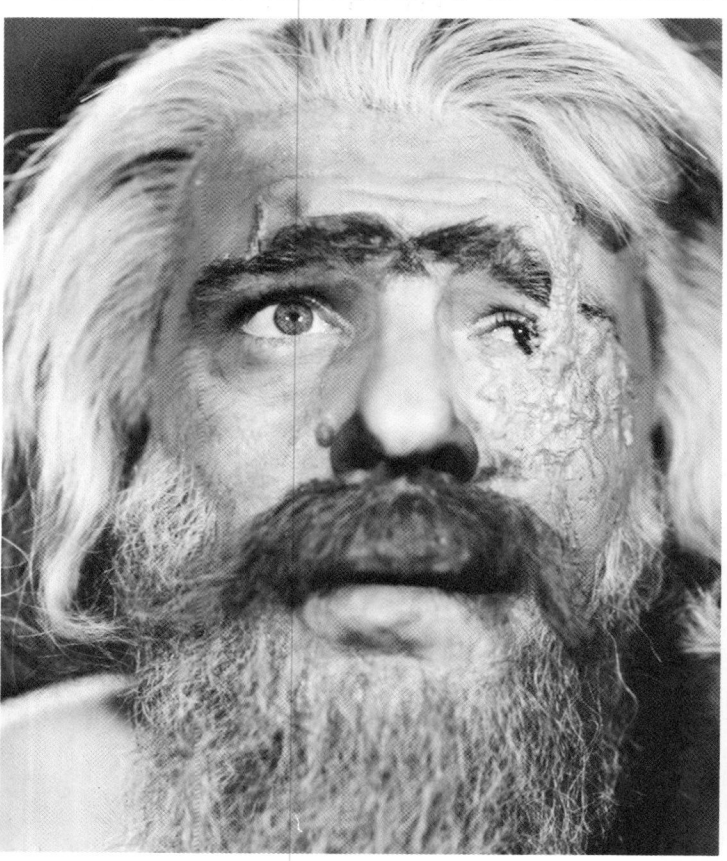

LON & SON...

```
MEMORIAM FOR LON CHANEY JR
```

The
Veteran Horror Star will, of course, have an issue of FAMOUS
MONSTERS OF FILMLAND
dedicated to him.

Any comments you might care to make about him for print would

be greatly appreciated.

Forry Ackerman
Forrest Ackerman

RESPONSE from VINCENT PRICE:

Lon Chaney, father and son, junior and Senior, how many wonderful memories of excitement and entertainment those names, that name, evoke. I never knew the father but from what I've read of him and being a great fan of his when I was a boy, I remember his gentleness. The same was true of the son. Working with him was a totally professional experience and added to it this feeling of gentleness now with his passing adds another wonderful memory to a long career.

Vincent Price

MISCEL*LON*EOUS...

One Million Years B.C. (Before Chaney). Lon as a caveman in very early appearance.

Just Plain Lon.

MR. WU on the Gong Show.

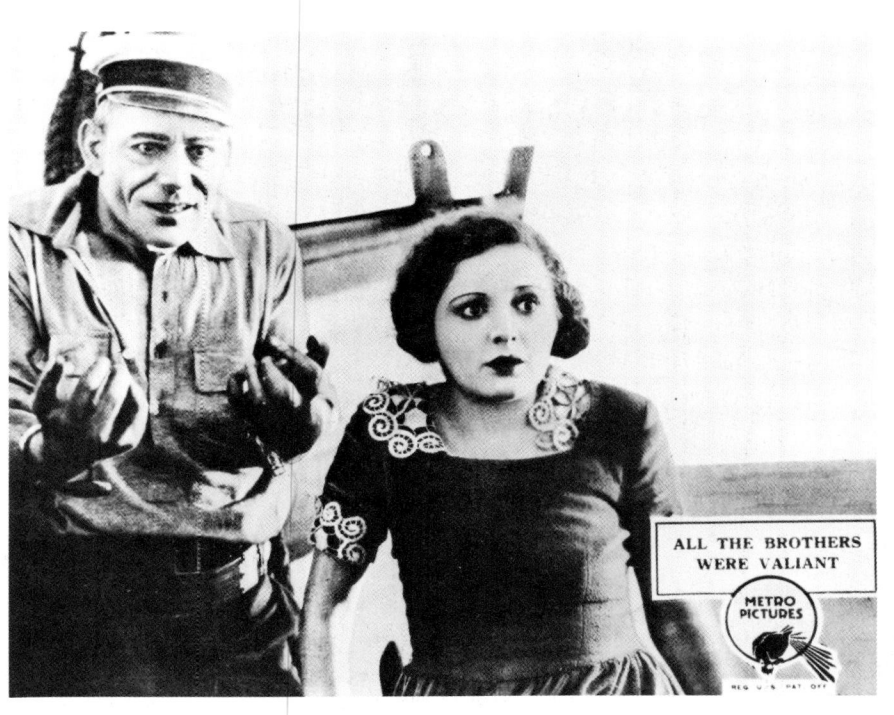

A Valiant Performance. (Three scenes).

Climax of the Talking Version of THE UNHOLY THREE.

THE BLACKBIRD.

THE PENALTY.

Six scenes from ACE OF HEARTS.

A BLIND BARGAIN (1922)

If you don't recognize these five faces by now, you better apply for a Full Modo instead of a Quasi Modo.

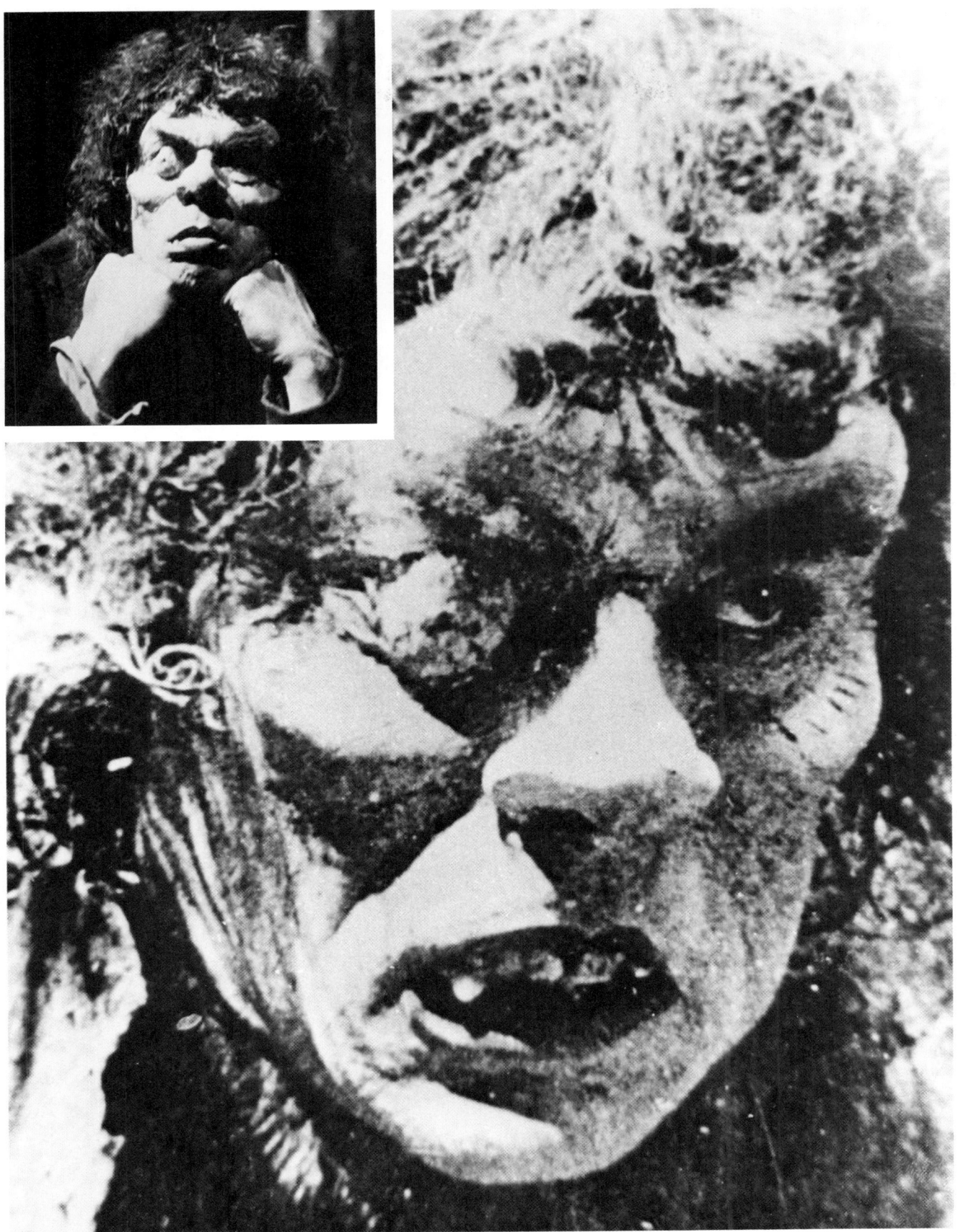

Forrest J Ackerman reviewing the Chaney photo file.

ADVERTISEMENT FOR MYSELF

(With a Nod to Norman Mailer)

DEAR DIARY:

(Not that I really keep one.)

My part of the book is finished: 13 Jan 83.

I thought it would be a labor of love but it turned out to be a nightmare of numbers. That's because, while I love words, I *hate figures,* and arranging the material in order seemed tantamount to tackling years of income taxes day after day. It was something like preparing a book with *six times* the content of MR. MONSTER'S MOVIE GOLD, *13 times* the contents of the filmonster magazine I edited for 25 years.

I won't bore you with the details but getting everything numbered correctly gave me a Kongsize headache. It's not possible for me to retire to a room and lock the door and turn off the phone and work uninterrupted for 8-12 hours with plenty of space to move about and file things. Stills would pile up on both sides of the typewriter (fortunately it doesn't have a movable platen) and periodically they would slide off onto the floor and get all mixed up. At times I actually worked with a *lap* full of stills and magazines and notes. Figures had to be recorded in as many as four places to keep everything straight and every once in awhile I'd foul up my system by failing to note down a number. During the creation of this book I was simultaneously editing an issue of *Famous Monsters,* agenting for 150 sci-fi literary clients, ghost-revising a movie book, curating my museum, answering the incessantly ringing phone, showing interested individuals the 300,000-piece collection...

Around New Years it became evident the publisher who had the book under contract could not get it published by Chaney's 100th birthday so I requested all the material back, added half a dozen articles to it, cropped 1000± photos myself (something I had not planned on doing) and the new publisher, printer, I, et al have performed at a frenzied pace in order to meet the deadline. If there are booboos, please consider the circumstances.

I've probably forgotten something.

Oh, yes: paying bills.

I said I wasn't going to bore you.

I lied.

Sorry.

Perhaps I can make it up to you.

How would you like to:

OWN THE *SECOND* LARGEST COLLECTION OF CHANEY SR. STILLS ON EARTH?

Approximately 1150 STILLS can be yours!

Some are originals from 50-65 years ago, others freshly minted copies from original negatives. All standard size 8x10 stills. Probably more than half appear in this book. No matter how fine the reproduction, however, there is nothing like owning an actual photograph for detail and sharpness. I found in selecting the 1000 stills for this book, that I had over 1000 duplicates. Of some stills there are two copies, a few even three. I have no further use for them, now that I have produced this volume.

So I am going to auction the 1100± photos.

The minimum bid for this magnificent collection is $5000. No, that's not a misprint; I *know* it should be $50,000 but I don't think there's a buyer who could afford upward of that figure. I'm prepared to accept that the collection will have to sell for far less than it's worth—but a semi-duplicate set is of no use to me and someone who would appreciate it should be enjoying it instead. Terms available if you are not prepared to pay the entire sum in one lump.

Bids will be accepted till Lon Chaney's 1984 birthday: April 1. At that time the three highest bidders will be informed and will have one last chance to up their bids to what will be the winning figure for the lucky bidder. As the owner of the collection will acquire a number of fine duplicate photos, they will be given the addresses of the five runnerup bidders so that those Chaney fans may have an opportunity to purchase some of the extra stills and the owner will have the opportunity to recoup some of his/her expenditure.

Besides all the more common titles (PHANTOM, HUNCHBACK, WU etc.) there are stills from A BLIND BARGAIN, LONDON AFTER MIDNIGHT, THE MIRACLE MAN, NIGHT ROSE, TREASURE ISLAND, THE PRICE OF SILENCE, etc. Some as early as 1916. Also candids. A truly incredible collection, a half a century in the building. I hope someone purchases it who truly appreciates Chaney and doesn't buy it for an investment—although its value can only appreciate...and rapidly.

Bids should be mailed to me at the following address. I simply don't have time to engage in fan-type correspondence about Chaney but egoboo is always welcome in case you like the book and would care to let me know. If you have some extraordinary piece of information to share or some rare Chaneyana, you will very likely receive a response, if not always immediately. I am planning further books about Karloff, Lugosi, Lorre, Rains, Veidt, Wegener and—inevitably—*METROPOLIS*.

FORREST J ACKERMAN
2495 Glendower Ave
Hollywood CA 90027

By Forrest J Ackerman

THE DAY Lon Chaney died it came to Mrs. Roberta O'Toole like a banshee that this actor's death was to influence her life in some fateful fashion. Lon Chaney was not merely a movie star but more like a living member of her family. He was Timmy O'Toole's idol, just as young Tim was the shamrock of his Mother's eye.

All the time she was undressing Timmy for bed, worry-thoughts niggled and naggled in Mother's mind. How should she break the bad news to him? He was sure to be shocked. It was worse than the Christmas when parents finally nerve themselves to tell their youngsters that...there *is* no Santa Claus.

Would her Mother's instinct tell her the right moment? Or could she skillfully maneuver it some way? It would be cruel to leave him to learn about it at school tomorrow from one of the members of his Monster Club.

LETTER TO AN ANGEL

The solution offered itself quite naturally. Timmy, the pajama fly neatly buttoned up over his plump little bottom, knelt by his pillow and said his good night prayers. After the family names and the President, he concluded: "And God bless Douglas Fairbanks, and Mary Pickford, and most of all God bless Lon Chaney". Then he turned and kissed his Mommy and clambered into bed.

"Tell me a ghost story," he said. "With Lon Chaney in it."

Mother hesitated.

"Timmy—" she began. Her voice held a strange sound in it, moist and minory, like the time his little puppy, Clover King, had been run over. Sensing some tragedy about to enter his fife, Timmy hugged his cloth-and-stuffings replacement to Clover.

"Timmy—Mommy has something to tell you. About Mr. Chaney. You know, people don't live forever. Especially people who work very hard. And Mr. Chaney—he died today. He—"

She said no more but helplessly regarded in mute horror what she had done to her little son. With all the love and best intentions in the world she had not been able to protect him from this moment. His china-blue eyes had gone saucerwide. His naturally pale face had visibly whitened. Unconsciously he clutched Clover around his muzzle. His nose wrinkled, his face squeegeed up and his breath escaped irregularly, as though he had the start of a sniffly cold.

"Lon Chaney...died? He *died?*" Disbelief, soul-deep, clogged Timmy's throat.

"Yes, dear. In the newspaper it said..."

"Show me!" His voice held a tone of Doubting Thomas, insisting to touch the wound in the side of his risen Master.

Mother moved into the front room, grateful for a momentary escape from her grim ordeal. "Jerome, have you got the paper handy?" Father handed the paper to Mother.

"How's he taking it?"

"Hard—worse than we thought."

Mother returned to the bedroom. Timmy sat up straight in bed, like a martyr about to lose his eyesight. "Show me!" he said. "Show me where it says!"

Mother pointed to the headlines. The type was very large. WORLD MOURNS CHANEY. There was a montage covering half the front page: Chaney as Quasimodo, as THE PHANTOM OF THE OPERA, as the slant-eyed Oriental MR. WU, as the Pagliacci of HE WHO GETS SLAPPED, as the contorted cripple of THE MIRACLE MAN. August 26th 1930, and Lon Chaney, the master of makeup, "the man of a thousand faces," was dead of cancer in a Hollywood hospital.

Timmy held the paper in his hands a long, long time. It trembled slightly. Mother said nothing. She saw tears forming in his eyes. She sat helplessly by, not knowing what to say in this crisis, what gesture of comfort or understanding to offer.

Then she saw something else forming in Timmy's eyes: resolution. He threw off the bed covers.

"Timmy! Whatever are you doing?"

"I have to get dressed, Mom."

"Dressed?" At this time of night? It's nearly quarter of nine, dear. Whatever for?"

"Something."

"Well—" Mother hesitated. An appeal to authority: "I don't know what your Daddy will say. Perhaps I'd better go ask him."

Mother left the room in indecision. Timmy was busy shrugging back into his coveralls.

Mother went directly to Father. Father put down his pipe. "Timmy is acting funny," she said.

"In what way?"

"He's getting dressed. I can't think whatever for."

"Dressed? Let's see."

Mother trailed Father to Timmy's room.

Timmy was sitting at his writing desk. He had torn a page from his Big Five notebook. He was laboriously printing something, nervously licking the pencil lead from time to time. When he was finished, he volunteered to show what he had written to Mother and Father.

Dear Lon Chaney. Don't be lonely tonight. I am praying for you, and missing you. I will never forget you. Please answer this if you can. Your best Fan. Timothy O'Toole, 5327 Citrus Avenue, Los Angeles, California.

"Now I need an envelope. And a stamp. An airmail stamp."

Wordlessly, with a look of incomprehension to Father, Mother fetched Timmy his envelope and stamp. Timmy folded the note neatly twice, inserted it in the envelope, licked the flap, sealed it and printed on the cover: LON CHANEY, HEAVEN. Then he affixed the big red-and-blue five-center.

Again he found use for his parents. "Dad, have you a flashlight?"

"Why, what for, son?"

"I want to find my kite."

"At *this* time of night?" asked Mrs. O'Toole.

"Please—it's very important, Mother."

"What do you want with your kite tonight, Timmy?"

"I need to send this message, Dad."

"To Lon Chaney? With your kite?"

"Yes."

Mother turned away to stifle a sob.

"Don't you think it's a little late, son?"

"Gosh, it's already after 9 o'clock. Dad, what time do angels go to bed?"

"Why—I really don't know."

"I guess grown angels stay up pretty late," suggested Mother.

"Then I have to go."

Mother went to the closet and brought back Timmy's warm green pullover. "I want you to put this on if you're going out into the chilly night air," she said. Gently she pulled the sweater over Timmy's head, and down over his little humped back.

In the dark garage Daddy chased eerie shadows away with the pale beam from the Ten Cent Store searchlight. The amber ray fell on Timmy's homemade goblin mask with its hollow cucumber nose protruding like a tapir's snout and its mass of excelsior hair dyed blood red with Rit. The light touched his penny-a-day lending library of a baker's dozen of *Ghost Stories* magazine with their spooky covers.

Outside a chorus of crickets stridulated their night-song: *crikadee...crikadee...crikadee.*

Illuminated in turn were Timmy's "genuine" aborigine boomerang, procured from the catalog of the mailorder novelty house in Kansas; his precious personally scissored and pasted scrapbook of Lon Chaney pictures; the gunpowdery smelling shells of burned-out fireworks, still saved from the Fourth as fine mementoes of an exhilarating evening of pryrotechnics; and, at last, hung up on a ten-penny nail, his dusty kite. The bad tear in it would need repair before it could take to the sky again. Mother's brown stickum paper could take care of that.

A big Daddy Longlegs, his nocturnal affairs disturbed by this unusual activity in his domain, and sensing danger, hastily began to descend from the web he had industriously spun over the kite.

Don't step on it—it may be Lon Chaney!

If every kid in the country took the publicists as seriously as Timmy, no flack artist need ever worry about his promotion being successful. *Yes,* Timmy was convinced, a man who could make his legs disappear, who could grow a hump on his back *and take it off again* (that was a trick Timmy hoped to accomplish when he grew up), who could look like he was blind, who could throw real sharp knives with his toes and hit the bull's eye, who could slide down a tight-rope on his head—who was to deny that such a god-like man might not also make himself look like a gorilla or a scarecrow...or even a spider?

Timmy, his own shadow wavering like some supernatural spectre, reached with a finger and cautiously picked Mr. Longlegs' web-strand out of the air. Gently he let the old grandfather down onto the oily gravel, watched him scuttle away to safety behind an empty orange crate. Then Daddy lifted down the Hi-Flyer.

They took the kite into the house. Mother insisted on taking it back to the backporch and dusting it off. Its rent was patched. Then Timmy took a safety pin and attached his envelope to the tattered tail of the kite—a couple of Father's Day ties that had seen better days.

Son and Father set out hand in hand for the ball park. Mother was agitated but Dad had nodded his browfurrowed quick short "don't interfere" nod, so she bided her counsel and contented herself with calling after them, "Try not to be too long, Daddy. Timmy isn't used to the night air and it's long past his bed time."

"Alright, dear."

"And *don't* let him overexert himself. The doc—"

It was hard work to get the kite into the air; there was very little breeze stirring that night. Dad stood on tiptoes and held the kite as high as he could but every time Timmy would run off with it, it would abruptly nosedive to the ground, threatening to crack its wooden skeleton.

"Hadn't you better let me try, son?" Dad offered after Timmy had made half a dozen unsuccessful trial runs; but, no, Timmy had to launch it himself. It was *his* message and he was responsible for getting it delivered.

At last a vagrant breeze caught the kite and the ball of string unwound in Timmy's hands as the Hi-Flyer took to its medium and chased toward the clouds. Finally the string came to its end and only the stick was left.

The kite bobbed about in the vault above like a high flying phantom and Daddy thought he saw something flutter from its tail but he couldn't be sure. Little Timmy was panting from exertion, the freckled forehead of his flushed face spattered with perspiration. Mother wouldn't approve; in fact, Daddy wasn't too pleased with the situation himself. After about half an hour of the kite flying, Jerome O'Toole tentatively suggested, "Don't you think it's about time to reel it in, son?"

"Just 10 minutes more," Timmy said. "The message has a long way to go."

Moonlight made a white shield of the kite.

Minutes passed in silence till, "He was a wonderful man," Timmy said. "He could do anything. I'll bet not even Dunninger or Thurston or *Houdini* ever could do Lon Chaney's tricks—like making a hump disappear,"

"Yes," said Jerome O'Toole, avoiding to look at his son's forever-crooked back, "he was a great man."

When they reeled the kite in a few minutes later, the message was gone.

On the way home they passed Dorschkind's Drugstore, which was still open, and Dad said, "How about a double-decker cornucopia?" But Timmy replied, "I'm not very hungry tonight."

Mother tucked an exhausted boy into bed a second time that night. "Do you think he got my message, Mama?" Earnest eyes looked searchingly to Mama for confirmation. Mama, her own eyes shiny bright with unshed moisture, bent and kissed her son on his sweet little mouth. "I'm sure of it, darling. Now, go to sleep—and pleasant dreams."

"Goodnight, Mommy. And God bless Lon Chaney".

Long after Timmy had been taken by the sandman Mother sat by his bedside and peered inwardly at the cinema of her own mind. She saw again his seventh birthday, when LONDON AFTER MIDNIGHT had been playing at the neighborhood theater and he had preferred treating all his friends to the show to having a party at home with games and prizes and all the trimmings. She had given him a dollar bill and he had proudly stepped up to the box-office window and pushed it through the wicket to the cashier. *"Ten* tickets, please!" Then he ushered his little pals and girlfriends into the lobby, down the aisle single file, and as near the front as he could possibly get. It gave Mother a headache to sit that near but she endured. She shuddered at the memory of the bone-white face Chaney effected as the London monster, with his eyes popping like olive pits out of hard-boiled eggs, and the scary teeth that sent shivers up her spine in retrospect. The man always frightened her but Timmy couldn't get enough of him. Cora and Fifi, the next door twins, however, were paralyzed with fear, and Mrs. O'Toole had to take them home before many reels had unwound.

She would never cease feeling jittery at the memory of that living death's-head that Chaney had somehow created in THE PHANTOM OF THE OPERA. She had actually shrieked right out loud in the theater and buried her head, embarrassed, on Father's chest when Mary Philbin slipped the mask off Chaney as he sat playing the organ. His outraged visage had been horror incarnate: bulging, bloodshot eyes fatigued with violet semicircles beneath them; the grotesquely exaggerated mounds of the cheekbones; the hooked-up flaring, porcine nostrils; the rotted, jagged teeth, like the rim of an enameled tincan top opened with a ragged knife; the scraggly strands of dead gray hair hanging like soggy serpentine from the incredible dome head...But little Tim had screamed in pure delight and clapped his hands—and insisted on returning for the Saturday matinee. He was there Sunday too, sitting through two complete showings, fortified only by a bag of jujubes and an Abazaba. That Timmy! That precious little tyke!

Mother shook herself from reminiscing. She patted Timmy's tousled head, presed a kiss to his soft young cheek, then went to the adjoining room and bed.

Timmy had a sore throat and running nose the next morning, which was a drizzly day anyway, so Mother decided to keep him home from school. He sat impatiently looking out the front window at the porch, waiting for the mailman. When he saw the rubber raincoated figure coming up the street, letter bag under arms, he ran and stood anxiously waiting by the door.

"Have you anything for me, Mr. Post-Toastie Man?" Timmy inquired expectantly.

"Why, no, 'fraid I haven't, young fella. Just for your Pop. How come you aren't in school?"

"Timmy has a cold coming on, I'm afraid," said Mother, arriving at the door to receive the mail. Pressing Timmy to her side she managed to suggest, "Maybe there'll be a letter for you tomorrow, dear."

"Who's he expecting to hear from? Little early for Christmas," said the Post-Toastie Man as he departed.

"An angel!" Timmy called after him.

The carrier halted momentarily in his tracks, looked back, chuckled, then continued along his route.

Timmy passed the rest of the day thumbing through his scrapbook for the thousandth time. Here was a bald Lon Chaney, confined to a wheelchair, in WEST OF ZANZIBAR (where the delicious Abazabas with their peanut butter centers came from)—yet here he had regained use of his legs and, in fact, was throwing knives with his feet!

This picture always made Timmy laugh: Lon made up like a *woman!* Imagine, a kind white-haired old lady, old enough to be his own Gra' Maureen! That was a real funny one—Lon Chaney pretending like he was a lady. That was about the only thing Timmy *wouldn't* want to be.

Now look at those fingernails, so long they looked like those icicly things they called skalactites or something. Their length meant he was a very rich Mandarin and didn't have to work, so he could let his fingernails grow. Sometimes, and for the same reason, Timmy wished he were a Mandarin.

But most of all Timmy wished he knew Lon Chaney's secrets; how, from a hunchback just like Tim, Lon could turn himself from Quasimodo into a wonderful clown with a back as straight as a wooden school ruler.

That night Mother and Dad had a serious talk about their Timmy lad. Mr. O'Toole was of the opinion the boy would forget about his tragic loss and the letter in a couple of days and everything would return to normal. Mother wasn't so optimistic. "What would you think of writing an answer to Timmy?" Mother put forward the suggestion timidly.

"What! Me? Pretend to be Lon Chaney?"

"You could just say, 'Thank you for your kind wishes,' or something like that," Mother persisted.

During the night Timmy developed pneumonia. He tossed and turned and it hurt Mother and Dad to the heart to watch their son roll restlessly back and forth on his curved back.

In the morning the doctor thought Timmy might have to go to the hospital. The youngster insisted he would *have* to stay home and wait for the mail. Lon Chaney might want to hear from him again. Now that he was dead, he might even reveal his secrets—at least to his greatest admirer.

Timmy's spirits declined visibly when the mail came that day and there was no letter for him. Mother called Dad home from work at noon time and they had a hurried conference, as a result of which Dad agreed that he would write a letter from Lon Chaney that evening. That it was delivered the next day was too much for the broken-hearted O'Tooles to bear, because—

Timmy died in his sleep shortly before midnight.

The mightiest and most majestic of all clocks, which tolls the time in Heaven, has a bell of supernal perfection fashioned of purest gold with tongue of solid silver. As it pealed forth the hour of 12 throughout the Kingdom, Timmy O'Toole approached the Pearly Gates. He did not even notice as St. Peter swung them wide for him: his gaze was intent on the angels, and he was seeking one in particular as the harps played promises of Paradise and the Heavenly Choir sang "Hallelujah!" to welcome this big-hearted little soul into the Father's Mansion.

Then Timmy's heart leapt right into his throat. *Timmy recognized HIM.* His beloved idol sat on a magnificent throne and he wore the most impressive makeup of all. He was giant tall; and a tremendous beard, bright as the sun at the equator, flowed from his infinitely kind face to the floor of polished ivory. And an astonishing circle of shimmering light shone over his head—a thrilling effect that Timmy had never seen in any movie.

"Come here, my boy," *he* bade him, and he spoke with the resonant volume of the mighty organ that always accompanied his pictures.

"Lon Chaney!" Timmy cried with a cry of ineffable joy and sprang forward and leaped into his lap.

And the Good Lord's eyes were bright with understanding as He laid His arm 'round Timmy's shoulders. And Timmy's back miraculously straightened and his hated hump disappeared as God enfolded him but Timmy did not even notice he was free of his deformity.

His face was turned upward in adoration.

"Lon Chaney!" he breathed.

And God smiled.

"Lon Chaney!" he breathed.
THIS PHOTO was not retouched to illustrate the climax of "Letter to an Angel". I've had it ever since Timmy was a tiny tot. I'll probably never know who chose to turn Lon Chaney into Santa Claus but the concept seems to fit in so snugly with the conclusion of the story that I felt the artist's rendition belonged here. All that's missing is the halo but even the Christmas tree decoration above Chaney's head suggests something celestial.

LON CHANEY SHALL NOT DIE!

"That's all there is to life, folks:
Just a little laugh,
A little tear."

—Prof. Echo